W9-CLO-698

*L*ook beyond the trademark big hair, and well, the other obvious big traits of Dolly Parton, and you marvel at the heart of a big-time star who emerged from the humblest of backwoods roots. . . . With a candor rarely found in show business or anywhere else, she bares her soul's joys and sorrows and scars with an earthiness that can bring laughter, tears, and blushes. . . . She holds nothing back."

—*Boston Herald*

"Dolly Parton imparts a happy message: You just can't offend this dynamite country singer."

—*San Francisco Chronicle*

"Parton details most everything: growing up in extreme poverty, why she chose not to have children, plastic surgery, friends who've tried to blackmail her, and her inspiration for her record-breaking hit, 'I Will Always Love You.' One of her most personal revelations is about her 18-month struggle with depression."

—*Atlanta Journal/Constitution*

*D*olly is a charmer, and so is her memoir. Call her book an entertainment."
—*The Chattanooga Times*

"Her book tells one of the most remarkable stories in show business, that began in a one-room cabin in East Tennessee and led to million-selling records, hit films, [and] a TV series. . . . Her book is one of the more honest music autobiographies to be published."
—*Memphis Commercial Appeal*

"Dolly Parton is one of those pop-culture icons who could only have been made in America. More gaudy than Elvis, more down-home than Loretta [Lynn] and more busty than anybody . . . The stories of her adult life are as funny, honest and embarrassing as those of her childhood. . . . [She] is a genuine American original. Her book only underscores how good she really is."
—*Lexington Herald Leader*

*S*he shows a glimpse of her soul."
—*USA Today*

"In this inspiring autobiography, Dolly reveals how she got to where she is today, her no-nonsense attitude and the down-home philosophy that has helped her from the start. . . . Dolly reveals with humor and honesty the real woman behind the superstar who still considers herself a simple girl from the country."
—*Sioux Center News* (Iowa)

"An inspiring, tell-it-like-it-is autobiography of one of America's best loved stars. In it Ms. Parton tells the rags-to-riches story of her life with honesty, insight and an unfailing sense of humor. . . . Ultimately Dolly is about this remarkable woman herself."
—*Collierville Independent* (Tennessee)

ATTENTION: ORGANIZATIONS AND CORPORATIONS

Most HarperPaperbacks are available at special quantity discounts for bulk purchases for sales promotions, premiums, or fund-raising. For information, please call or write:
Special Markets Department, HarperCollins*Publishers***,
10 East 53rd Street, New York, N.Y. 10022.
Telephone: (212) 207-7528. Fax: (212) 207-7222.**

HarperSpotlight

DOLLY

MY LIFE AND OTHER UNFINISHED BUSINESS

———

DOLLY PARTON

HarperPaperbacks
A Division of HarperCollinsPublishers

The book *Dolly* by Dolly Parton is available on tape from
HarperAudio, a division of HarperCollins*Publishers*.

If you purchased this book without a cover, you should be
aware that this book is stolen property. It was reported as
"unsold and destroyed" to the publisher and neither the
author nor the publisher has received any payment for this
"stripped book."

HarperPaperbacks   *A Division of* HarperCollins*Publishers*
10 East 53rd Street, New York, N.Y. 10022

Copyright © 1994 by Dolly Parton
All rights reserved. No part of this book may be used or
reproduced in any manner whatsoever without written
permission of the publisher, except in the case of brief
quotations embodied in critical articles and reviews. For
information address HarperCollins*Publishers,*
10 East 53rd Street, New York, N.Y. 10022.

A hardcover edition of this book was published in 1994 by
HarperCollins*Publishers.*

Cover photograph © 1994 by Patrick Demarchelier. Dolly's
hair by David Blair; wardrobe by Tony Chase; makeup by
Bobbe Joy.

First HarperPaperbacks printing: June 1995

Printed in the United States of America

HarperPaperbacks, HarperSpotlight, and colophon are
trademarks of HarperCollins*Publishers*

❖ 10 9 8 7 6 5 4 3 2 1

*I dedicate this book to my God,
my family, my friends, and my fans*

SPECIAL THANKS

Thank you, Buddy Sheffield, for your talent, inspiration, humor, love, and devotion. I thank you, too, for the use of your computers, the one on your lap and the one on your shoulders. I love and appreciate you more than you might ever know.

Thanks, Gladys Carr, for being the world's greatest editor and for all the hours you've spent sifting through the coal mines of my life trying to make me shine like a diamond. (Thanks to your wonderful staff as well.)

Thank you, Mort Janklow, for all the years you spent as my literary agent, trying to find me the best publisher for the most money. Thank you for doing that and for seeing it through.

Thank you, Sandy Gallin, for finding Mort Janklow for me and for keeping after him; and for keeping after me to write this book. I know it was for the commission, as you know all there is to know about my life, but I love you anyway.

Last and certainly not least, thank you, Jim Morey, Mark Kiracofe, Judy Ogle, Don Warden, Teresa Hughes, Jason Pirro, David Blair, Tony Chase, and Susie Glickman, for your special contributions to this project as well as to my life.

FOREWORD

*O*nce upon a time and far, far away, back in the hollers at the foothills of the Great Smoky Mountains of East Tennessee there lived a little girl with yellow hair, blue-green eyes, fair skin, and freckles. She loved to read almost as much as she loved to dream. She read everything she could get her little hands on, the Bible, *The Farmer's Almanac*, *The Funeral Home Directory*, the directions and descriptions on the garden and flower seed packets, all medicine bottles, catalogues, any and all kinds of mail, school books . . . but mostly she loved fairy tales. So I grew up to be a fairy princess of a sort, more of a Cinderella story, the rags-to-riches kind.

I always loved books. I don't remember learning to read, it was just something I always did. I was hungry for knowledge, I guess, and information; I was a curious kid. I still am.

~

I love to write stories. I wrote stories back then, not just songs, but long, involved stories. Even when I was in school and was supposed to give a book report, I would make up the story, make up the fictitious author, then get up and talk about it. Of course, the teachers never heard of it and they must have known I made it up. They gave me good grades for creativity, I am sure. On the occasions when I was asked about the book, the library, and the author, I would just say it was a book my grandpa had or one I found at my neighbors'. I was also a creative liar.

This book was harder to write, as I had to tell the truth because I lived it. Some writer once said that writing your life story is the hardest thing you'll ever do. I believe that now, although it didn't register with me until I started to write my own. It sure takes a lot out of you. It stirs up every emotion possible. I often had to stop because I couldn't take it anymore. Sometimes I would laugh out loud. Sometimes I'd cry uncontrollably from memories brought forward that had been buried for so long. Sometimes it would be like wading in a beautiful clear clean mountain stream; well, that was the happy times. When the water would get muddy, those were the harder times. Then I'd get completely marred up in the mud, and that was the worst of times.

I made it through, and I must say I'm glad it's done. Like lines from one of my songs:

No *amount of money could buy from me*
The memories that I have of then;
But no amount of money could pay me
To go back and live it through again.

⌒

That's from "In the Good Old Days When Times Were Bad." My life has been far better than it's been bad. I've had heartaches, headaches, toothaches, earaches, and I've had a few pains in the ass; but I've survived to tell about it.

My life has been a coat of many colors, to quote another song of mine, but I wouldn't change a thing. I just hope you get as much out of it as what I tried to put in it. I tried to be as honest and open as I could be without completely hanging myself or somebody else. You may like me more, or you may never like me at all; but you will know who I am and what I'm about.

I know you'll go straight to the gossip parts first (I would, too). But after you've read those parts a few dozen times, please start at the front and read the whole story. It would mean a lot to me, and hopefully it will mean a lot to you as well.

Love,
Dolly

PROLOGUE

anuary 1946, the coldest day of the year. A biting wind blows the snow sideways through the remote hills of East Tennessee. The snow sticks to the sides of the trees and to the weathered walls of the house, little more than a shack, and blows up through cracks in the floor making long white rows like designs on an icy chenille bedspread. By the hearth, a worried young man stokes a fire, trying to raise the temperature and his hopes. His wife, a mere girl, lies in a crude bed, sweating in spite of the cold. Even though this is not her first childbirth, it is a difficult one. The doctor has been sent for.

Some distance away, a little horse chooses his steps carefully as he makes his way along a mountain ridge in the blinding snow. It's as if he knows his passenger is important. One wrong step, one icy rock, one animal burrow hidden by the snow and the little horse might stumble. The doctor might be thrown. The baby and even the young mother might not make it.

The horse steps true. The doctor arrives. Mother and baby come through all right.

The girl in the bed was Avie Lee Parton. The young man was Robert Lee Parton. The child born that day was Dolly Rebecca Parton. Me. I have always believed that God guided that little horse's steps that day, just as he continues to guide every step I take.

There have been other books written about me, and much of what I have done or achieved in life is a matter of record (pun intended), so in this book I will try to outline the events in my life that shaped, touched, or warped me or otherwise made me who I am. I am not saying that my life is one that other lives should be patterned after. Actually, I think it's a big mistake to try to pattern yourself too much after anybody else. We are all individuals. Just like snowflakes, no two of us are alike, and that, to me, is the beauty of it. I hope to tell in this book how I have become the best Dolly Parton I can be, largely through trial and error, I can assure you, but it is up to you to be the best (your name here) you can be. If I can help in any way, then I feel good about taking your money for this book. If I don't help, I still feel okay about taking your money because I think you will at least be entertained. Besides, I need the money. As I always say, "It costs a lot to make a person look this cheap."

I

I was born January 19, 1946, in a one-room cabin on the banks of the Little Pigeon River in the Great Smoky Mountains of East Tennessee. I grew up poor—very poor. In fact, my daddy couldn't afford to pay Dr. Thomas for delivering me, so he gave him a sack of cornmeal. I have often joked that I have been raking in the dough ever since. Being born poor is something I am neither proud nor ashamed of. I have found that poverty is something you don't really realize while you're in it. At least not if you're a kid with a head full of dreams and a house full of loving family. Lord knows ours was full. My mother got married when she was fifteen and had twelve kids by the time she was thirty-five. I was the fourth child, after my sister Willadeene and my brothers David and Denver. Coming along later would be Bobby, Stella, Cassie, Larry, Randy, the twins, Floyd and Freida, and my baby sister, Rachel.

My mama and daddy always gave us everything they could, and all of us kids knew and appreciated that, although it was never spoken. There's a funny thing about mountain folks. There's an awful lot that is never said out loud. I can remember very few times when one member of my family said the words "I love you" to another one. That doesn't mean it wasn't communicated. It's a kind of silent speech that says, "Thank you, Mama, for the hot butter beans," in the same way that a father might say to his son, "Nice going, you plowed a good straight row" by giving the boy a light punch on the shoulder. It's kind of an eye-to-eye and heart-to-heart language that in some ways I think is deeper and truer than the regular oral kind because you have to pay closer attention to the one doing the "talking."

My daddy was a sharecropper. That means we didn't own the land we lived on. We farmed it for somebody else in return for a share of the crop. In a hard land that is stingy about giving up much of a crop, that share doesn't come to a whole lot.

The land belonged to an old woman named Martha Williams. We called her Aunt Marth, even though she wasn't related to us. In the same way love doesn't have to be spoken to be expressed, a person doesn't have to have blood ties with you to feel like part of your family. As for me, I couldn't have loved her more. My earliest memories are of Aunt Marth. I was often left with her when I was little. She was a good friend to me, and she made me feel special. Her big house was not far from our little cabin, and even as a little kid, I could go there on my own. I can remember climbing up the steps to her porch. I couldn't have been more than two or two and a half, and I had to struggle up the steps one at a time.

I guess one reason I remember Aunt Marth so vividly was that her house was always filled with strange sounds and smells, the things that trigger our memories the most. She had terrible asthma, and she used to cough and wheeze something fierce. Sometimes she would even cry because of the pain and because she got so desperate for breath. She would also burn some kind of strange brown substance in jar lids placed around the house. The stuff gave off an eerie smoke, and in those days before electricity came to that part of the woods, the house could get really spooky in the late afternoon. I later learned the smoke was to help her breathe.

Between the smoke and the coughing and wheezing, I was frightened many times, but I would never run away and leave Aunt Marth. Even though I was just a toddler, I always felt like she needed me there as much as I needed her. Maybe that's part of what made me feel special.

There were fascinating and delightful sights and sounds around Aunt Marth's house too. She had a great big spinning wheel in her living room, and I was quite taken with it. I used to stand and watch her spin yarn for hours. That wheel seemed as big to me then as a Ferris wheel would now. It's funny how we remember things we knew when we were kids. Sure, we're small, and that could make them seem bigger, but I think it's more than that. I think it's partly because of the wonder we experience at learning new things. I hope I never lose that wonder.

Aunt Marth was a dear, sweet soul. She would make gingerbread and hoecakes, and she would always share them with us kids. To poor kids those things seemed like the riches of Solomon, and we loved her for it. They tell me I used to go running up to her on the porch and the first words out of my mouth would be, "Ain't you got no gingerbread?" Even if she didn't have gingerbread, there was always one special treat I could count on. Aunt Marth would

sit me on her knee and ride me up and down as she
would sing:

> Tiptoe tiptoe, little Dolly Parton
> Tiptoe tiptoe, ain't she fine
> Tiptoe tiptoe, little Dolly Parton
> She's got a red dress just like mine
> She's got a red dress, she's got nine
> She's got a red dress just like mine.

I can remember being amazed that Aunt Marth
knew a song that had my name in it. It never occurred
to me you could put anybody's name in the song.
And, after all, I was special. Why wouldn't there be a
song about a special little girl? That was the first song
I was ever aware of, and it was like a drug to me. I
used to clap my little hands and squeal, "Sing it again,
Aunt Marth, sing it again!" And she usually would,
unless she got to coughing and wheezing too much. It
didn't bother me at all that I didn't have a red dress,
let alone nine. If Aunt Marth said it, it must be true.

When I was about five, we moved away from Aunt
Marth's place. The men moved the household belongings on a sled pulled behind our mule. I don't know
exactly how far it was, but to a kid it seemed like a
long trip. I said good-bye to Aunt Marth and toddled
off behind the sled, holding on to my Aunt Tude's
forefinger. I remember tripping over rocks and cow
ruts and fighting my way through briars and constantly asking, "Can't we slow down?" But in the
mountains there is a certain pace that survival sets for
you, and it can't be changed for one dreamy little kid
being dragged unknowingly through a threshold of life.

Life at the new house (new only to us) didn't seem
that different to me, but the difference was a great one
for my daddy. For the first time he wasn't a share-

cropper. As I recall, he bought this place for five thousand dollars. He was determined to build a better life for all of us. The place has always been known in my family as "over in the holler." It was overgrown. The fences were all down. The roof leaked. Making something out of this was going to be more work than sharecropping ever was. But Daddy did it.

David and Denver weren't really big enough to help very much, and it seemed as though uncles and the like were pretty scarce during working hours. Daddy worked long, hard hours, but the old place finally began to shape up. One of our favorite family stories tells about a preacher who stopped by one day while Daddy was hard at work. This particular preacher was never much of a help to anybody and seemed to show up only when he was out beatin' the bushes for money. Well, this snooty parson in his starched collar stopped by the fence while my daddy was sweating and groaning trying to get a stump out of the ground, and he said, "Hello, Lee, this is a right nice place you and the Lord have here." Daddy wiped the sweat from his brow with the back of his sleeve and said, "Yeah, well, you should have seen the som'bitch when the Lord had it by hisself."

I have often joked that we had "two rooms and a path, and running water, if you were willing to run to get it." I can remember being excited when we would move into a new house because there would be new newspapers on the walls. Poor folks would use newspapers like wallpaper. They helped to seal the cracks and make the house warmer in the winter, but to us kids they were something new to read and new pictures to look at. We would go all over the new house reading an episode of "Dick Tracy" or "Blondie." Sometimes you'd have to climb way up into a corner or stand on your head to read something that had been pasted on upside down. Some things got overlapped, so I can remember having to peel part of the paper off the wall to see how "Snuffy Smith" turned out.

If there's one positive thing about being poor, it's that it makes a person more creative. None of us kids ever had store-bought toys to play with when we were growing up. When I tell kids that now, they always say, "What did you play with?" I usually tell them, "I played with Denver and David and Bobby and Stella and Cassie . . ." How can a Nintendo compare to that?

I don't know when he found the time, but Daddy would sometimes make us little toys out of wood. He was a real good whittler, and he would make us little cars out of rubber bands and old thread spools. You'd wind them up, and off they'd go across the dirt in the yard. I can still hear the sound one of our old spool cars would make clattering across the boards on the front porch.

Mama made us things too. Once she made me a doll out of a corncob. She made it a little dress out of corn shucks and used corn silk for hair. Daddy got the poker hot in the fire and used the tip of it to burn two black eyes into the corncob. I thought she was beautiful, and I named her Tiny Tasseltop. The first song I ever wrote was about that little corncob doll:

Little Tiny Tasseltop,
I love you an awful lot
Corn silk hair and big brown eyes
How you make me smile.
Little Tiny Tasseltop,
You're the only friend I've got
Hope you'll never go away
I want you to stay.

Well, what did you expect for a little kid?

We kids were forced to be creative. I was, anyway, and I guess I did a fair share of forcing the others to go along, but we all had a good time. There is a plant that grows in the hills that we called "poke sallett." I believe it's actually poke salad, but we neither knew nor cared about that. The green leaves of the plant are actually edible (it's cooked like any other greens), but nobody ever gets hungry enough to make a meal of it except poor white trash. Naturally, I am familiar with the taste.

The most fun for us kids were the pokeberries that grew on the stem of the plant. They are dark purple, and when you mash them, the juice is like a dye. We used to paint our skin with pokeberries so that it looked like we were wearing bracelets or wrist-watches. Sometimes we would paint what we called "Jesus sandals" onto our feet. We would dress up in gunnysacks for robes and carry tobacco stakes as our walking sticks and go gallivantin' all over the country-side pretending we were the disciples, or at least some kind of biblical types. We felt real holy, but somehow our kinship with Jesus was lost on Mama when we came home with those awful purple stains all over us.

Another thing we loved to do was to catch June bugs and tie them to a string. I'm sure it was more fun for us than the poor weighted-down June bugs, but we had a ball flying what we called our "'lectric kites." You tried to get a real good fat June bug with a lot of lifting power. Sometimes you could just fanta-size about him being able to lift you right off the ground to where you could soar up among the clouds and look down at the trees and the fields. That kind of blissful thought would sometimes come to a sudden halt when your June bug would sacrifice his leg in the name of freedom and buzz off across the pasture. In the blink of an eye you could go from being a kind of daring Smoky Mountain astronaut to being just a kid with a bug leg hanging from a piece of thread. I'd like to take this opportunity to publicly thank all of those five-legged June bugs for those dreams, fleeting though they may have been.

I was always fascinated by things that flew, especially hummingbirds and butterflies. Maybe it was because I envied the freedom they had. To me, a hummingbird seemed to have the power to buzz right out of the holler, right across Locust Ridge and out into the real world. I bet he could be in New York City by afternoon if he wanted to. It was easier for me to imagine a hummingbird doing that than it was to imagine New York City. I had no concept of how far away it was or what it was like. I only knew that it was somewhere else, and that meant more to explore, more to learn, more to build dreams around. And that sounded good to me. I suppose that's why I used to try to follow them.

A hummingbird is a hard act to follow, darting this way and that without an instant's notice, sometimes even flying backward. That, coupled with the fact that when you're looking up trying to keep your eye on a darting bird, you're bound to occasionally run into a tree or the side of the house or a brother or sister or some other thing that gets in the way of such a dizzy attempt at adventure.

One day I got to follow a butterfly. I guess it was a monarch, with beautiful iridescent orange wings and velvety, coal-black wing tips. I would get as close as I could to it and hold my hand up to where I could feel the breeze from its wings, but I was careful not to touch it. I knew that holding it would make the color come off of its wings like powder on my hands and that if I did that, the butterfly wouldn't be able to fly anymore. I used to imagine it was some kind of magic powder that gave them the power to fly. Maybe if I had enough of it to rub on me, I could fly too. But that would mean hurting an awful lot of butterflies, and I wanted them to fly. I'd just have to watch and fly with him in spirit.

He and my spirit must have flown a long way from home without really paying attention, because I got lost. That was okay at first. I thought if I kept walking sort of in big circles, I would eventually find something I recognized. That was actually fun, seeing places I had never been. I would find a patch of dandelions on one hill, on another a devil's snuffbox, as we called them. These were little mounds that grew low to the ground. I believe they're related to mushrooms. In the summer they get dried out so that the outside is like a piece of dark brown paper and the inside is filled with powder that puffs out like a dragon's breath when you stomp it.

To somebody who has never stomped a devil's snuffbox, that might seem like vandalism. Anybody who has seen one, especially as a kid, knows they just have to be stomped. Now that I've learned more about it, I know that the "snuff" is actually spores that help make more devil's snuffboxes on other hills for other kids to stomp. But at the time, I just knew they needed stomping.

If you accept that a kid is just another one of God's creatures, like a fox or a blue jay (and I don't see how you could do otherwise), you have to believe that it is part of the divine plan for the snuffboxes to be made the way they are and for kids to stomp them, just like bees pollinate the flowers. If God is going to depend on a kid to spread snuffboxes, he would naturally make the stomping both fun and guilt-free, and that is just what it was. So I would stomp one and squeal with delight at the brown puff and then see another one through the smoke and take off to do my God-given duty on the next hill. Of course I didn't know I was doing the Lord's work, but I took to it with such zeal you would have thought I did. My work took me even farther from home.

When it began to get dark, I got scared. When I couldn't see any sign of a light or hear anything other than the wind and the whippoorwills, I was petrified. I called as loud as I could, but there was no one to hear me. The trees were only silhouettes now. And the bushes, which my butterfly and I had swooped through so happily earlier, now began to look like hunched-over hairy things lying in wait for me in the night. The snuffboxes I had stomped so gleefully became shadowy unknown things I wouldn't dare step on or even get near.

I stopped in a small clearing as far as I could get from unfriendly bushes, and I thought for a minute or two. After some consideration, I came up with a plan: I cried. It didn't really help anything, but I figured if my poor bush-riddled body was going to be found in the morning, I was going to let it be in a pool of my own tears.

Finally, when all seemed lost, I sniffed back a tear just in time to hear a familiar sound, one my mind associated with a friend. It was not a human friend, but I was in no position to be choosy. It was the sound of the bell worn by our milk cow, Bessie. At the moment, its clanking sounded to me like angels banging on some kind of heavenly cymbals.

I ran toward the sound and got to where I could see Bessie's hulking figure coming up the hill. I waited for her to come by, but she was in no mood to wait for me. She knew there was a bucket of feed waiting for her at the house, and she was a cow on a mission. I knew that attached to her bucket of feed would be my mama, so following Bessie became my mission. Bessie was not aware of my plan, so she had no intention of slowing down to accommodate my stubby young legs. As she passed by, I reached out and grabbed the leather collar Daddy had fashioned to hold Bessie's bell and held on for dear life. I soon became aware of exactly how dear my life was.

As I flailed like an unwanted necktie against the cow's neck, Bessie dragged me through briars, into rocks and stumps, and under low-hanging limbs. Those bushes that had only seemed scary were now a real threat. As they slowly flayed my skin away, I began to think how shocked Mama would be to see Bessie coming home with a kid skeleton hanging on to her bell strap.

What blood I had not left on the hackberry bushes in the holler rushed to my heart as I caught the first glimpse of the kerosene lantern Mama was holding as she called Bessie, "Sook, sook!" When I was finally dragged into the yard, I thought Mama would be thrilled beyond words to see my bruised and bloodied carcass. She must have been, because she didn't use any words as she administered a few extra bruises to my butt with a hickory switch.

I have to admit that switch actually felt good. As soon as the licks had been dealt out, Mama held me tight as I cried. I could see tears in the corners of her eyes too. If you had asked her why she whipped me, she would have said it was because I hadn't come when she called me. Any parent knows that what she was really saying with that switch was, "You scared me half to death. You have to feel pain now so that you'll remember this in the future." At that moment, we were both just thanking God that I had a future.

Some childhood pains you get over very quickly. Others you never do. I remember one day back in that holler like it was yesterday. Mama came in one morning and said, "Y'all get dressed. We're going over to Aunt Marth's house." Well, I was jumping for joy. I hadn't seen Aunt Marth in a long, long time. I couldn't wait for her to see how much I had grown, to tell her what I had been doing, and to sing her some of my songs.

The trip to Aunt Marth's didn't seem nearly as long as it had when we moved. Maybe it was because my legs were three years older. Maybe it was because my excitement carried me along. Anyway, we soon got to Aunt Marth's, and I went running up to the steps. I could bound up them two at a time now, and I went flying into the house with the screen door banging behind me. I noticed there were some folks I didn't know in the kitchen, but I wasn't there to meet them. "Aunt Marth!" I called as I ran into the living room.

Just as my foot crossed the threshold, something hit me like a shot. There was a strange feeling in the house. I stopped in my tracks as I saw a coffin in the middle of the room with its lid propped open. I wish I had stopped a little sooner. From where I was I could see that the pale, cold corpse inside was Aunt Marth. I stood frozen. This couldn't be. She was my Aunt Marth. She was my special friend. I needed her. She needed me.

My knees finally thawed, and I turned to run. Just as I did, I was met at the door by some of the boys in the family. When the adults were looking, they acted respectful, but when they had gone, they pushed me up close to the coffin. I didn't want to look, but they held my face up to the edge. They told me they had cut Aunt Marth open and drained out all her blood and replaced it with embalming fluid and stuffed her full of cotton and alcohol.

It was the most horrible description I have ever heard. Of course, that was their intention. They explained that they were going to put her in the ground and that worms would crawl in and out of her body and eye sockets. They kept on until I got sick to my stomach. But that was not the worst of it. Two of them held my hand and made me touch the body. I was too horrified to cry as my hand felt the cold, clammy skin of the person who had been so dear to me. But I more than made up for it later. It had a spirit-shattering effect on me that I have never quite outgrown. To this day I will not go to funerals, and I cannot look at a dead body.

What makes children do such horrible things to other children? I suppose it's mainly ignorance. All they wanted was to make me squirm and cry for the moment. I can't believe they knew what they were really doing and how deep that emotional scar would be for me. That was my first experience with death. I got over the boys' meanness, but the sense of loss I felt that day was one I am still not at peace with, and one that has revisited me at other times in my life.

Back to life as usual in the holler, a form of meanness showed up in me. Some might say that meanness begets meanness, but I'm not sure that's true. I believe you could take a kid and raise him in a vacuum and never show him anything but kindness, and there is still a certain kind of devilment that is going to enter that kid's mind. Of course that theory could never be tested because it would be unkind to raise a kid in a vacuum in the first place. That sort of inevitable meanness must have been what led me to torment the chickens that ran in our yard. The floorboards in our cabin were so far apart, a kid could feed the chickens bits of bread or crackers through the cracks—and one kid did.

That in itself should have been fun enough. But then up steps that youthful meanness that adults make tolerable by calling it mischief. I figured that if the chickens could be lured into pecking up through the cracks, a little girl with quick fingers could grab them by the beaks and hold them above the ground for a few seconds, causing them to thrash about and beat their wings as if they had been set upon by the devil himself.

This plan was successfully carried out enough times to give every chicken in the yard a sore beak and a wisdom about sticking her nose into cracks. I used to tell myself it somehow made them better prepared for the future. It is that same kind of childlike innocence that creates such an excuse for devilment that also chooses to believe a chicken has much of a future in the first place.

Of course if my daddy ever caught me at it, many a sore chicken beak would be avenged on my backside in short order. I don't mean, as some celebrities have, to claim that I was abused. None of us kids were. We were not beaten. We got plain old Tennessee butt whippin's. And in truth, we deserved them.

When one of us had done something wrong, the rest would rather die than tell on the guilty party. I don't know if that was out of loyalty to brothers and sisters or some unspoken code of the mischievous that made us keep silent knowing the same service would be afforded us when we were the one who "done it." Whatever the reason, our failure to cooperate with the party of the second part (the one holding the belt) usually meant we would all end up getting spanked. If we had taken a minute to think about that, we probably would have figured out that the loyalty we were drawing interest on in that unspoken kid bank was not really doing us any good if it was intended to be insurance against getting our butt beaten for some future offense. This way, we were bound to get whipped not only for that future one but for every present one as well. Still, the code was followed, and I supposed there was some kind of integrity in it, if not the clearest of logic.

I would always want to be the last in line. My plan was to run around to be first in line before Daddy got to me, but that never worked. You'd think a man with that many kids would lose count just once in his life. Being in last place, and being a sensitive kid, I ended up feeling every blow to every other kid just as if it had landed on my butt.

Daddy used to spank us with a leather strap. But when Mama whipped us, she would send us out to pick out a switch. We would try a crude form of mountain-urchin psychology by choosing a big, dangerous-looking stick that Mama wouldn't have the heart to hit us with. We'd go out to fetch a switch but come back with a limb that would be better used as a fence post. Our psychology usually backfired when Mama would only get madder and go out herself and pick out one of those reedy little sting-your-butt-bad switches.

2

Animals always were a big part of our lives. It seems like a pointless thing for kids to get attached to something like a chicken that is going to eventually end up on the dinner table, but we did it anyway. We had one favorite chicken, which we named Penny. Human beings all have distinct personalities, and I believe that animals do too. It's harder for us to distinguish them because for the most part their personality traits are subtle. At least they usually are. Not so with Penny. This scraggly-looking red hen could only be described as goofy. If she had been a human being, she definitely would have been institutionalized. If anybody ever dropped anything, she would snatch it up and take off running. She would run with it all day long, and nobody could stop her.

I remember one day when Rachel was a baby. She was sitting in the yard with her bottle, and somehow the nipple came off and fell to the ground. Penny one-hopped it like some kind of feathery shortstop and took off running like a chicken with a nipple in her mouth. Rachel started in squalling like a banshee. Mama said, "Lord, we got to get that nipple back. It's the only one we've got!"

Well, we all took off after that crazy chicken. We chased her around the barn, over hill and holler, but she always stayed a few steps ahead of us. The boys started throwing rocks at her, and we tried various ways of heading her off. But she seemed to be enjoying it. I can't remember how the nipple was ever rescued because I fell on a piece of glass and cut my knee almost to the bone. I still have the scar from chasing that stupid chicken.

I don't remember it myself, but my family swears there was a time when I was caught sucking a sow. I was about three years old, and we had a sow who had fewer pigs than she had nipples. Well, she was lying under a snowball bush with her litter and there was an empty place at dinner, so I fell in with the pigs and got myself a nice, plump teat. I was soon discovered and quickly removed from the sow with considerable embarrassment, more to my mama than to me. I don't know that there's anything to it, but some have suggested that there could be some connection between that incident and the way I developed later in life. If a sow's objective is to fatten up her offspring, then she would have been mighty proud of the way her temporary one turned out. There was a time when I definitely became a hog.

I'm sure that my sucking on the sow was prompted more out of wanting something to do than by any particular craving for hog's milk. We were always trying to find something to do. One thing I enjoyed a lot with my sisters was playing house with moss. There was a kind of thick, green, luxurious moss that grew in the shady places up in the hills. We would take it and cover stumps and pretend they were upholstered chairs and sofas. We would also cover the ground with moss for carpet. Even today, I would be hard-pressed to find carpet that beautiful. I have never ceased to be amazed by nature. Anybody who spends any time at all observing nature has to believe there is a God.

My mother had a way of making little games out of things that might be unpleasant or even frightening to us kids. I will never forget one day at the old house on Locust Ridge. Daddy had gone away for a few days on some kind of trip, and Mama was left way back in those woods with all of those kids to tend to. This particular day the sky began to turn yellow, and it looked stormy. I know Mama was worried, but she wouldn't let us know it.

She gathered us all in the house and said that we'd play a new game. She had us take the couch and some other furniture and turn it upside down and put it up against the wall. The boys especially liked this part of the game because they got to do something they would have gotten their butts beat for under normal conditions. Then Mama said, "Let's all pretend that there's a big storm coming, and let's crawl up under the couch to take cover." Of course this wasn't pretend at all, but she made us feel like it was. And that kept us from getting too scared.

After a while it got a lot easier to pretend there was a storm. The wind blew like mad, and we could hear tree limbs snapping and things blowing by the house. Our house was between two mountains, so tornadoes hardly ever came through our little valley. But this one had managed to touch down in our little holler like some kind of angry giant sticking out a dark black tongue.

Mama knew it was bad. She said, "Now, let's all pray that the storm will pass over us and leave us unharmed." And pray we did. Those of us old enough to know what was really going on prayed like we'd never prayed in our lives.

The noise was horrifying. It sounded like a train was running over our house. After a while the noise stopped and the wind stopped and we went outside to see what had happened. The storm had done a lot of damage. It had uprooted trees and torn up crops and blown down fences, but our little house had been completely skipped over. If praying really did help, I always thought it must have been Mama's prayers that were actually answered. Hers certainly deserved to be.

As glad as we were to be alive, we were sad to find that all of our little animals had been killed, all of our chickens and ducks and things. All of us kids were heartbroken. Sometimes it makes you feel a little better just doing something, so we made a little graveyard and buried them all. If the truth were known, that's probably the real reason behind human funerals too. We had our little animal funeral, and Denver preached. Denver always wanted to do the preaching. I'm sure Mama would have loved it if he had actually become a preacher, but I'm afraid it was just like me sucking the sow—he was just looking for something to do.

Partly because it was something to do and partly out of a sense of adventure, we once undertook to dig to China. I admit to being the instigator. I was always reading. I loved books, and I would read anything I could get my hands on. I had read something about China, and it seemed like the most different and fascinating place I could ever imagine. Of course, even then I had dreams of leaving the Smokies and traveling the world. So any place that wasn't Locust Ridge was exotic to me.

I was going around talking about China, and somebody told me that if you dug far enough, you could come out in China. Well, that was all I needed to hear. I convinced the other kids to help me, and we started digging. We picked a spot up on the mountain. I can't imagine why. You'd think if we were going to dig all the way to China, we would have at least given ourselves the advantage of starting in the lowest holler we could find. Kids gullible enough to try to dig to China in the first place are not likely to think of that. Besides, being up on the mountain made it kind of secret and special.

We started a hole, and we dug at it for months, any time we could get away. We dug with tin cans and knives and forks and just about anything that would move a little bit of dirt. Of course every day I was just convinced we were going to break through to China any minute. One of my brothers insisted that if we did make it to China, we would all be standing on our heads, but the rest of us pooh-poohed that notion. We did, however, have considerable discussion about what the "Chinamens" would be like. What would they think of us? Would they kill us? Of course I was willing to risk being killed to see China. I thought surely if we could dig all the way there, we could deal with a few billion Chinese.

Needless to say, we did not quite reach China. The hole we dug did seem like quite an accomplishment in itself though. We thought it was huge. I went back there as an adult, and the hole was not nearly as impressive as I had remembered it. In fact, someone had put a little gate across the opening and was using it for a doghouse. Maybe if we had started in the holler, who knows?

Even now, looking back on it, I think digging to China, or at least the attempt, was important for us.

The excitement we felt anticipating our destination was real even if the plan was flawed. At least we made the effort. No bunch of kids ever had more fun digging a doghouse.

It doesn't surprise me that someone had the good sense to make our "China" hole into a doghouse. After all, it was there. In those mountains, even today, if something is there, you find a way to use it. I believe that philosophy has made me what I am today. It is not just about survival, but about trying every day, literally every minute, to make things a little bit better. The whole family might work for days to clear trees or move rocks or whatever it took to scratch out enough farmable land to plant one extra row of corn. But from that day on, the Partons would be one row of corn richer. Yes, I said richer, for riches are in the mind and spirit of the one eating the corn. When you think about it, gold has no real value at all. It's too soft to make tools out of, and you can't scrape enough of it together to make a good cooking pot. On a scale of real worth, it can't possibly compare to the gold in a good fat ear of corn that pops when you bite it, or even the gold in the homemade butter you roll the corn in. That is especially true when the dirt and calluses on the hands holding the corn were earned honestly by helping to grow it.

When I think about survival and the things Mama and Daddy did to keep us all alive and reasonably healthy, I am aware that it was not just their wills and wits that kept us going. It was a legacy passed down from every mountain dweller who had ever learned anything about surviving hundreds of years before, starting with the Native Americans. Other than the land itself, this was the most important thing parents had to leave their children, and my parents had learned it well.

There was one day when this passed-along treasure became very important to me, although I did not realize it at the time. Every spring, around May 1, Mama would let us shed the shoes that had held our feet prisoner all winter and run all over the hills barefoot. The word barefoot still conjures up a sense of freedom as I remember the feel of new grass between my toes. We would start out with new, white, tender feet that had been steamed soft by drying snow-damp socks by the fire. By summer's end, we would tramp back into the house with older, wiser feet, brown and tough like shoes with toenails on them, feet that had slapped their way across flat creek stones and dug makeshift ladders up clay banks, feet that scoffed at field stubble and laughed at cockleburs.

But on the day we declared our independence from shoes, Mama would make us go all around the house and yard with a tub and collect all of the broken bottles, can lids, and other hazards that had gone unnoticed under the snow, trodden down by our indestructible brogans and now posing a threat to our new bare spring feet. We had gathered almost a full tub of debris when I noticed some broken glass on the other side of a fence. I climbed the fence, and as I jumped down on the other side, my foot came down on a piece of metal that had been part of a plowshare that was partially buried in the dirt. My foot was severely cut. My toes were dangling, barely hanging on. I thought I would be crippled for life. I might well have been if Mama hadn't known exactly what to do.

In the hills at times like that, especially when a child is threatened, everyone stops what they are doing and joins in the effort until everything possible has been done to help. This took a great effort by several people. I remember a group of men holding me. I know one was Daddy and some were my brothers, but I know that some men from among the neighbors were there too. Why did it take so many strong men to hold a little girl? Because of what Mama had to do.

First, she put kerosene on the cut to fight infection and packed it with cornmeal to stop the bleeding. Then she took the same needle and thread she used for making quilts and sewed my foot back together, without benefit of anesthetic. I screamed and cried and fought mightily, but the men held me still. Mama's hands, the kerosene, and the cornmeal all did their work. I have complete use of my foot today because Mama knew what to do. I have often wondered who first learned those things, over how many generations. What mountain man or woman, long since dead, do I owe for my toes?

It occurred to me that in the future it would make more sense if we collected the trash *before* we took off our shoes. I suppose that was my contribution to the legacy.

I wish I could claim to have added to the legacy with regard to farming, but the truth is I hated to work in the fields. I don't know if it was out of dread of physical work itself or because the work took me away from my songwriting and dreaming, but I would do anything to try to get out of it. I would sometimes pretend to be sick, but Mama would just feel my forehead and look down my throat and send my lying butt to the fields. Sometimes, if I insisted, she would threaten me with castor oil. But I would rather have put up with a few moments of absolute hell than suffer all day long. So, I would agree to take it. Well, that was all Mama needed to hear. If I was willing to take castor oil, I had to be lying about being sick. If I was really sick, I would fight that spoon as if it were the devil himself.

I knew that my older sister, Willadeene, had a problem with nosebleeds. If she got too hot, her nose would bleed, so she got to stay at the house. Of course that didn't mean she didn't have to work. She did a lot of the housework and took care of the younger kids. She was like a second mother to us all.

I figured what worked for Deene could work for me, so I used to try to give myself a nosebleed. A nosebleed would be perfect. It would be graphic and horrifying, all that red blood streaming down my face. It was sure to bring out the "poor child" reaction and get me a one-way ticket back to the house. Once I got back to the house, I could write songs, or sing songs, or sing about songs, and most of all get on with my all-important dreaming. I would go behind a tree where Daddy couldn't see what I was doing, and I would hit myself in the nose as hard as I could. Sometimes I came close. I got to where I could smell blood, but I never quite managed a work-stopping nosebleed.

In the midst of the direst poverty and despair, the human spirit, especially that of children, will find some hope to cling to, some promise of a better day. That had to be what our Uncle Dot Watson, who was married to my mother's sister Estelle, was playing on when he put us up to "growing a pony." We had all kinds of animals on the farm, but we never had a pony. A pony, after all, would eat feed and have to be taken care of and not really contribute anything to the survivability of the family, except for providing the kids with a little fun. We used to dream about having a pony and how wonderful he would be and the freedom he would give us to hop on his back any time we felt like it and traipse across the hills and hollers like wild Indians.

Uncle Dot was living proof that the spirit of mischief that naturally crops up in a kid does not necessarily end with adulthood. He knew we wanted a pony, so he told us that we could grow one. "How, Uncle Dot, how?" Why, by planting pony seeds, of course. A pony seed to anybody else would have been a horse turd, but to a kid who's ready to believe anything with such great promise, it sounds like a simple and workable concept. We set out to find the very best pony seeds. We studied turds for hours, talking about how well shaped that one was or what a good, strong pony this one would make because it had a lot of hay fibers in it. We planted our horse turds and weeded them and watered them religiously. I guess we honestly expected one day to walk out and find a row of fine, healthy ponies. When nothing happened, we would wonder if we had watered them too much or planted them too close to a tree. And all the while Uncle Dot would listen to our questions and give us advice. He always said we should be ready with a rope because the ponies came up really fast once they got started.

Of course we never grew a pony, but we had a fine "herd of turds." The experience didn't really hurt us any, and I guess the adults had a lot of fun at our expense. We had some too, and that was, after all, the idea behind having a pony in the first place.

The whole pony-seed experience reminds me of the story about the little boy who was such an optimist that it got on his brother's nerves. The brother decided to break him of it, so one Christmas he hid the little boy's real present and put a sack of horse manure under the tree instead. On Christmas morning, the brother was surprised to find the little optimist digging excitedly through the sack saying gleefully, "With all this horse shit, there's got to be a pony here somewhere!" I guess we were all optimists and didn't know it. In those hills there are worse things to be.

I can remember always having a desperate need to bring something fine or beautiful, or at least different, into my life. At school there were these colored chalks and crayons. The teacher would write with the chalk on the blackboard, and I used to think to myself, "I could draw on the barn with those and make something really pretty." I also thought that if I could just get those crayons home where nobody could see me and I wasn't embarrassed, I could paint something real nice. That's why I took a box of crayons and two pieces of chalk one day while everyone had gone out for recess. I hid them inside my shirt when nobody was looking. I put them in a hollow tree trunk near the school yard, planning to come back for them after school was out.

A little girl had seen me hide them, and she told on me. I had always been afraid of the teacher. I was born in January, so I started school when I was five. The teacher was a big man, and he used to whip the boys with a razor strop. He would stand at the front of the class and wave that big leather strop around and say, "You be good to me and I'll be good to you!" I guess he was intentionally trying to scare us. It worked. The man looked like a giant from where I was sitting, and I could hear that razor strop slicing through the air just over my head. That was my first experience with school, and it scared me to death.

After school that day, I went to the old hollow tree to get the crayons and found the teacher, glaring at me, razor strop in one hand and my pitiful stolen colors in the other. I closed my eyes and waited for the thick piece of leather to come down on me, but it didn't. I would have preferred being beaten to what happened next. The teacher called all of the other kids together, and they watched as he took hold of my shoulders and shook me. "Do you all see what Dolly has done? She has stolen!" he railed. I was terrified and embarrassed. The teacher made such a big thing out of it. I felt completely worthless and vile.

I got in trouble again when I got home. We had always been taught not to steal (that was one bit of Bible teaching Daddy agreed with Mama on), and I was harshly punished for what I had done. That whole experience gave me a negative feeling toward school that I never really got over.

I can remember some worthwhile experiences associated with school though. When I got to the stage where I was growing out of my tomboy years and starting to take an interest in boys, I had a young, good-looking teacher named Bud Messer. He was the kind that young girls would always have a crush on. I was taken with him because he seemed to be such a fine gentleman, which, aside from Dr. Thomas, was a pretty rare thing in those parts. He tried to teach us manners and social skills.

I remember once going to a pie supper. That was where each girl baked a pie (my mother baked mine) and brought it to a social, where it would be auctioned off to the boy who bid the most for it. The boy who bought your pie had the right to sit with you while the two of you shared it. It was a sweet old country custom, and I guess it was a way of getting around shyness. It was a lot easier for a boy to act like he really wanted a certain pie than it was for him to admit he was interested in the girl who came with it. This was at the time when I had first met my dear friend Judy Ogle, and we went to this pie supper together. My pie was bought by Dewey King. I don't remember how much he paid for it, but I do remember he had to bid against a couple of other boys for it. This was the first indication I can remember that boys were interested in me, and I was touched by that.

Although I'm not quite sure where. Dewey seemed determined to have my pie at any price, and I was impressed by that as well. He had a twin sister, and they both had snow-white hair. He was the prettiest thing you'd ever want to see.

Well, Dewey and I sat down to eat our pie. I guess I was chewing with my mouth open, so Bud Messer came over and sat with us and tried very discreetly to tell me to close my mouth when I ate. "It's nice for the young ladies to chew with their mouths closed," he said. I was a little embarrassed, but I was also proud that I had learned something. I felt so grown up that I could sit there and eat like a lady.

I was anxious to get home so that I could tell the other kids, even the ones older than I was. I felt like it was my duty to help bring them the finer things in life. None of us Partons had ever had any table manners. We would sit at the table and smack our food like a bunch of possums in a mulberry bush. Well, when my chance came, I got a little confused. I had learned that I was not supposed to talk with food in my mouth and that I was supposed to chew with my mouth closed. When I became the teacher rather than the student, it came out as "You're never supposed to chew with food in your mouth." Needless to say, my manners lesson didn't have much of an impact on my family of smacking possums, other than to bring on a healthy round of laughter.

I remember my mother making an attempt to civilize my father. He had been drinking and had come home stewed to the gills and was peeing off the porch. Mama was naturally mad at him and seized this opportunity to chastise him. "Lee, I don't want you peeing off the porch," she scolded. "You're setting a bad example for the children." It was not within the bounds of the man/woman relationship of that time and place for her to criticize the drinking that had caused him to pee off the porch, so she had to confine her complaint to the act itself. The fact that she had brought the children into it was to justify her lack of tolerance and to play off of the regard she knew my daddy had for doing right by his children. I don't know how much of that my daddy thought about before he answered: "Fine, Avie Lee, I won't pee off the porch," and he calmly got down off the porch and began to pee up onto it.

3

Even when a day's work was over for us kids, it wasn't over for Mama. In fact, it never was until she went to bed. I was never quite sure when that was because she was always up and working when I went to sleep. It seemed like she always had a small baby and was pregnant with another one. We used to say she "had one on her and one in her" for all of her young life. People have often said that we put Mama up on a pedestal, to which I always reply, "Shoot, that's the only way we could keep Daddy away from her!"

Mama had a way of sensing which one of us kids needed a little extra attention, which one might be a little down. One way she had of treating this was to make stone soup. She would announce that we were having stone soup for supper and send us all out to pick out a pebble. We would scour the countryside looking for just the right rock, just the right degree of smoothness, the right weight and color. We took it seriously, as if the stones actually had some power to make the soup better. I suppose if that many kids believe a rock can make soup taste better, it can. I always looked for streaks and patterns in my pebble. I would sometimes follow Daddy as he plowed the fields and pick through the fresh, warm dirt for the shiny rocks that would be turned up. I went out every day knowing that some real treasure would come to the surface that would pay the way out of poverty for all of us. That dream did come true in a way, and I have never felt naive for having dreamed it. On these days behind the plow, I would pick out rocks that seemed to have that stone-soup magic feel to them and squirrel them away. So when Mama put out the call, I would usually just head for my stash.

When we had all found a rock and come back to the kitchen, Mama would look at each stone and talk about its merits and how well each child had done in discovering it. Then, without fail, she would choose the rock found by the neediest of us. She would scrub it clean and then put it in the old black kettle as it boiled on the stove. Of course she would put in tomatoes and okra and potatoes and onions and salt pork. She would explain to her wide-eyed brood of rock collectors that these things just added a little extra flavoring to the natural goodness of the stone. I can remember the feeling of having my stone picked to go in the soup. It's a warm feeling, a sense of being needed, and of knowing, or at least believing, that you have had a hand in feeding your whole family for a day. In that sense, there was magic in those stones and a lot of wisdom in that mother.

Mama used to make quilts on a big old quilting frame by the light of a kerosene lamp. All us kids would sit around and watch her and listen while she sang old-timey mountain songs or told Bible stories. I will never forget the sound of her lone voice resounding sweetly off the stones of the fireplace as she sang:

Farther along we'll know all about it
Farther along we'll understand why
Cheer up my brother, live in the sunshine
We'll understand it all by and by

She had ways of making us go to bed and (the more difficult problem) stay in bed. She told us scary stories about "ol' Scratch Eyes" and "Raw Head Bloody Bones." In all my life I have never seen or heard of anything more horrifying than the image I used to have of Raw Head Bloody Bones. Mama would tell us that Raw Head would get little children who didn't go to bed when they were supposed to. Even those among us who were old enough to suspect she might be making all of this up didn't want to risk it. If we were ever slow in getting to bed, all Mama had to do was sneak outside and scratch on the window screen one time and we would all hit the covers like ground squirrels diving into their burrows. It is no wonder so many of us peed in the bed. Who was going to get up to use the slop bucket when Raw Head Bloody Bones might grab you by the ankles the minute your feet hit the floor?

My mother was not the only one who planted scary notions in kids' heads. I can remember hearing some of the old folks talk about "haints" and tell some of the old tales that had been passed down through generations. Maybe parents always had trouble getting their kids to go to bed. Or maybe it was just human nature to create horrifying stories so the real horrors of survival in such a place didn't seem quite as frightening.

Not all of the horrors were imaginary. There were

bobcats in the woods that would sometimes let out blood-curdling screams in the night. I later learned that those screams are quite often a part of the bobcat's lovemaking. Of course, knowing that gave them a completely different kind of fascination for me. Worse than the bobcats were the panthers or, as the mountain folk say, "painters." I don't know how many of them actually exist, especially these days, but there were stories of how they had reached through cracks in the wall and grabbed babies from their cribs. Certainly some of the old houses had cracks in the walls big enough for that. Even the adults seemed to be scared of the "painters." I don't know if any of those baby-snatching stories were true. I do know, from my knowledge of the way things get stretched as they are passed on, that anything anywhere close to a story like that would be enough to give rise to at least a hundred better ones.

Although I was too young to understand a lot of what was going on at the time, I now know that Mama had a lot of health problems, which I'm sure were not made any easier by having a baby every nine months. She and Daddy had other problems too, as all couples do. Sometimes he'd be gone for days at a time. Sometimes Mama would get to telling a story or singing a sad song and she'd start to cry. Then we'd all cry. That's what being a family is all about—sharing good times, misery, boredom, whatever. Those things brought us all closer.

Everybody knew that Mama sewed and made quilts, and they also knew we were poor as Job's turkey. Different people would save scraps of cloth and bring them by the house in boxes or bags. That's how quilting got started—it wasn't so much out of design but as a way to use every scrap.

One fall when the wind began to get that chill to it

and the first wild geese could be heard in the evenings honking their way south, Mama began to make me a coat. A lot of times when she made something out of patchwork, she would try to find scraps that matched as close as possible so that it wouldn't be so obvious. But she knew me and my personality, so she decided to make my coat out of the brightest, most different colors she could find. This was going to be a colorful coat with no apologies.

It's a lot of work to tailor a coat for a child and line it all by hand, even if you cut it all out of one piece of cloth. You can imagine how much work it took to make one out of little pieces. I knew she was making it for me, so I watched her almost the entire time. She told me the story from the Bible about Joseph and the coat of many colors. Joseph's coat was given to him as a sign that he was loved and special, and I felt the same way about mine. I watched how she folded every edge of every little piece under and sewed it with close stitches so that there wouldn't be any ragged seams. When there are so many kids in a family, you can imagine how a mother's time has to be divided up among them. So to see my mother spending this much time to do something just for me was special indeed.

As soon as it started to look anything like a coat, I would beg her to let me put it on, and I would strut in front of the fire in it like some kind of patchwork peacock. I could tell the other kids were getting jealous, probably not so much of the coat as of the attention I was getting from Mama. I started to understand how Joseph's brothers got so jealous of him that they put him down a well and sold him into slavery. Aside from Denver, I don't know if any of the other kids would have actually sold me into slavery, but I could easily be in for a few spiteful pinches or hair pullings. I didn't care. After all, it was me they were being jealous of—me and my beautiful coat. And it was beautiful.

I remember the night Mama finished it. I wore it around the house until she made me take it off and everybody got sick of telling me (with my none-too-subtle prodding) how beautiful it was. That night I almost never got to sleep. It was worse than Christmas Eve. I couldn't wait to wear my coat to school the next day. It wasn't really cold enough for a coat yet, but Mama let me wear it anyway. She could see it was no use trying to dissuade me, so off I went down the path, lickety-split. It's the only time in my life I have ever been anxious to get to school.

I burst through the school doors like a multicolored whirlwind, wondering just how many people I could find to admire my coat. I was so proud of it. I wanted to be seen in it. I wanted to be noticed. "See my new coat?" I said to one boy. "New," he sneered, "it looks like a bunch of rags." My heart sank a little, but he was just one boy. Surely the others would see how wonderful and special my coat was. My heart sank further as other children poked fun at me and my coat. Soon it turned into a whole room full of mocking faces; laughing, pointing, jeering at me . . . me and my coat. I wanted to tell them the story Mama had told about Joseph and make them understand how special, how singular, how beautiful . . . but they would not hear it.

My heart was broken. I couldn't understand the cruelty, the ignorance that made them laugh at me that way. The teacher came in and noticed I was being picked on, so she tried to help. "Don't you want to put your coat in the cloakroom?" she suggested, but I would not. They would not shake my pride in my coat, my love for my mother, my faith in myself. I would not have it. I would sit there and be hot and wait them out. I would wait until school was over and walk proudly from the building wearing my coat like a banner of pride. I would walk with my head high into the autumn afternoon and show my coat to God. He would know how special it was, how special I was. He did. He liked the way it looked with his autumn leaves. He admired the way it complemented his evergreens and the rich brown earth of the path. He watched carefully to catch glimpses of it from his side of the clouds as I marched proudly home. He loved the way it looked on his Dolly Parton.

As painful as it was, that experience at school that day was a great blessing to me. It was what inspired me years later to write the song that has become my signature piece. "Coat of Many Colors" is still my favorite song that I ever wrote or sang. It also was a big hit, and that did a lot to help me forget that early pain. It's amazing how healing money can be.

After the song had become a hit and had done so much for my career, I wanted to go back home and repay Mama for all the love she had sewn into my coat. I said, "Mama, let's go to Knoxville. I'm going to buy you a mink coat." Mama is the type of person who is somewhat uncomfortable about somebody making her an offer like that. At first she came back with a joke: "It's bad enough we have to eat little varmints. I don't want to have to start wearing them." Then she took on a more serious tone as she said, "Shoot! Where would I wear a mink coat, to a pie supper? Give me the money instead." So I did.

The beginning of school was also the time for Daddy to get us all a new pair of shoes to wear throughout the fall and winter. Transportation was a big problem, and Daddy was not about to try to drag all of us into town with him. He usually only went about once every six weeks or so, and it was easier for him to just ride our plow horse by himself. So he would get out his knife and gather up a bunch of straight sticks, and then he would call each of us kids to him one at a time to have our foot measured. He would lay a stick along the length of each little foot and make a mark on it. Then he'd cut the stick and mark it with the name of the kid it had been cut for.

Off he'd go with his pile of sticks, either to town or George Franklin's store, and he'd put the sticks inside the shoes until he found a pair to fit each of us. When we thought it was about time for Daddy to be getting home, we would begin to look for him up the trail. Then finally we would all pretty much gather in the yard waiting to catch the first glimpse of him, eager to find out what kind of shoes we would get.

There was really not much chance we would get anything other than brogans. These were sturdy, high-topped leather shoes that usually had three or four pair of eyes in the bottom part and then several hooks up toward the top. They would take a lot of punishment, which was indeed what was in store for them from our brood, so it was fitting that we have them—although they often weren't quite fitting in terms of size.

Daddy would finally come up the old road toward the house. By now we could barely make out his silhouette in the evening shadows as he and the horse plodded along with the shoes tied together in pairs by their strings and slung over the horse's neck like saddlebags. Of course, we wanted to just start in grabbing, but Daddy would systematically take the stick out of each pair, look at the name on it, and hand that pair to the kid for whom they had been prescribed.

We put them on and laced them up and commenced clomping around the house in a ritual that, fortunately for Mama's nerves and the mice under the old floorboards, only happened once a year.

If anyone's shoes didn't fit, he or she would never tell Daddy. The prospect of having to stretch a pair of shoes a bit or wear extra socks or lace them up real tight seemed preferable to having Daddy take them back to be exchanged on his next trip. We would all rather have ill-fitting shoes than wait six weeks for another pair, so when asked how they fit, we always said, "They jist fit me, Daddy. They jist fit me fine." A kid can deal with blisters on his feet a lot easier than he can learn patience.

If the shoes didn't fit, odds were nine to one that they were too big. That is in part because it's impossible to put a stick into a shoe that's too short for it and in part in keeping with the belief that mountain people had, my daddy among them, that kids should "grow into" things. That philosophy, along with the hated practice of handing clothes down, was the cornerstone of "po' folks" economics. The way those old brogans held up, two or three kids might "grow into" the same pair.

Having the new shoes meant that we could wear them to school with dignity. At least they were new and store-bought rather than old and homemade.

There was one occasion when my embarrassment about being poor caused me trouble. My brother Denver was mean. He's my brother and I love him, and I wish I could say he was "high-strung" or "moody" or make some other excuse, but the fact is he was just plain mean. We were close to each other in age and were always thrown together at school and elsewhere. This proximity caused us to fight like two ill-tempered badgers whose tails had been tied together by a mischievous child, perhaps a mean little boy like Denver.

It should be noted that Denver has softened over the years. We are good friends now, and he even named his daughter Dolly Christina in my honor. Back then, though, the only thing he wanted to honor me with was a black eye.

I have to say on his behalf, though, that he was honest. Denver was in the same room with me in school, and this galled him. By this time we were taking a bus to a public school where there were a lot of kids who were much better-off than we were. On one particular day, in health class, the teacher asked each of us to stand up and tell what we had had for breakfast that morning. As I sat waiting for my turn, I became more and more embarrassed about the fact that all we ever had for breakfast was biscuits and gravy. Other kids were recalling glorious breakfasts of eggs, sausage, bacon, orange juice, and all kinds of things that seemed wonderful and luxurious. I hated my biscuits and gravy. I wanted to gag them up and poverty along with them.

I was not above a creative stretching of the truth to get me out of an uncomfortable situation. When it came my turn, I made up a list from what the other kids had named of all of the things that sounded the most appealing. "Oh, I had eggs and waffles and orange juice and sausage and cornflakes . . ." I went on. Even as I made up my dream breakfast, I could feel Denver's eyes burning holes in my back. I had forgotten he would be next in line. Damn alphabetical order! I knew he wouldn't lie, especially not to save me. "What's he going to do?" I worried, even as I wrapped up my imaginary menu.

I finished detailing a breakfast good enough for three rich kids and then sat down to await my fate at the hands of the hatefully honest Denver. I was going to be showed up as a liar—worse yet, a poor, gravy-biscuit-eating liar.

"And what did you have, Denver?" asked the teacher. I cringed. He stood up quickly and said simply, "I had the same thing she had." This of course was the truth. He had in fact had the same pitiful biscuits and gravy I had.

For a few moments, I allowed myself to think that my brother had actually come to my rescue in a tight spot, but then his fist grinding into my back told me I was living in a dream world. Not only did he beat on me on the way home, he also told Mama and Daddy that I had lied at school, causing me to get a whipping when I got home.

I was often accused of tattling myself. I can say in my own defense (because I am the one writing this book and not Denver, nah nah nah nah nah), that I didn't tell things out of a desire to get others in trouble—at least not most of the time. I usually told out of sheer excitement and my inability to contain anything I found interesting.

Once Mama and Daddy had gone to town and left Willadeene in charge. We looked all over the house for something to get into, and finally discovered that we had cocoa, sugar, butter, and milk—all the makings of chocolate candy. A committee was formed to pester Willadeene into making the candy. It did its job well. After about thirty minutes of "Please, Deene, please," she gave in on the condition that nobody tell Mama and Daddy. Of course we agreed to this. This was one sweet-starved group of young'uns that would have agreed to have some of their less favorite body parts amputated tomorrow for the promise of chocolate candy today. Personally, I never cared that much for my left foot anyway.

I watched every step of the way as my sister made the candy, made twice as delicious by the illegal nature of it. The chocolate smelled so good as it was brought to a boil and then poured onto a plate that eager if none too sanitary fingers had helped to butter. Of course we never really let it set properly. Mama and Daddy would be coming home, but that was just an excuse for the fact that we just couldn't wait. First, the chocolate that remained in the pan had to be spooned and licked up and fought over until no trace remained. Then there was that glorious plate full of goo. It was spooned and fingered and slid off the plate with the aid of the butter into one urchin mouth after another. Willadeene, all the while, was nervous about the whole operation. She knew she would be the one held responsible if our sweet secret was discovered. She carefully washed the pot and the spoons and the other implements of illegal confectionery. She even smelled them for chocolate "giveaways" after they had been dried.

The cleanup had just been finished when Mama and Daddy pulled into the yard. Willadeene surveyed the house for any signs of the candy-making and was in the process of fanning the smell out the back door with her apron when she was shocked to hear me in the front yard. I had rushed to the car as soon as the doors opened and offered loudly in my most confident voice, "Mama, Deene didn't make no chocolate candy." Mama would not have even needed the traces of chocolate in the corners of my mouth to know exactly what had gone on. We were punished, but they couldn't remove the satisfying swell of chocolate candy from our stomachs, and all in all, it was easier than an amputation.

I can remember what a wonderful thing candy was then, or any kind of sweets. I used to think that when

I became a star, I would have candy and cakes and pies any time I felt like it. One need only look at the width of my butt in *The Best Little Whorehouse in Texas* to know that I kept that promise to myself, at least for a while. Wouldn't it be something if we could have things we love in abundance without their losing that special attraction the want of them held for us.

4

From time to time, into our little world
between the mountains would come heaven on
wheels. Green's Rolling Store it was called. Most folks
called it simply "the peddler." It was a rusty old
schoolbus, although there was little of the original
vehicle showing to give it away. But to us it might as
well have been Disneyland. We could hear it coming
for miles. The road to our house was deeply rutted,
and the old bus would creak back and forth, banging
the pots and pans on its sides in a kind of "here comes
candy, ain't it dandy, wish I had a nickel handy"
rhythm.

Once the peddler had pulled into our yard, the
caked-on mud would crack, the doors would open,
and a kid could step inside. Everything in the world
was inside that schoolbus, or at least everything worth
knowing or caring about. Baby Ruths and needles and
thread, Butterfingers and bathtub stoppers, row upon
row of store-bought perfection. Our favorite thing
was a Sugar Daddy because it lasted so long. You

could suck on it and pull it into a point and make the sweetness stay with you until bedtime, even beyond. My mother will attest to this, having found many a kid with one glued to his or her hair with no choice but to cut it out with the scissors.

The peddler would take eggs or even live chickens in trade if you had no money. I can remember the chickens, tied by their feet to the outside of the old bus, looking quizzical but seeming to accept their part in the overall scheme of things. We were not above stealing our own chickens to trade to the peddler for something sweet in our mouths, even if it meant a board across our butts. Like the chickens, we had learned to accept life's trade-offs.

I guess I always had a streak of devilment in me. I think it was more due to curiosity than anything else. The problem was that curiosity included finding out just how far I could go without getting my butt beat.

My grandmother on Daddy's side was an invalid. Grandma Parton, who was always called Bessie, had some kind of inner equilibrium problem that caused even the simplest motions to make her sick. She had somehow acquired this condition during her last childbirth.

She always lay in bed and couldn't stand for people to even get near her because even their movement would make her queasy.

She and Grandpa Parton, who was called Poppy by all of us, lived up in the holler with my Uncle Leonard. He is married now with a house full of kids and grandkids, but at the time he was a bachelor and took Grandma Bessie and Poppy into his house to care for them. I loved him for that. I loved my grandparents, and they loved me. I was the only one of the kids that would spend much time up there. Most of them thought Grandma was just a griping old lady. I was the only one that could sit on her bed without it bothering her. I guess I just knew how to do it.

There were a lot of unpleasant things that Grandma had to have done for her. I guess that's another reason the other kids stayed shy of her. I probably would have too except for that curiosity and my inability to let sleeping grandmas lie. I just couldn't stand to see her just lying there. It seemed like somebody just had to mess with her to remind her she was alive. I took on that job.

She had to use a bedpan, and she would sometimes ask me to empty it. I would take it to the creek and clean it all out like a dutiful grandchild. But then I would hang around the creek and play with it like a white porcelain boat. I would lose myself in this play, and usually, by the time I got back, Grandma Bessie was in a hurry to have her bedpan back. Well, that creek, being a mountain stream, was cold as ice, and I would hand Grandma the bedpan literally frosted over. She would slide it under her and then take in a gasp that you would swear would suck the bedroom curtains in with it. I always pretended I didn't know what was going on, but I guess I knew enough to tell you about it now.

One of my other chores was to brush Grandma's false teeth. She was always so afraid I was going to break them. Teeth were hard to come by in those parts. Grandma had never been to a dentist in her life. The story was that the funeral home kept all of the teeth no longer needed by their "customers," and people who needed them would go down and try on sets until they found one that fit. I don't know if that was true, but I do know Grandma was very protective of her teeth.

I would be careful with them as I took them to the kitchen and scrubbed them good with toothpaste. But then my inner devil Dolly would take over. I'd put those false teeth over my own teeth and try to get them into my mouth. Of course they wouldn't fit all the way and stuck out like some kind of werewolf fangs. I would dance around Grandma's bed like a monster, making growling sounds. She would try to shield her eyes from my bouncy movement as she would shout, "Lord God, young'un, you're gonna break my teeth!" She'd reach out and swipe at me, which just egged me on because I knew she couldn't reach me. I guess that was the closest I had ever seen her to getting up and walking.

My visits with her weren't all devilment. I would clean out from under her fingernails and toenails and brush her hair, because I knew she had a lot of pride. She loved for me to do that. I'd massage her feet and do whatever I could to make her feel better. She used to reward me by letting me play in her big jar of Pond's cold cream. She always had Poppy save all the pretty flour sacks to make my school dresses out of.

Sometimes she'd order things for me out of the Sears, Roebuck catalog. She loved to sit up in her bed and look at the catalog, and she was always ordering something. I loved it when she'd send away for something for me, and I'd spend every day waiting by the mailbox until it came. I still love to shop out of catalogs. I guess I inherited that from my Grandma Bessie.

Those things she bought for me were among the very few store-bought things I ever had as a child. I can remember getting a whipping for drawing names at school. At Christmastime, they put all of the names in a box and everybody would draw one to see who he or she was supposed to give a gift to. Daddy always told us not to draw names, but what was I supposed to do? Everybody else in school drew one.

It was a traumatic thing, though. Even if I could

explain away not being able to buy someone a gift or, worse yet, give the person a really cheap or home-made gift, there was always the possibility that some-body would give me something really nice. This made me feel terrible—guilty, poor, and terrible. The worst thing about poverty is not the actual living of it, but the shame of it.

Still, Christmas was a warm, wonderful time for us. Snow has a way of making even a humble shack look magical and inviting. Christmas will always be certain images to me: the glow of the fire through the win-dows, the crackle of a pine knot burning, even the smoke that seemed to reach out and pull you by the nose into the house. One of my favorite things was to bring some of the snow in to make snow cream. Mama would send the older kids out with a pan and a big spoon to gather up the sparkly white stuff. The younger ones always wanted to take part in this, but it was generally known that their snow gathering would be too haphazard. Snow cream made from yellow snow is not quite the same. The official snow collec-tors would be very careful as to where the future treat came from. The purest snow could be skimmed from the powdery buildup on top of the woodpile or raked off the tin roof of the little springhouse.

The pristine crystals were brought inside, with much ballyhoo and fanfare, and the mixing process would begin. I always loved to be the one to stir the snow cream with the big wooden spoon as the deli-cious ingredients were added. In fact, there are some who claim I used to hide the spoon to make sure nobody else got that job. I will neither confirm nor deny that until I've had a chance to talk to my lawyer. The sugar and vanilla and milk would be stirred in, and there it was: snow cream, the closest thing we usually had to ice cream, but still better in its own way. Sometimes there would be hot pie or cobbler to spoon it onto, but the snow cream was wonderful all by itself.

I remember going with Daddy to get the Christmas tree. We used to fight over who'd get to carry the axe as we followed Daddy over hill and dale, looking for just the right tree. There were a lot of cedar trees that would be suitable, but it seems they only grew in certain places. It would have been much easier for us if there had been only one or two. Everybody had a favorite and would lobby Daddy to consider the finer points of that particular tree. In the end it was always Daddy who finally said, "This one." I would try to help drag the tree back to the house but was usually brushed aside by the bigger boys.

Once the tree was inside, we would sometimes find surprises like a bird's nest or the intricate mud houses built on some of the twigs by last summer's dirt daubers. These dirt houses didn't seem very Christmassy and would be broken away after being studied, but the bird's nest could stay. Maybe somebody would make some little eggs out of foil or dough, and it would become part of the decoration. All of the decorations were handmade. When it came time to string popcorn, Mama would give us one of her precious needles with the plea, "Y'all please keep up with my needle and don't poke anybody's eye out." With the popcorn that got eaten and stepped on, making these strings long enough to go around the tree could occupy a kid for quite some time.

My favorites were the gingerbread men Mama would make to go on the tree. We all knew they were delicious, but somehow there was some kind of unspoken truce that allowed them to hang in peace . . . at least until Christmas Day when the tree would more likely be decorated with gingerbread heads.

Christmas Eve there was always singing. Mama did most of it, but we all loved to sing along. She would always tell the Christmas story, and then Daddy would take us to the barn to see the animals kneel. The legend was that at the stroke of midnight, farm animals all over the world would kneel in honor of the newborn Jesus. Somehow we would always fall asleep before this happened. I suspect it was, at least in part, a way to get us to be still long enough to get sleepy, but it was a fine tradition anyway. Luckily there was something to get us to go to sleep. Otherwise, our excitement might have kept us up forever.

Dawn would break Christmas morning, and we kids would bolt out of bed like a covey of quail flushed by a double-barreled wake-up call. The race was on to grab your stocking and see what was in it. This was the one day, the one hour of the year when we experienced plenty. A Christmas stocking is a marvelous thing. You leave an empty, limp sock hanging there at night and then wake up to find it fat with promise, nearly bursting at the seams with rare and precious goodies. Here was a lesson in hope, faith, and fulfillment you could actually hold in your hands. It would have been easy to simply dump the contents onto the hearth and instantly wallow in the bounty of it all, but it was much more fun to feel. "This is an orange! This is a peppermint stick! I got chocolate drops!" went the excited squeals as the stocking fondling went on.

Somehow Mama and Daddy always managed for each of us to get one store-bought gift. Regardless of what it was, it was a thing of wonder to be revered, looked at with slow eyes, felt with tender hands, and relished for its newness. Best of all was that "it's really mine" feeling that could carry you around on a cloud for days, or until it was replaced by that "it's really broken" feeling.

The boys' gifts usually included fireworks, and they'd be outside announcing that fact to the world as soon as a match was found. For today, tin cans would become space capsules, finger-formed dams would be blown, and many a German matchbox would no longer threaten Allied troops. There was always somebody who protested that fireworks should not be a part of Christmas. Perhaps they were meant for New Year's, but nobody really expected them to last that long. In a way, though, they were the perfect salute to Christmas. They made a joyful noise, they spoke with a loud, sure voice. They were here for one soul-stirring burst of excitement and then they were gone, leaving only the glorious anticipation of next year.

We girls usually got a little pink plastic doll with its own white cloth diaper held in place by a tiny gold safety pin. That may sound really cheap, and I'm sure it was. But for us, just the fact that it was plastic made it different from the ordinary things we saw in the holler. There was no way this could have been home-made. Unless your home happened to be a sweatshop in Taiwan.

Those little plastic dolls instantly became the focus of whatever motherly instincts the Parton girls had. Of course we all had one, and they basically all looked alike. If you looked closely though, and of course we did, you could see little imperfections in the plastic that identified each doll. We "mothers" would get to know our dolls intimately. Inevitably, some-body's would get lost or eaten by a cow or thrown down a well by an ill-tempered brother; sometimes there would be a "baby snatching."

A fight would usually follow, consisting more of

accusations and name-calling than anything else. "That's my doll," the rightful mother would cry. "See, it's got two little extra globs of plastic on its left ear." On a good day, though, each mother would care for her own plastic treasure, and all would be well with the world. We would scavenge to find things to serve as a crib and bedclothes. The more industrious ones would even fashion clothes for the doll. I always liked mine just the way it arrived Christmas morning, in its special cloth diaper with the shiny gold pin.

Mama and Daddy had their own special way of sharing Christmas. At a time when they could afford nothing else, Mama had given Daddy a box of chocolate-covered cherries and a package of handkerchiefs. Every Christmas since then, she has given him those same two gifts. It has very special symbolism for them and helps them to appreciate much more fully the things they have now. At the time, all of that was lost on us kids. We were primarily interested in Daddy's chocolate cherries and whether or not he would share them. He always did.

My most memorable Christmas was the one for which I personally received the least. When Mama and Daddy married, he was only seventeen and she was fifteen and they were both poor. Daddy had never been able to give Mama a wedding ring. One Christmas he gathered us all together and explained to those of us that were old enough to understand that there wouldn't be the usual store-bought gifts we had come to expect. This year all of the money had gone to buy Mama a ring. There was instead one gift for the person who could find the ring where Daddy had hidden it. This set off a frenzy of searching. Every place that could accommodate a ring was looked into. Of course, all of this was accompanied by wild guesses as to what the one gift might be and confident proclamations of what each searcher would do with the gift once he or she had won it.

Finally, the ring was found. By this time, we had electricity so that now a string of garish bubble lights added to our tree decorations and our unending fascination. Someone found the ring, placed around one of those bubbling glass tubes, and rushed it to Mama. Everybody shared Daddy's pride as she slipped it on her finger and a chorus of very genuine "oohs" and "ahhs" went up. The "one gift," as it turned out, was a big box of chocolates that we could all share. That is Daddy's way. Those chocolates were so sweet they could make your teeth hurt, and so are the memories of that Christmas.

I never think about Christmas and candy without remembering how Denver would instantly take whatever candy he had and lick every piece. This was to insure that no one else ate it. He apparently didn't mind his own spit, but to the rest of us, it might as well have been cyanide. It seemed like there was always one person, usually Stella, who would hoard a piece of candy or two until everybody else had crunched theirs into oblivion. Then the held-back candy would be slowly and painfully licked in front of the candyless green-eyed horde with a gleeful kind of one-upmanship that is peculiar to brothers and sisters. This would always lead to blows and bring on some form of justice from Mama or Daddy always involving some kind of speech about the "true spirit of Christmas."

Denver needed no special occasion to harass and needle me. He was always beating the tar out of me, and I couldn't do much about it because he was older and stronger than I was. This was the first evidence of a sort of male chauvinism mountain boys don't necessarily grow out of, although they do tend to subdue it somewhat after two or three divorces. In response to this, I had begun a sort of early Appalachian feminist guerrilla movement. My tactics were simple—to strike by surprise and then run like hell. I was good at holding a grudge. Sometimes I would wait until hours or even days after Denver had beat me up and had forgotten all about it. Then I would strike with the swiftness and severity of a red-tailed hawk. I could sometimes get in a really good lick that would stun him long enough for me to haul ass.

One time, Daddy had just replaced the screen on the back door and Mama had taken this as a cue to spray the house for flies. She didn't want new flies or kids coming in during this, so she had locked the screen door. I was in my silently seething grudge mode with Denver. I saw an opportunity to give him a good, hard shot from across the back of the couch and then beat a quick retreat, using the couch as an extra obstacle in my favor. I seized the moment.

I caught him with a hard right that felt really good. It must have hurt him because it was hard enough to hurt my own hand. That was a good hurt, and I relished it as I ran for the back door. I hit the door expecting it to fly open, but it was locked. That new screen Daddy had put in was stretched as tight as a banjo head, and it knocked me backward, landing me on my butt on the kitchen floor. I cried, hoping Denver would take pity on me, but there was none in him. Talk about beating a dead horse: He gave me a beating twice as bad as the one that had inspired my sneak attack. I took the blows, but I still had that sting in my right hand that told me I had struck at least one blow for womanhood.

Womanhood was a difficult thing to get a grip on in those hills, unless you were a man. My sisters and I used to cling desperately to anything halfway feminine. For a long time I was a tomboy, but once I got a better idea of what it meant to be a woman, I wanted it with everything in me. We used to love when our aunts would come to visit. They had been out of the mountains, even to other states, and they knew so much. We thought they were incredibly sophisticated and worldly. Best of all, they had purses filled with lipstick and powder and eyeliner and all kinds of things we had no access to. This was the real ammunition in the battle of the sexes. They would sometimes let us explore these bags of ammo, and we would do so with all of the awe you would expect from art lovers touring a museum.

Even if we had been able to get those things for ourselves, Daddy would not have let us use them. He did not believe girls should wear makeup—at least not *his* girls. He thought it would make us look trashy and get us into trouble.

Maybe his trying to keep cosmetics and things from us had something to do with the intensity with which we wanted them, especially Stella and I. Maybe that has something to do with the fact that as soon as we got away from home, we practically made a career out of makeup and the other trappings of what we considered to be femininity. To paraphrase the Bible, "Bring up a child in the way you think he should go, and when he is old he will make you pay for it the rest of your life." Many a bellman struggling under the weight of my makeup bags has had to pay as well.

Still, our aim was not to consciously rebel against Daddy. We wanted those things because we felt they were a vital part of our personalities. We could see the pictures of the models in the newspapers that lined the walls of our house and the occasional glimpse we would get at a magazine. We wanted to look like them. They didn't look at all like they had to work in the fields. They didn't look like they had to take a spit bath in a dishpan. They didn't look as if men and boys could just put their hands on them any time they felt like it, and with any degree of roughness they chose. The way they looked, if a man wanted to touch them, he'd better be damned nice to them. Most of all, they looked like a man would want to—very much.

I had very carefully avoided letting the mountain philosophy of hard work become a part of the fabric of my being. I had, however, retained some of what I had learned about "making do." Once I had seen the actual materials in the purse museum, I could figure out how to improvise.

Lipstick was the most fascinating thing to me because it was red and got the most attention. Also, it went on the mouth, which I figured was about the sexiest part of a woman that was all right to show in public. For this, I used Merthiolate. Mama always kept a supply of it around to put on our cuts so that it would look stupid and burn like forty hells. If your lips were dry and chapped, and mine often were, it could sting like fire when you put it on. It wasn't exactly red, a little too orangey, and was truly capable of making us look trashy and bearing out Daddy's worst nightmares.

If we were lucky, we would have Mercurochrome. It was a truer red and didn't burn so much. The one thing they both had in common was their ability to stain the lips so that the color would last for several days. This meant that Daddy was bound to notice. "Where did you get lipstick?" he would demand through gritted teeth. "It's not lipstick, Daddy. It's my natural coloring," was always the plea delivered in spurts between frustrated wipes with a coarse wash-cloth. The first part of this was of course true and could, in a kid's mind, create a gateway of honesty through which the rest of the statement could slip without a hint of the remorse usually connected to a lie like some kind of illegitimate Siamese twin. The kind of spit-in-your-eye boldness this gives a kid's words only tends to make the adult more determined to exact penance—or at least scrub off the vile colors of rebellion, even if it means taking some of the lips off with it. The phrase "I'll wipe that smile off your face" never was taken so literally.

Next came face powder, or at least my substitute for it—flour. I didn't have anything to even approximate base makeup, so I figured the flour would help hide my freckles. I hated my freckles even before my brothers figured that out and used it to torment me unmercifully. My "powder" also helped to hide the dirt. I wanted to be feminine, but apparently not at the price of having to actually break down and wash my face. That would have seemed like an act of treason against all of kiddom.

Mama didn't relish the idea of our wearing makeup either, but I think it had more to do with the fact that it showed we were growing up and would be leaving the nest. That could have been what secretly motivated Daddy as well, but he was not the kind of man to let such a feeling show. Mama would make fun of my putting flour on my face. "What are you gonna do when you get hot and sweaty, break out in biscuits?" she would say with that "you're being silly, but you're mine and I love you" kind of look on her face.

After considerable experimentation, I found that the most reasonable facsimile I could find for eye makeup was to burn kitchen matches, lick the blackened ends, and apply the black paste to my eyebrows and lashes. My impatience to become a woman sometimes caused me to get a burned tongue. It took several matches to do each eye, and I have never been one who found it easy to wait for anything.

Finally, I would use the juice of pokeberries for rouge and sometimes to color my lips. It stained almost as badly as Merthiolate, and I went through several days of looking like a clown (and being told that in no uncertain terms by my brothers) before I learned the subtleties of pokeberry rouge. When the pokeberries weren't in season, the pain I endured for the sake of beauty was of a shorter duration, but more intense. I would simply pinch the devil out of my cheeks until they took on a red blush. This could give a more satisfactory look than the tricky pokeberries, but the effect wore off and my "rouge of pain" had to be reapplied on a regular basis.

The quest for beauty has always been a struggle for me. I can't remember anybody ever saying that I was one of the more beautiful children they had ever seen. I was a pale, skinny little thing with corn teeth and hair that was fine and close to my head. And then there were those hated freckles. You could not have said that I was "as cute as a speckled pup" without expecting the speckled pup to piss on your leg out of resentment.

My sisters all had beautiful hair and would get home permanents. Their hair would turn out wonderfully coiffed in that sort of white-trash, pose-for-a-picture-with-your-prom-date kind of way, but mine would just get frizzy. Leaving the solution on longer was not the solution. No matter what I tried it only made things worse. It was bad enough that I had doubts about my looks without that fear being reinforced. Of course I could always depend on my brothers to tell me how bad I looked, but in my mind I could write that off as meanness.

I sometimes even wondered if I was indeed my parents' child, since my sisters all looked so good. However, since it would require some hanky-panky

on my mother's part for it to be otherwise, I have no
real doubts. Even if she had the inclination, she never
had the opportunity. The old adage about keeping
your wife "at home, barefoot and pregnant" was
never carried out more conscientiously, although I
suppose my mother did wear shoes on most occasions.
Those old seeds of doubt about my looks have grown
into quite a bumper crop for many a makeup artist,
wig maker, and plastic surgeon.

Even if I was sure of my parentage, I still felt like I
didn't belong. I was just different and I knew it. A
person might think that a kid growing up with that
many others would never be lonely, but I often was.
Some kids make up imaginary friends, and I had my
own version of that. I called them my angels. I would
talk to my angels all the time. I felt safer because they
were with me. They understood why I had to sing,
why I had such dreams, why I wanted to climb aboard
a butterfly and wing my way out of the holler and
into a world that I knew lay beyond what I could see.

As the firstborn crop of kids got old enough to
have some responsibility, Mama would assign each of
us a little one in the next wave to help care for. This
helped to make us feel closer as a family. And I'm sure
it gave her just the slightest bit of relief from her burdens, which otherwise could have been overwhelming.
I was so excited when she told me that the baby she
was carrying was going to be "my baby." I had seen
how Willadeene had taken her duty seriously. She
held her designated baby, gave it its bottle, and
changed it. She really took care of "her baby." I was,
in this one respect, ready to grow up.

Mama got very sick. She had spinal meningitis and
took to her bed with a burning fever. Dr. Thomas was
sent for, and he had Mama taken to the hospital. This
scared us all because we knew the illness had to be

really serious for a Parton to go to the hospital. Mama's fever got so high that she had to be packed in ice. In spite of all the doctors did, she slipped into a coma. A great effort was made to hide the truth from us kids, but the doctor told a few relatives that there was no way Mama would live. Worse yet, if she were to live, the fever had been so high that she would no doubt suffer such brain damage that she would be no more than a vegetable.

I don't know how much of this Daddy knew. I know it was enough to give his face an ashen look I had never seen before or since. He was terrified at the thought of losing his Avie Lee. I know he really loved her. Whatever wrong he had ever done her he looked at as a weakness in himself rather than anything against her. How those weaknesses must have haunted him during those hours. Dr. Thomas says he left the hospital that night certain that my mother would not live until morning. But Mama's friends and relatives, and indeed her own cast-iron will, would simply not accept that.

People sat up and prayed for Mama all through the night. I remember Grandma Rena was among them. She clutched her Bible to her heart as she said, "Whatsoever ye shall ask in prayer, believing, ye shall receive." There must have been some powerful faith at work in that place. In the morning, my mother lifted her head from her pillow and asked for water. She had survived. She had lost her hearing in one ear, but she was alive and her mind was intact. The doctors had no medical explanation for what had happened. Dr. Thomas, who was also a Methodist minister, had no difficulty in declaring it "a miracle, an honest-to-God miracle." Mama's name is still in medical books, relating the incident of the woman who overcame what had previously been thought to be an unsurvivable fever.

When Mama was able to talk, she gave an amazing account of her near-death experience. Remember, this was many years ago, before that kind of thing became commonplace. Daddy and the others listened in awe as she told of going through a long tunnel, moving toward the brilliantly glowing white light at the end of it. Mama said she saw her family and friends all there waiting for her. But she heard us kids calling her back . . . calling her back to life. Well, we kids always did scream louder than anybody. I'm glad we won.

Our mother was very weak for a long time and was slow in recovering completely. I think this was in part because of the physical hardship her body had endured and in part because of something she knew. Mama had premonitions—"visions," she called them. They could be startlingly accurate. One night, years later, she sat up in her bed and said to Daddy, "Lee, get your clothes on. Denver's had a wreck at the Cove bridge." By this time, Daddy knew not to take Mama's sixth sense lightly, so he drove her to the bridge. There was Denver's wrecked car with the wheels still spinning. Denver had broken his neck and would not have survived if he had not been found early. In that remote area, he could easily have lain there all night. I don't know what gave Mama the power she had, unless it was that her care for her children was so intense that it could reach beyond the boundaries of time and distance.

I think it was care for me that made Mama so upset at what she "knew" about the baby she was carrying. She told Daddy that my unborn brother, Larry, would not live. He had been made "my baby," and she knew it would be harder for me than anyone else. Mama went into labor on July 4, and Larry was born on the fifth. The angels that had spared Mama called little Larry to be with them.

When Daddy came home and told us, I was inconsolable. I remember somebody saying, "Your baby is dead." I remembered when they had also said, "Your Aunt Marth is dead." I guess I was angry at God. Why was my baby dead? Why did everything that was mine have to die? I couldn't eat. I couldn't sleep. For the first time in my life, I couldn't sing. I wouldn't leave Larry's grave. I would take a lantern up on the hill and sit there most of the night talking to him and crying.

Finally I came to some understanding. We had a picture of little Larry in his coffin. My family has kept it, and we have always considered him a part of the family. I remember looking at that picture and knowing that the body I was looking at was not my little brother. I remember an old song called "That's Not the Grandpa I Know" that is about that same thing. I came to think of his spirit as something apart from his body, something not bound to that grave that I kept mourning over but set free to live a perfect existence in heaven. Finally, I got the feeling that Larry wanted me to shut up and let him get some sleep. "Get off my grave and get some sleep yourself," I thought he was telling me. I took his advice.

In my childlike way, I came to understand that death is only frightening to those of us left behind. I made peace with that idea, and with God, and I went on with my life. I sang again, now with a voice made richer for having known loss.

I have often been asked if the story of "Applejack" is true. Essentially it is. I took some poetic license with the song, which is my right, but the basic facts are there. There was this old man who lived all alone in what could only be called a shack by the side of the road. He had a name, but folks called him Sawdust because he kept sawdust on the floor of his shack. I don't know if he chose to be alone or was just left alone because nobody wanted anything to do with him. I have to admit he did smell awful. You could be driving in a car and pass him on the road and smell him—with the windows up. Maybe for him that was a kind of people repellant. If it was, it worked.

People tend to fear what they do not know, and what they fear they dislike. All kinds of rumors circulated over the hills about the old man. He had a bunch of old, mangy dogs, and some said he had sex with them. While there was no doubt he slept with them, it is not likely the relationship was actually consummated. More likely, he was a hunter. He would almost have to be to have enough to eat. He didn't farm much, and he never went to town.

There was one time when he sent away for a mail-order bride. I suppose that in itself shows that he didn't really want to be alone. If only he had sent away for a case of soap at the same time. Anyway, after a while this woman came to live with him. She was large and unsightly, but I can still imagine the shock she was in store for. The woman had a grown daughter, and right away rumors started to fly that the old man "did them both."

It seems like they stayed for about eight or nine months, and then they disappeared. Naturally, the rumor mill kicked into high gear. Of course the old man had killed them. The only disagreement among the rumormongers was as to whether or not he had fed them to the dogs or eaten them himself. This is actually not too far removed from the stories of "Raw Head Bloody Bones" and other mountain tales of horror. People will create monsters. I suppose if everybody in the world looked exactly alike except for one person who had brown eyes instead of blue, that brown-eyed man would be the devil incarnate. Most likely, he put his mail-order bride back in the mailbox along with her daughter.

There were times when I had to walk by Sawdust's house, to get to church or to visit relatives. I had heard all of the stories, and at first I avoided him like everybody else. He could be frightening-looking. His long hair and beard were matted, and his teeth were not pretty—either one of them. Then, one day as I made my way down the hill, I heard some pretty good banjo picking. As I stepped past a grove of trees and into the clearing, I could see that the music was being played by old Sawdust himself. Suddenly, the old man looked completely different to me. I believe there is a bond that unites all musicians, and somehow I felt an instant kinship with this unlikely person. The face could have uglied a squirrel to death at forty paces, but the foot was stomping out a rhythm, and that was good enough for me.

Every day after that, I would stop to listen and watch him play. Naturally, I would start in singing. He would break into something I knew, like "Shady Grove," and I would sing and clap or beat out the rhythm on the porch rail. I was having a grand time, and Sawdust loved it too. More and more he would be out on the porch when he knew it was time for me to come by. Of course, I was always hoping to be upwind of him, but the stories he told fascinated me so much I would have stood the smell anyway. He had been in the war, but more important to me, he had been places. He had been on ships and crossed oceans and seen foreign countries. He taught me songs and chords on the banjo, and he taught me it was all right to be different.

5

All my life, at least from the time I have been able to grasp more of life than my own toes in my crib, I have been driven by three things; three mysteries I wanted to know more about; three passions. They are God, music, and sex. I would like to say that I have listed them in the order of their importance to me, but their pecking order is subject to change without warning. In my heart of hearts, I always know that God comes first. But in my body of bodies, some other urges can be absolutely irresistible. For the moment, since I am writing and am therefore primarily a spiritual being, I will try to deal with them in their rightful order.

Like everything else in my life, I found God in my own unique way. Lord knows there were those who tried to find him for me. From the time I was born I was carried, led, pushed, or dragged into church every time the doors opened. I felt a need for God and always wanted to have a relationship with him, but I was the ultimate nightmare for a fundamentalist

Christian out to save souls. I was a kid with her own opinions.

My Grandpa Owens was a preacher, and my mother was a devoutly religious woman. I could see that the way they worshiped God worked—for them. They were good people and lived their lives the way I thought a person should. So I had no problem with wanting to be like them in that way. I guess what I resisted was the way God was presented. I can remember seeing the pictures in the Sunday-school pamphlets that showed him as a big old scary thing. He might be a frightening old codger with long hair and a beard, blowing the winds out of his cheeks, or the vengeful God with a fiery look in his eyes, shooting lightning bolts from his fingers to strike down us sinners. If you're a kid who is naturally afraid of old men and lightning, is this somebody you'd really want to know?

Now, of course, I can see that this was no accident, for fear was indeed the tool often used by the well-meaning soul savers to bring those less opinionated to redemption. It was effective, even on me. A good preacher could work up a sweat delivering the standard fire-and-brimstone sermon. With his voice reverberating through the rafters of one of those old country churches, it would send chills up your spine.

"Are you prepared to meet God? You could be killed on the way home today. Are you ready to be judged?" I guessed I had damned well better be ready to be judged, because it was obvious I was going to be every day of my life. To me, it seemed like a lot of people took the Bible too literally. But at the same time they were selective in which parts they clung to with such conviction. It seemed to me like the part about "judge not, lest you be judged" got kind of swept under the rug.

I also felt that they had misinterpreted the words "God-fearing." Maybe this was because the Bible had been translated from Hebrew. Maybe it was because many of the people passing on the word of God couldn't read or write. They were limited by what they were told was truth by other illiterate people, who had been told it by others, and so on. I can remember one very fat woman in the church. She had lost some weight, and people couldn't help but comment on it. "Yeah, I been fastin'," she said, "just like Jesus, I fasted for forty days. Of course, I eat at *night*." I supposed she'd get those familiar fasting headaches, take two ham biscuits, and go to bed. Her fasting for forty *days* is an example of how literally some people took the Bible.

I remember one particular case of this that had me confounded for the longest time. There is a Bible verse that reads, "Whosoever shall call his brother a fool is in danger of hellfire." This was taken very literally. That meant that I could call any of my sisters a fool with complete immunity, but if I should even accidentally call one of my brothers a fool, I would burn in hell. This was quite a scary proposition, because I had a lot of brothers and any one of them at any given moment could act like a fool. Now, I never called anybody a fool that didn't deserve it. By the same token, if someone did deserve to be called a fool, I felt it was my duty to do so. This kept me constantly walking on the brink of the fiery pits of hell.

There was also a great catchall commandment that could make just about anything a sin: "Honor thy father and thy mother." Anything you did or said that went against what your father or mother wanted you to do or say could be construed as dishonoring them, and therefore a sin. This was the one situation when I used to turn the literal translation of the Bible around to work for me. "It says honor," I would say, "not obey." This of course did not keep me from getting my butt beat, but it did allow me to sniff back my tears with a healthy sense of righteousness.

Looking back, I truly believe that what I have done with my life has brought honor to my father and mother. And I feel I have done right by both them and God in that respect. I now also believe that "God-fearing" actually means "God-respecting." But at the time the fear was real.

I can remember sitting in church and listening to what a worthless sinner I was, and feeling so ashamed without giving much thought to what I had to be so ashamed of. What has a six-year-old kid done that justifies being burned in hellfire? Any time I asked questions like that I was always told I was too young to understand. It seemed to me that should work both ways. I should also be too young to be punished for something I didn't understand. Then I was told that just the fact that I was questioning things was a sin in itself—blasphemy. There's a good way to explain something to an inquisitive kid. Give them a word they can't possibly understand, one that sounds like "blasting" something . . . or, worse yet, like something you might accidentally do with some body part without knowing it.

In searching my soul for the terrible sins I had committed, it was the area of body parts that seemed to be the most likely key to my deserving to be burned in hell. Well, here comes sex ahead of schedule. I guess as honorable as my intentions might be, it is going to be impossible to write about my three passions without mixing them together in the same way they overlap and intertwine within me. Nature, which is God, is going to have its way.

As a kid, you might have told a lie or two or maybe

taken some small thing that wasn't yours, but these don't seem to be capital offenses. So, it must be sex that condemns you to hell. Not that you've had sex or anything close to it, but somehow just being aware that it exists feels like a grievous sin in itself. The fact that you might have actually thought about doing something, or touched your brother during a community bath or yourself in your bed at night must be your "great sin."

The sex drive being as difficult to resist as it is, and having been so branded as evil, can give a thinking child a sense of helplessness. "I'm being driven steadily toward hell by a force beyond my control." So you try not to even think about it. That, of course, is like the old problem of trying to count to ten without thinking of a banana. Of course, under those circumstances, you can think of nothing but bananas. Every boy in those hills had a banana.

I was always aware of boys at church. The custom for many of the men was to take the women and children to church and then stand outside under the trees and drink while the weaker ones got the religion they needed. After all, they were men and needed nothing but their own wits and muscles.

Of course, it was also customary for each man to get converted from time to time and go through an intense but usually brief period of crying and begging the Lord, and most likely his wife, for forgiveness. I guess it wasn't unmasculine for the men to get their religion in these short, intense doses. I suppose also that most of the women had relationships with God that were more constant and committed, much like their relationships with their spouses.

Among the most prominent under-the-tree drinkers were a pair of characters named Red and Clarence. They were two of the biggest drinking carousers around, but when the spirit hit them, they could get very religious. Once Red had decided he had received the "gift of tongues," a common practice in our Pentacostal church. He went to church a few times and would, on impulse, stand up and go into seemingly meaningless strings of syllables, to which the believers would respond with "Bless him, Lord." The story is that one day Red and Clarence were downtown in a truck belonging to one of them, and Red looked out the window and was reading a sign, somewhat haltingly. "E-CON-O-MY-AU-TO-SUP-PLY, Economy Auto Supply," Red sputtered, to which Clarence, assuming his friend had gone into "tongues," quickly came back with, "Bless him, Lord."

That story circulated through the ranks of the church membership and was the source of great laughter for a time around the Parton household. It became something of a running joke that would crop up whenever anybody said anything that could be mistaken for "tongues." Sunday morning, getting ready for church, a brother would say, "Come tie my bow tie," and some smart-aleck sibling would shout, "Bless him, Lord," and the rest of us would join in, all pretending to be caught up in the spirit.

Young boys were dragged to church the same way I was. But since they were destined to become men, they were given more leeway. I suppose when they started growing pubic hair they were allowed to wander out of church before the service was over to take their places outside, as if training to be men. Much of their training apparently involved staring back into the church at us girls.

It was the custom after church for the boys and girls to do some limited socializing, flirting, and so on, while the women gossiped and the men smoked and spit. This flirtation, however, was limited by the distance the boy could get the girl to walk into the woods, the couple's ability to escape the gaze of the adults, and the girl's own boundaries.

So there I sat, trying to be holy, praying for forgiveness for sins I couldn't put my finger on, repenting for things I had put my finger on, and all the while being aware of the boys looking at me, the woods behind the church, and the possible combinations of all of these things. The devil and I certainly had one thing in common: We were both horny.

I often went down the aisle when the choir sang and the preacher made his final frightening plea. I would get down there and pray, but I never felt like I had really found God and didn't want to publicly make a commitment until I had. I used to watch the others in the church, especially some of the women, who would get worked up into an almost trancelike state and raise their hands and shout at various times during the sermon. They seemed genuinely in tune with God in their way, and I wanted to know what it was they felt.

There was one man who struck me as being very different. At the time, we were going to an old church with a high ceiling and exposed rafters. Sound would resonate from the old seasoned wood in a haunting way. The man's name was Curt Dockery. At times during a service he would stand up and sing. He would just feel led to sing and get up, no matter what was going on at the moment. Everyone knew to expect it, and they would stop whatever they were doing and listen, because the man's voice was strong and rich and sincere. He would get a certain look in his eyes, then rise and let out with "I am a poor wayfaring stranger." There was a real reverence in his voice. I could tell he was singing directly to God. Of all the people I knew, he seemed to have really made contact.

I truly wanted to receive salvation, and I prayed long and hard for it. For some reason, though, I didn't want the boys looking at me while I prayed. In fact, I didn't want anybody looking at me. It was too personal a thing for me to do in public. That is why I prayed on my own, in private places.

I finally found one place that became very special to me. It was an old abandoned church. It had been "the chapel" in Caton's Chapel, the little community we lived in. Most of its windows were broken, and its old floorboards were buckled and dusty, but to me it seemed like God still lived there. Ironically it had become a place for all types of sin and vice. Boys would meet there to shoot craps or drink beer and moonshine. Couples would use it at night for sexual encounters. Boys and men fought there. There had been more than one stabbing. And yet, for me, God still lived there.

I would often play in the space under the floor of the old chapel. I can still smell that soft, cool dirt. There were the telltale cones built by the doodlebugs. I would lean close and say into them, "Doodlebug, doodlebug, your house is on fire." The sound of my voice would cause the soft dirt around the hole to vibrate, making the doodlebug think he had trapped an ant. He would betray himself with a flick of sand, and I would move in for the capture.

It was while playing under the old porch that I sometimes found the gold foil packages that had contained condoms (I had never heard them called anything but rubbers). I used to put the two sides back together and pretend they were gold coins. I knew exactly what they were and would never dare to take these "coins" home. It was because I knew what they were that I was fascinated by them. I knew what had come in this package, what it had been placed around, and what it had ultimately been placed into. That to me held more mystery and attraction than real gold would have.

Inside the old church, the drawings on the walls were more testimonies to youthful sexuality. I spent a lot of time looking at them, studying the way the sexual organs had been drawn and at times trying to add to them.

Also inside the church was an old piano, with a cracked sounding board and rusting strings, that had been left behind when the congregation moved on. So, here in one place was God, music, and sex. My fascination was complete. I picked up the flat pieces of ivory that had been the tops of the piano keys and kept them as treasures. I once took some strings from the soprano section and affixed them to an old mandolin I had found in our barn. It was more like a dulcimer, really. And when I strummed it, it sent up a droning sound that I could sing to. I wrote a lot of songs with that old mandolin.

And so I would sing hymns to God for a while and look at dirty pictures for a while and pray for a while, and one day as I prayed in earnest, I broke through some sort of spirit wall and found God. Away from the stares of the boys and the mothers and the preachers, I had met him not as a chastising, bombastic bully but as a friend I could talk to on a one-to-one basis. He is our father, after all, and that's the kind of heavenly father that made sense to me. Here in this place of seemingly confusing images, I had found real truth. I had come to know that it was all right for me to be a sexual being. I knew that was one of the things God meant for me to be.

I also knew that my dreams of making music, of traveling outside the Smokies and pursuing a greater purpose, were not silly childhood ideas but grand real schemes ordained and cocreated by my newfound heavenly father. I was validated. I was sanctified. I was truly reborn. I was happy. I thanked God long and loud for having shown himself to me. I sang with a strength and conviction that only God, and possibly Curt Dockery, could have understood. The joy of the truth I found there is with me to this day. I had found God. I had found Dolly Parton. And I loved them both.

On my way home that day, I was on a cloud, or at least I felt like it. My happy feet danced on and kicked up the dust of the old road. On my way, singing and shouting, a man came along in an old A-model truck. "Where are you going so happy on this fine day?" he asked. I gave no thought to my answer. It came from me as if it were the obvious truth that anyone could easily see. "I'm going to paradise," I said. The man chuckled and drove on. How could he have known he had just talked to a twelve-year-old girl and God all in one breath? I will never forget the feel of my feet on that happy road. The dust seemed beautiful to me. Poverty and doubt did not exist. I knew God. I knew where paradise was. It was ahead of me.

I couldn't wait to tell Mama that I knew I was saved. I begged her to let me be baptized right away. Some of the women in the church were against it. They didn't think a twelve-year-old girl who had found God somewhere other than at the front of the church service knew what she was about. Mama instinctively knew how genuine my conviction was, and she allowed me to be baptized by Brother L. D. Smith in the Little Pigeon River.

I remember getting up very early that day and putting on the white dress Mama had prepared for me. I was filled with a sense of awe and reverence as I waded out into the flow of the river. I knew the symbolism of being lowered into the water to signify the death of my old, sinful self, then raised up to be born into a new righteousness. That symbolism was lost on some of the boys who had gathered on the river bank to witness this sacred rite.

When I was twelve, those body parts that were destined to become my calling card in life and the reference point for many a joke by late-night talk-show hosts were already well in evidence. My white cotton dress became somewhat transparent in the rushing water, and the boys on the bank were moved to shout "Hallelujah!" This seemed inappropriate to some of the attending church biddies who had seen through this sudden groundswell of religion among the boys as surely as the boys had seen through my dress. I thought it was altogether in keeping with what I had learned in the old chapel and my relationship with my friendly God. He wouldn't have given them to me if he hadn't wanted people to notice them.

6

Music, I suppose, will be the thing that sustains me in the time of my life when I am too old for sex and not quite ready to meet God. It has always been an essential part of me. Since I have been able to form words, I have been able to rhyme them. I could catch on to anything that had a rhythm and make a song to go with it. I would take the two notes of a bobwhite in the darkness and make that the start of a song. I would latch on to the rhythm my mother made snapping beans, and before I knew it, I'd be tapping on a pot with a spoon and singing. I don't know what some of this sounded like to my family, but in my head it was beautiful music. I loved to hear the wild geese flying overhead. I would get into the music of their honking and start to snap my fingers to their cadence and sing with them. I think I was especially drawn to them because I knew they were going somewhere. They had good reason to sing. They were free to go with the wind, to make the world their own. My song connected me to them. They took part of my spirit with them wherever they went.

My sisters were musically abused. That is the only way I can think of to describe what I put them through in my constant search for musical satisfaction. Stella and Cassie were my chief victims. Of course, I was always the star, and I made them sing backup. I would use any kind of promise, threat, or coercion to get them to do what I wanted. "Oh, I'll do your chores if you'll just sing one more verse," or "I'll tell Mama about your boyfriend if you don't sing one more verse," or, "I'll just die and it will be your fault if you don't sing one more verse."

There was one period of time when I just knew I had hit upon a surefire formula for instant stardom. I would have my reluctant backup sisters sing in pig Latin. Brenda Lee had not thought of this; what a silly oversight on her part. This was going to be the biggest thing that ever hit radio, TV, or the special live stage that would surely be built so that the entire world could hear us sing, "E-shay, as-way I-may est-bay end-fray." (Translation: She was my best friend.) I had made up all of the parts, and I wanted to hear them. It was of no consequence to me whether my sisters wanted to sing them. It simply had to be done. Even today, if I start into one of our old arrangements, Stella and Cassie will chime in with their parts. I had them so drilled. Somehow pig-Latin backup singing never caused quite the stir I expected it to; we never even made it onto "The Ed Sullivan Show." Stella and Cassie are probably just as glad that it didn't.

When I was forced to pursue my musical dreams on my own, I would whang away at my old mandolin with the piano strings. I started getting pretty good with it, within its limitations, and people started to notice. Of course, that was exactly what I wanted. I was never one to shy away from attention. Finally, my Uncle Louis began to see that I was really serious about wanting to learn, so he taught me guitar. He gave me an old Martin guitar, and I learned the basic chords pretty quick. This was like manna from heaven to me. At last I could play along with the songs I heard in my head. Mama's family were all very musical, and I used to worry the heck out of all of them to "teach me that lick" or "play this with me." If Daddy had found it hard to get me to work in the fields before, now even he began to realize it was a fruitless undertaking.

I would sit up on top of the woodpile playing and singing at the top of my lungs. Sometimes I would take a tobacco stake and stick it in the cracks between the boards on the front porch. A tin can on top of the tobacco stake turned it into a microphone, and the porch became my stage. I used to perform for anybody or anything I could get to watch. The younger kids left in my care would become the unwilling audience for my latest show. A two-year-old's attention span is not very long. So there I would be in the middle of my act, thinking I was really something, and my audience would start crawling away. I was so desperate to perform that on more than one occasion I sang for the chickens and the pigs and ducks. They didn't applaud much, but with the aid of a little corn, they could be counted on to hang around for a while.

Some of the others would sometimes take part in my shows, but it seems like they always complained about my hogging the tin can. Stella would usually be the comedienne, and then Denver would come on and preach. Of course, I was the star.

There were times when I got to perform for real people, who actually wanted to hear me. Several of us

Parton girls had a sort of a singing group that would perform at different churches around the area. By this time we had a car, and Daddy would drive us to the various churches on Sunday evenings, or for Wednesday-night prayer meetings. In keeping with tradition, Daddy wouldn't actually attend the church service. It was his custom to sit in the car, or under the trees if it was hot, and have a drink or two while the preaching went on. He used to like to stand and look in the window or in the front doors of the church while we girls were singing. Whether he would admit it or not, he was pretty proud of us.

I'll never forget this one night when Daddy had taken us way out to a little church up on a high ridge. There was no kind of instrumentation, and the hymns were all sung a cappella. During the preaching, there was a little more shouting from the congregation than usual. When it came time for us to sing, we were introduced by the preacher, a wiry little man with kind of a fiery look in his eyes. We stepped to the front and took our places on the old wood-plank platform to one side of the pulpit. Softly, I sung a note to get us started because it was decided I could come closest to hitting a key that we could all sing in. We began our songs, just as we had planned. I was aware that the pastor was on the stage behind us, but I didn't think anything of it.

After a while, I could feel Stella nudging me in the ribs, trying not to be noticed. I looked at her, and she motioned with her head slightly back toward where the preacher was standing. He seemed to be totally wrapped up in the spirit, nearly in a trance. I didn't think too much of it, until I spotted a familiar sight—the back markings of a snake, a cottonmouth moccasin. I had seen them in the woods, usually scurrying across the path toward cover. They were afraid of me, and I was afraid of them. And up to now, we had always managed to keep our distance from each other. Here, apparently, they were a part of the worship service. I could see now, out of my peripheral vision, that the preacher had a full grown cottonmouth by the back of the head and it was twisting and coiling all around his forearm.

Some members of the congregation were reaching out as if they wanted to touch it. The preacher was getting more and more worked up, and he reached into a wooden crate by the pulpit and took out two more snakes. This time he seemed to be holding them much more carelessly. He lifted them near his face as if daring them to strike.

We sisters just kept on singing, unconsciously moving away from the snakes until we were very near the front of the platform. Just then, I noticed something that struck a note of fear in my heart much greater than that inspired by the snakes. My father had stepped into the back of the church to hear his little girls sing. Whatever he had been drinking didn't impair his ability to see exactly what the preacher had in his hands. Just at that moment, the man and his snakes took a step toward the congregation, thus toward us.

Daddy had seen enough. He charged down the aisle like a wild boar through a thicket. "You get them Goddamn snakes away from my kids!" Daddy bellowed with a force in his voice I had never heard before. It was amazing how quickly that preacher broke his trance and paid heed. He had heard the voice of a higher power, in this case a really pissed-off redneck. Daddy swooped us up and out the front door before we had time to think about what was happening. We didn't even stop singing until we were almost down the steps into the churchyard.

We were glad to be out of there, and I at least was proud that Daddy had come to our rescue. But Daddy obviously felt terrible about it. On the way home in the car, he got to feeling especially bad. "Goddamn! I can't believe I said Goddamn in church!" he muttered to himself. He finally got so upset he had to stop the car and get out in the woods and, in his way, ask God's forgiveness.

I couldn't help thinking how badly Mama had always wanted Daddy to walk down the church aisle and declare himself. Now he had certainly done that, although not I'm sure the way Mama had in mind. There are many different beliefs in this world. There are those who believe that their faith will keep poisonous snakes from biting them, and others who believe in protecting their children from danger, no matter what. There are also those who believe that on this occasion, their father did the right thing.

And now, on to sex, that other great drive in my life that I am dealing with in third position, even though there have been many times in my life when it has wrangled its way, without too much resistance, into first place.

I have always been aware of sex. On a farm it is hard not to be. There were always animals who were more than willing to do their part for sex education. A kid is naturally curious when one animal gets on top of another one and begins humping. But with older brothers or sisters around, these acts are likely to be explained in no uncertain terms to a child at a very early age. I didn't mind the explanations because I was dying to know everything I could.

Some of us were more than curious about sex and the farm animals. Once we had a calf whose mother was unable to nurse it. Daddy had fashioned a bucket with a large nipple on it to hand-feed the calf with.

The story goes that one of my brothers (I don't know which one, or even if the story is true for that matter) figured out that it wouldn't be too difficult to substitute himself for the nipple. One time my father walked in on this particular act of animal husbandry. "Damn, Daddy," the boy said without blinking an eye, "are you just gonna stand there and let this thing eat me up?"

If you've ever been hunting or camping or just gone for an extended walk in the woods, you are probably familiar with that special kind of horniness that can overcome a person in such a setting. There is something primal about it, something that goes back to a time when we were climbing all over the trees like monkeys and climbing all over each other any time we felt like it. If you know that feeling at all, you can understand a little bit about how it was to be a bunch of kids going through puberty and living in the woods. Maybe it's not quite right to say we were going through puberty. It might be more accurate to say it was going through us like Sherman's army through Georgia.

From the time I knew sex existed, I wanted to know everything there was to know about it, and I wasn't shy about asking. We had aunts, uncles, cousins, and friends who were a few years older and had been out in the world a little bit. They would tell us anything we wanted to know. As the saying goes, "That's the great thing about a sense of humor and a sex drive, you can't wait to share it with everybody else."

I was always very open-minded about sex, and I'm glad that I still am. I have always loved sex. I've never had a bad experience with it. I am a very emotional person, and to me it's another way, a very intimate and wonderful way, of showing emotion. It was never dirty to me. After all, God gave us the equipment and the opportunity. There's that old saying "If God had meant for us to fly, he'd have given us wings." Well, look at what he *did* give us.

People often ask me how my mama and daddy did it in the house with so many kids. I don't really know, but the evidence speaks for itself: They did it. Once when Cassie and I were playing around Mama and Daddy's bed, I found Mama's diaphragm between the mattresses. I had no idea what it was. I knew what rubbers were, and I thought surely it must be one. I thought my daddy must have a really short, big, round one. It was a most unsettling mental image. Now that I know what it was, I can't imagine what Mama did with it unless she drank coffee out of it. Lord knows she didn't use it for its intended purpose.

I don't know if the following story comes under the heading of sex or not. It is a little kinky and quirky, and to this day I am not quite sure of the underlying reasons for what happened.

One of the first people to appreciate my singing was my sister Willadeene. She used to tell me that I sounded "better than Brenda Lee," and of course to me this was like throwing biscuits to a yard dog. Willadeene got married at sixteen to Arthur Blalock, Jr. There's a southern custom of calling boys who are juniors Junie or June, so everybody called him June Blalock. While he was dating Willadeene, he would come to our house to pick her up, and she used to love to have me sing for him. The old abandoned chapel was at the foot of the hill our house sat on, and June would usually park his car down there and walk up to the house. Willadeene always wanted me to be singing in the old chapel when June drove up because it echoed and sounded really pretty. I was flattered that she was proud of my singing and wanted somebody she cared about to hear it.

That is why I have difficulty explaining what happened one evening. There was a swing on the hill above the road up to our house, and if you got a good push off from the bank, you could swing out over the road. Well, June was coming for Willadeene, and she had sent me down to the old chapel to sing for him as usual. For some reason, I got halfway down the hill and took a detour up the bank to the old swing. Something possessed me to take my panties off and start swinging out over the road. When June came up the hill, I pulled my dress up and swung right out so that my butt was right in his face. Then I sang at the top of my lungs:

> *On top of Old Smokey*
> *All covered with grass,*
> *Look here, Junie Blalock,*
> *At my naked ass!*

He was embarrassed, and of course Willadeene was mortified. She snatched him into the house and banged the screen door behind them. Of course, I did what any young lady in my position would have done. I modulated up one key and sang it all over again.

To this day, I don't know exactly what prompted my performance on the swing. I could be feisty and kind of crazy. Maybe I was jealous that my sister had a boyfriend. Maybe I had gotten all of the attention I could from him with my singing and had simply moved on to the next level. I don't know, but I do know that there are many who would say, and rightfully so, that I have been showing my ass ever since.

There's something about growing up in such limiting surroundings that will make you do crazy things. Maybe it has more to do with growing up than the surroundings. My brothers would fight. It didn't really matter what the fight was about. Once it had begun, it became a matter of one's manhood having been challenged, and no satisfaction was possible until somebody was bloody or at least had welts raised somewhere above the neck. David and Denver were big boys, and my mother couldn't handle them when they got into a real knock-down-drag-out. If they were outside, this was not a big problem; Mama and the rest of us would just kind of go along ahead of them as they tossed and tumbled through the yard, picking up sharp implements that they might fall on or, worse yet, use as weapons.

Once, though, they got to fighting in the living room and seemed as if they would lay waste to the entire house. Daddy would have nipped this in the bud, but all Mama could do was cry and scream and pray—all at the same time. "Lord, don't let those boys break my chairs! Boys, in the name of God, don't hurt each other!" As if by divine intervention, the thing that ended the fight was relatively harmless. One brother knocked the other into the stovepipe of the old wood-burning heater. It was in the springtime, so the heater wasn't in use, but the black cloud of soot (we pronounced it "sut") that spewed from the old stovepipe got the boys' attention. Before long, they were laughing rather than fighting, each at the sight of the other completely blackened. The whole living room was blackened as well. But Mama, so glad the damage hadn't been worse, couldn't help laughing too.

We all cleaned up as well as we could and went to school that day. It wasn't until later when we saw one another in the light of midday at recess that we realized our nostrils were all perfect little black round holes. There was also "sut" under our fingernails and forming inky borders that looked like hair nets around our foreheads. The evidence both on our bodies and in the living room made the fight impossible to keep from Daddy when he got home. If the original intention of the boys had been to inflict pain on each other, that was accomplished.

I suppose it was good that my brothers fought each other. As it turned out, they would need the practice for a much less forgiving enemy. There was a family of kids that went to the same school we did, who for some reason began picking on the Partons. At first it was just the usual scrapes that a kid might ordinarily get into after school, but it got more and more serious. It got to where every day they would be waiting for us by the path home to beat us up. Some of them were really big kids, adults really, who had been kept back in school several years. David and Denver were tough, but they just couldn't stand up to a bunch with more and bigger boys. I had always had fights with my brothers and sisters, but this was different. As heated as fights with Denver could sometimes get, I always knew deep down that he was my brother, that he loved me and would never really hurt me. With these people I didn't know that. In fact, the most frightening part of all was that I knew the opposite of that. They hated us, and they really wanted to hurt us.

We would come home beaten up every day. We stayed sore and bruised all the time. Daddy cut a new path for us to use going to school, and that worked for a day or so, but our tormentors found it and soon they were waiting by the new path every day to beat us nearly senseless. Finally, Daddy had had enough. He and David and Denver walked down to the other family's place. Daddy's intent was to talk to the parents of the other kids and see if they could do anything about what had been happening. He did make it clear, though, that he meant for it to stop.

The other family was actually several families living in one house under deplorable conditions. It was hard to tell whose kids were whose, probably even for them. It was understandable that they could feel anger, but I have never understood why they chose to take it out on another poor family not much better off than they were. It must be akin to that anger that makes people in a riot burn their own neighborhoods. I don't know why they had originally taken such a dislike to my family. Maybe one of their boys had had his sexual advances spurned by one of our girls. But the feelings obviously ran very deep.

They attacked Daddy and the boys. Daddy was a big man who could hold his own against great odds. But even he was not prepared to be set upon by a gang of five or six, including at least one woman. Another bunch had cornered David and Denver and were beating them badly. Daddy says he got to the point where he was fearful for his life and the lives of his sons. He fought back mightily. He hurt two or three of them enough to take them out of the fight, including a woman who Daddy says was trying to beat him with something that looked like the handle of a hoe. Even at that, he had not intentionally hurt the woman, but in trying to defend himself he had broken her nose, and incidentally one of his own fingers, which is still crooked to this day. Daddy managed to break free enough to get the boys out of the spot they were in. Some of the other family ran to the house, presumably to get guns, and Daddy and his sons ran for home.

I will never forget the sight of Daddy, David, and Denver coming home all bloodied and beaten. This was the man I thought was unbeatable. He was the highest authority I had ever known. He was the one we all went to for protection. Yet here he was, bloody and struggling for his life. When I first experienced an earthquake many years later, it affected me in almost the same way. I had come to depend on Daddy to be there, strong and all-powerful, the way we come to depend on the earth to be solid, stable, and constant. Seeing my father this way shook the very ground that my childhood security had been built on.

The terror on my mother's face told me the danger was not over yet. She and Daddy both knew that the next likely thing to happen would be for people to show up at our house with guns. Deputy sheriff Wiley Noland lived several hollers away. It was determined that David and Denver could get there faster by going over the hills than anybody could using the roads. They lit out. They had both been hurt, but they understood the urgency. They must have had wings on their feet. They were back in a short while with the deputy, who went to the other house and was able to stop the dispute, at least for the moment.

The next part of the saga was almost comical. The woman with the broken nose had decided to sue Daddy in civil court. I don't know what she expected to get from him, but with that same "blood from a turnip" kind of logic, Daddy countersued. Daddy and Mama had to go to court, and the proceedings drew a big crowd. The incident had become known as a feud. In local circles it had taken on the legendary status of the Hatfields and McCoys. This was in part because the stories had been greatly exaggerated, but primarily because people had very little else to talk about.

Daddy is an honest man, and as he told his story I'm sure the court could tell that. Witnesses for the other family couldn't seem to get their stories straight. One would tell a version of the story that Daddy's attorney could use to poke holes in another one's story, and on it went. Finally, the woman with the broken nose pulled a dramatic fainting spell on the witness stand. The judge threw the case out of court. That feud went on for many years, but I am happy to say that those people are now good neighbors of mine and all of the Partons.

7

My Grandpa, Reverend Jake Owens, was a rock of our family. His real name, Jacob, naturally enough, comes from the Bible, as did everything he ever thought or did. He never had a drink of alcohol or smoked a cigarette. He never even overate or did anything else to excess. He loved his Lord and he loved his family.

Almost from the day he was born he felt the call to preach. He began preaching when he was seventeen, years before he was actually ordained. There were few ordained ministers in our parts anyway. If a young man felt led to preach the gospel, he just let it fly. Many of them couldn't even read or write. They just watched other people preach and then copied the way they did it. My Grandpa Jake was much more educated than most. He was a music teacher of sorts and even taught public school as a substitute.

He was loved and respected by everyone who knew him. I cowrote a song with my Aunt Dorothy Jo

called "Daddy Was an Old Time Preacher Man"
about Grandpa Jake.

> *Daddy was an old time preacher man*
> *He preached the word of God throughout the land*
> *He preached so plain a child could understand*
> *Yes, Daddy was an old time preacher man*
> *He told the people of the need to pray*
> *He talked about God's wrath and Judgment Day*
> *He preached about the great eternity*
> *He preached hell so hot that you could feel the heat*
> *Yes, Daddy was an old time preacher man*
> *Aunt Leanona would get up to testify*
> *And we'd sing "In the Sweet By and By"*
> *Then we'd sing, "I'm on My Way to Canaan Land"*
> *Yes, Daddy was an old time preacher man*
> *Daddy worked for God, but asked no pay*
> *For he believed that God provides a way*
> *We never had a lot, but we got by*
> *Guess it's 'cause the Lord was on Daddy's side.*

That song was one of the biggest duet hits Porter
Wagoner and I ever did. My grandpa did preach so
hot you could feel the fires of hell. I suppose I got
much of my love for God and music from him. In
return, I gave him a fit when it came to my tight
clothes, bleached hair, and makeup. He was just sure I
was doomed to hell. He would call me Jezebel and
then shake his head and say, "Lord, the devil must
have made you wear your clothes that way and bleach
your hair like that." And I'd say, "No offense,
Granddaddy, but I did this all by myself. The devil
had nothing to do with it."

I was not the first one in the family to cause
Grandpa Jake to raise an eyebrow. For the most part,
my mother's family, the Owenses, are vagabonds.

They live to play music and will let nothing, earning a living, for example, stand in the way of that. My father's people are hardworking, relatively no-nonsense farmers. I am a part of both of them and feel very fortunate that I am. I got the best parts of both worlds. Daddy always loved music, but he never really thought it could put any food on the table.

The Owenses, my Uncle Bill, for example, always genuinely believed that there was a huge fortune to be made with little or no effort, if not today, then certainly tomorrow. It was as if the Partons fed me and the Owenses served up a dessert of dreams. I take great joy in making music, and it is what I truly live for. On the other hand, I have learned to make it work for me so that I can live quite well while I'm doing it.

Daddy would have understood planting watermelon seeds after the last frost and then having the satisfaction of sitting back under a tree in July and eating the sweet melon. He would appreciate knowing you started with a plan, saw it through, and then enjoyed the fruits of it. Mama would have the same kind of understanding about planting a bunch of dreams and watering them with sweat and tears. Of course they would bear fruit. It's the nature of things. It was the Owens in me that made me plant the dreams, but I probably would not have had the will to put out the sweat and tears without the Parton.

Uncle Bill began to take a real interest in my talent. Of all of my musical relatives, he was the one who took his music the most seriously. He aspired to make records of his own as well as to have his songs recorded by known artists. His full name is Billy Earl Owens, but it was usually shortened to Bill. I always liked to call him Uncle Billy. He was the only person back in those days who had the same vision as I did.

He had shown many a kid a few chords on the guitar, but none of the others had the patience and discipline I did. When he taught me a chord, I not only learned it, I added to it. I made a lick out of it, then wrote a song to it. He was impressed with my determination. He was willing to work hard, sacrifice, whatever it took to follow his own dream. So we joined forces.

As the fourth one down, I had always felt somewhat misplaced in our big family. Nobody paid me very much attention. At least it seemed that way to me, since I needed so much of it. Billy paid me a lot of attention. He was a great visionary and really thought I had potential. That was nice by itself, but for once here was somebody who wanted to help me develop my talent. He was my first and special angel of that kind. It was Bill who brought me to the attention of Cas Walker.

Cas was quite a character. He had started out selling produce from a wheelbarrow, rolling it from house to house, and eventually opened a store. His business had grown to the point where he had stores all over Knoxville, in Kentucky, and in Pennington Gap, Virginia. He had become a multimillionaire by selling his groceries on radio and TV. Cas was real opinionated. He would go on his show and rant and rave about politics, usually taking a much more liberal view than that of most people around those parts. Those who didn't agree with him would spit and cuss as they sat whittling outside the courthouse, but there wasn't much they could do about it. Cas had the money. It was his show. He had paid for the time, and he could do as he damn well pleased with it.

He was a local celebrity, and everybody around had his own little Cas Walker impression. When he was on TV hawking his groceries, he would point with his middle finger so that it looked like he was giving people the bird as he would say, "It's not three dollars, it's not two dollars, it's a dollar and a half!" Folks used to laugh at the way he would point because they thought he didn't know he was doing it. I was never quite sure. Cas was that much of an individual. If he wanted to go on TV and flip people off, he would do it.

Cas always told the story about the time I was introduced to him. Uncle Bill wanted to get me on Cas's radio show, so he managed to get me backstage to meet him. I remember looking up at him and thinking how different he was from the men I had known in the mountains. Cas tried to "dress down" so as not to alienate the common (grocery-buying) people, but there were still little things that gave away that he was a very wealthy man. I stood there about on the level with his belt buckle, which seemed to a poor kid from the hills to be a thing of almost unimaginable richness, looking up at Cas in his starched white shirt.

He said hello and then kind of "garumped" as if I should say something. I choked back my butterflies and finally managed to say, "Mr. Walker, I want to work for you." He shook my hand and said, "Well, you've got a job." He told me, "A lot of people come to me and say, Mr. Walker, I want a job, but you said I want to work for you. You're hired because you're the first one that ever wanted to work."

I started out singing on the radio. The show was broadcast live in the middle of the day from a little auditorium there at the radio station, WIVK in Knoxville. There was room for an audience of about sixty or so, and people would crowd in off the street when the show started. When time came for my first show, I stood there backstage with my Uncle Bill, trying to breathe. It's funny how when you're nervous even normal bodily functions require worry and effort. I could hear the sound of the people kinda buzzing out there, waiting for something to happen.

It was at that very moment that everything came to a head for me as a performer. My insecurity came face-to-face with my ambition. My shyness banged head-on into my need for attention. This was what I had always wanted, and yet there was this fear. I'm not quite sure if it was the fear of failure or of success. Maybe it was both. I was either going to do this thing, and do it for the rest of my life, or not at all. I was introduced. I looked at Uncle Bill. He looked back as if to say, "I can't help you now." I knew it was up to me.

Somehow, I walked out to that microphone and began to sing. My voice was thin and tentative at first, but I got more and more confident as I went along. By the last verse, I was belting the song out at the top of my lungs, singing with joy just the way I had done on top of the woodpile. I sang as if it would be my only chance ever to sing for a crowd like this or on the radio. For all I knew, it could be.

I finished my song, and the crowd exploded with approval. They cheered and clapped and stomped their feet. It was as if they were saying, "Yes! Yes, Dolly, we love your singing. Yes, Dolly, we love *you*!" And this time they didn't crawl away.

At that very moment I fell in love with the public. This was what I had always wanted—no, needed. It was the attention I had longed for. I knew what they were giving me. Now I had confidence in what I had to give them. They shouted for an encore. I didn't have one. I had only prepared the one song. I looked at Uncle Bill, who was onstage with me, grinning like a mule eating saw briars from behind his big red electric guitar. I couldn't hear him over the crowd, but I could see his lips forming the words, "Sing it again!" I did. They loved it again. So did I. I finally knew what a star was. I wasn't one yet, but I knew that I would be, and that I would have that love affair with the public for the rest of my life.

Looking back, that audience probably responded to me as much because I was ten years old as out of admiration for whatever talent I had. But it was just the boost I needed to keep me on the road to my dream.

I sang on television before my family ever owned one. I used to get five dollars a show, and I thought that was really big money. When you consider that my Daddy would sometimes work all day in a sawmill for the same money, it was. After I had been on for a while, Cas would take me with him when he took his show to different towns around the area. I remember playing at the Pines Theater in Sevierville. That was like playing for my own home folks, and I was really proud.

Cas would do all kinds of stunts to bring people to the shows and ultimately into his grocery stores. He used to have what was called a "greasy pole." It was like a telephone pole that had been sanded down real smooth and then greased up with lard. It was as slick as a two-dollar lawyer and almost impossible to climb. At the top of the greasy pole was a cash prize for anybody who could reach it. I decided to give the greasy pole a try.

I was still pretty much a tomboy then. I felt confident in my climbing ability, but I also had a plan. First I got myself good and wet, then went out into the parking lot and rolled around in the dirt. I thought if I could get enough sand and dirt stuck to me, it would give me better traction going up the pole. When my turn came, I ran over to the pole and started up. A few people laughed and must have thought, "Who is that dirty kid?" But as I began to make headway up the pole, the laughter turned into shouts of encouragement. With all the grit I could muster (including that stuck to my jeans) I shinnied up the pole and triumphantly brought down the prize—two hundred and fifty dollars.

The cheers of the crowd soon turned into disgruntled muttering. Somebody had recognized me as one of the performers on the show, and this created quite an outrage. People were angry that I had won the money. Not only had I used what they considered to be an unfair advantage, but in their minds, I shouldn't have been eligible. They began to cry that the whole thing had been fixed. That was when Cas Walker showed what a high-minded, strong-willed individual he really was.

"How could a greasy pole be fixed?" he shouted down the crowd. "Either you can climb the damn thing or you can't." He went on, "Nobody said you couldn't roll in the dirt. If this young lady is smart enough to do that, she deserves the money. Hell, it's *my* money! I didn't expect to have to give it away at all. This girl has taught me something today, and that in itself is worth two hundred and fifty dollars." With that, he shook my hand, and the crowd, although not altogether happy, had to accept the fact that I was the winner.

Two hundred and fifty dollars was big money in Sevier County, Tennessee, in 1956. Mama and Daddy couldn't believe my good fortune. I thought about what to do with the money and finally hit upon what seemed to be the perfect use for it. I would buy the family a television. This was the perfect answer. It would benefit all of us. It would bring excitement and contact with the outside world that we had never known. Not least of all, my family could finally see me sing on "The Cas Walker Show."

Until that time, all our family ever had was an old battery-operated radio. We couldn't listen to it as much as we wanted to because we had to save the battery, but we could hear the Grand Ole Opry sometimes. The radio had to have a big copper grounding rod that was driven into the earth outside the house. Sometimes it would start cutting out and whistling. That meant that it wasn't properly grounded and one of us would have to go outside and pour water on the grounding rod until it would get clear again.

No one could have anticipated the impact that television would have on our family, neighbors, and relatives. There is a movie called *The Gods Must Be Crazy* in which a Coke bottle falls from an airplane and profoundly changes the lives of a tribe of Bushmen. My TV had the same effect on that bunch of hillbillies. It was bad enough that all of us kids started watching it the minute it signed on. The station in Knoxville only had programming for about eight hours a day. Up until it came on, there would be this old black-and-white test pattern with all kinds of little lines and numbers on it with the head of an Indian chief in the middle. When we first got the TV, my brothers and sisters would sit and watch that for a long time until the station would sign on. There were cartoons and things in the afternoon, but the real attraction was "Gunsmoke."

When it came time for "Gunsmoke," the whole family would be glued to the set. Relatives and neighbors began coming over. Before long there would be as many as twenty-five or thirty people crowded into our house trying to see a pitiful, snowy nineteen-inch black-and-white TV.

If they had just watched "Gunsmoke" and then

gone home, it might not have been so bad. But they wouldn't leave. They would sit, or stand, or lean and watch that TV until it signed off with the "Star Spangled Banner." Then that familiar test pattern would come on again. I'll be damned if some of the "po' asses" who hadn't had good seats for "Gunsmoke" wouldn't stay and watch the test pattern for a while.

Daddy was undone. "I can't have these people in the house all night," he complained, "I got to work!" At first he would try to drop hints. "Well, let's you and me go on to bed, Avie Lee," he would say aloud for everybody to hear. "I think these people want to go home." This didn't work. It was as if these people had all become addicted to something that was beyond their power to give up. "Get out of my house!" Daddy would yell. Mama would just swear that he had offended friends or relatives and that they would never come to our house or speak to us again. But next "Gunsmoke" there they were, as if they had no memory, no sense whatever of being bothersome, and no intention of leaving.

Even if I felt I had become a star, Daddy was still a farmer who had to get up with the chickens every morning. "That damned TV has got to go!" he said plainly and emphatically. We all recognized that tone of voice. When Daddy used it, there was no room for discussion. The TV was sold. I would have to go on being a TV star without my own family being able to see me.

I was a feisty kid. I don't know who coined the phrase, but it used to be said of me that I was "smart enough to know everything and dumb enough to say it." That is one description I have never attempted to dispute. The guys in the house band of the TV show used to have fun kidding with me. Once they got together and made up some excuse as to why they weren't going to play for me. I bowed up and said right to their faces, "You will play for me too. You wait 'til Mr. Walker gets here. You'll play for me, and you'll be damned glad to do it too."

It got harder and harder to go to school after I became "locally famous." There were those who resented me, and they weren't at all subtle about showing it. One day, some of the more hateful ones locked me in the cloakroom. At first I thought they were just kidding around, but when they hadn't let me out after about ten minutes, I began to cry and beat on the door. Of course, when somebody locks you in a closet, that's exactly what they're hoping you will do. That added to their enjoyment.

I don't know how long it was before somebody let me out, but it seemed to me like an eternity. I remember the dank, musty smell of that old closet and the sweaty smell of the coats. Worst of all, it was dark. I began to imagine all kinds of terrible things that might be surrounding me in my prison. I started to feel like I couldn't breathe. I thought if I didn't get out of there, I would die. I don't know if it was the treatment itself or the hate I could sense behind it that made this such a horrible nightmare for me. To this day, I am afraid of the dark and I sleep with a night-light on.

All the while, I kept on singing on the Cas Walker shows, on radio and TV. Uncle Bill or some other relative would drive me to Knoxville. I can remember Aunt Estelle going with me to a place where you could make your own record. It wasn't like a professional studio or anything. It was more like a little booth where you watched the record being cut as you recorded it. I remember the discs were made of a black waxy stuff. When it was turning, the part that was cut out by the needle would come off in a long, fine string that looked like black hair.

I will never forget how excited I was when I heard that I was going to get to make a real record. One of my uncles, Henry Owens (brother to Bill and Louis), performed under the name John Henry III. This was just something he made up. There never was a first or second, but that was and is his stage name. Aside from performing where he could and doing some recording, he was in the service at a base in Lake Charles, Louisiana. He lived next to a recording studio and had made friends with its owner. Uncle Bill had been down a couple of times, and he thought it would be the perfect opportunity for me to cut my first record. He sent for me to come to Lake Charles.

When I heard about it, I was barely able to contain myself. I was walking the same hills and hollers I had known all my life, but everything seemed different to me. That other world that I had always known was out there waiting had finally sent me an invitation. I would run up a hill almost expecting to just keep on going, to run out onto the clouds and come down in a whole new world. Some people say the anticipation of a thing is a greater joy than the thing itself. I was a great argument in support of that theory.

Suddenly my anticipation and joy came to an abrupt halt. There was one problem. The recording studio was in Louisiana. I was in Tennessee. I was twelve years old. There was no one to go with me. Uncle Henry had sent a bus ticket for me and for somebody to accompany me, but there was no body to fill that other seat. The trip would take several days, and none of my hardworking aunts or uncles could spare the time. There was never any question that my mother might go and leave so many other kids at home.

Not ever having been one to give up, especially when something is important to me, I made it my business to find someone who was available—my Grandma Rena. Available is all she was. Grandma Rena knew less about the world outside Sevier County than I did. What little travel she had done had all been under the protection and guidance of her husband. She was not at all confident she could look out for herself on such a trip, let alone me. I begged and pleaded and guilt-tripped and cried until finally she gave in.

Mama had that "I'm not so sure about this" look on her face as she said good-bye to me that morning. I assured her we would be fine. After all, the bus tickets were already bought. Somebody would put us on the bus and meet us at the other end. Grandma Rena was just for company.

They say that our memory for smells is centered in the part of the brain that developed first in evolution, and that is why a smell can take you back to a place or time quicker than just about anything. I don't think I'll ever forget the way the inside of that bus smelled. It was a combination of diesel fuel, Naugahyde, and people who were going places. The steady purr of the engine and the slight vibration on our feet seemed comforting, even, to some extent, to Grandma Rena. To me it seemed like a big, friendly animal of some kind, one that was going to carry me in its belly and deliver me to a new and exciting place, like Jonah and the whale.

My big friend pulled out of Sevierville with a puff of smoke and a settling of rednecks and luggage, and we were on our way. As we got to where we could no longer see the familiar mountains that had been the background of my entire life up to that point, the only question to me was whether or not the anticipation would kill me before we got there. As we crossed the state line into Alabama, I remember being a little disappointed that there was no actual line, just a sign by the side of the highway. Still, I was in another state, on my way to make my first record. Grandma Rena dozed off, but I wanted to see everything. Although so far, Alabama didn't look much different from Tennessee.

After a few hundred miles, the roadside held a little less fascination for me, but we were still heading for Louisiana and my record. We got off the bus to stretch our legs and use the rest room in Birmingham. When we came back, we were not prepared for what we saw. There were a dozen buses, and they all looked just like the one we had been on. Which one was ours? Which one was my Jonah's whale? We only knew we were going to Lake Charles. None of the signs over the buses said Lake Charles. Did we go to Mobile? Did we go to Meridian? We didn't know.

Grandma Rena got upset. She sat down and started wringing her hands in worry. Then she started to cry. I didn't know what to do either. Should we get on one of these buses? Finally I went to the ticket window and was very honest with the man there. "Mister, me and my Grandmama are lost, and we don't know what to do." He looked at my ticket and told me which bus we were supposed to be on and which sign to find it under. By the time we got there, the bus was already gone.

Now Grandma Rena was really upset, but I promised her I would get us to where we were going. There were telephones at the bus station, but neither of us had ever used a phone before. I knew which bus we were supposed to be on. We would simply wait until another one came. While we waited, we both got very hungry. I asked a couple of people, "Are you gonna finish those potato chips?" or "Can you afford an extra candy bar?" Grandma Rena didn't want me begging, but we had to have something to eat. Finally, some kind people noticed the situation we were in and offered us some food.

Looking back, perhaps I should have included food when I was outlining the driving forces in my life. I have always loved to eat. If I were asked to create one sentence that involves God, music, and food as they all relate to my life it would have to be: Thank God I have been able to sing for my supper.

We finally got on the right bus. And this time we stayed on it. With the time we had lost, the trip took over thirty hours. I still remember the overwhelming feeling of relief when the bus passed a sign that said Welcome to Lake Charles.

The little recording studio was called Gold Band Records. The man who owned it was Ed Shuler, a Cajun man whose studio had produced a number of records, including "Sea of Love," which had done pretty well. I made my little record, "Puppy Love," which was written by my Uncle Bill Owens and me. The flip side was "Girl Left Alone," which Uncle Bill and Aunt Dorothy Jo had helped out on.

It was exciting making the record and hearing it played back over the big speakers in the studio. And there was a surprise I hadn't counted on. Ed Shuler had a son named Johnny who was about my age. He was dark with what I would later come to know as "bedroom eyes." I had never seen anything like him. I had known boys back home, but they were for the most part rough country bumpkins. This boy was so handsome and well kept. And the way he talked was so different, with a hint of a Cajun accent. I was really taken with him, and apparently he was with me as well. He was my first real love.

Johnny and I spent every minute we could together, sometimes sneaking off and sitting under the big live oak trees behind the studio. I had never seen trees like that, heavy with Spanish moss and with branches reaching out so far and coming so low to the ground. Everything was so different from anything I had ever known, especially this boy. He was so sweet and gentle with me—and he really knew how to kiss. He would hold my head in his hands and kiss me till my knees went weak. My life changed quite a bit on that trip.

Uncle John Henry drove me and Grandma back home. On the way we passed a roadside stand that had a stalk of bananas hanging outside. I begged Uncle Henry to get me one. I had never had a banana in my life, although I had thought about them. I raised such a ruckus in the backseat that Uncle Henry finally bought me the whole stalk. They were the greatest thing I had ever tasted. I ate bananas all the way home. Even though I got sick as a dog on them, I still remember it as a pleasant experience. I had eaten bananas, been to three different states, been loved by a dark-eyed Cajun boy, and made myself a record. I felt like a woman of the world if ever there was one.

8

My little record got some play on the radio, and I kept on singing on the Cas Walker show. During summer vacations and any other time I was out of school for a few days, I would go to Knoxville to live with my Aunt Estelle and Uncle Dot Watson (yes, the same guy who got us to plant horse turds). This way I could do both the TV and radio shows. I would take the bus from Estelle's house and get off at a bridge they call the Viaduct, near the JFG coffee plant. I can remember the wonderful smell that would come wafting through the doors when the bus would let me out. I probably love coffee so much today because of that.

The bus got me to the theater quite a while before I had to be there. There I was, just my guitar and me. It was the second of these that got me into trouble. The guitar was just an innocent accomplice. Actually, I started out quite innocently as well, but temptation got the better of me. It wasn't long before I had the guitar out and was playing and singing. I was just playing for myself, but after a while a few people started to gather around.

This one couple, who looked like they were from out of town, stopped and heard one whole song and part of another. The lady smiled and chirped, "You sing real purty, honey." "Thanks," I said, without missing a strum. "Isn't she good, Hubert?" the woman went on, this time giving her husband a poke in the ribs with her elbow. The man just kind of nodded and grunted. The chirpy woman was now through with subtle hints. "Well, aren't you going to give the child a quarter?" she asked the man, giving him a much harder poke in his side. The man must have been used to this, because he obediently took out a quarter and dropped it into my guitar case like a setter trained to drop a quail at a hunter's feet. For a second I thought to myself, "Daddy wouldn't want me beggin'." Then a couple of other suckers dropped coins in the case, and I thought, "Daddy's back home, and I want a Jiffy burger."

Jiffy burgers were wonderfully greasy little sliders from a place near Aunt Estelle's house. I wanted them more than anything. To me, they represented everything that mountain life wasn't. The problem was I only made twenty dollars a week (I had gotten a raise) and gave Aunt Estelle half of that for my board. And I had already been caught taking Aunt Estelle's laundry money to buy these burgers. So if old, purple-haired ladies wanted to fork out the cash, it was all right by me.

At first I was uncomfortable with the idea that the people who were giving me money thought I was needy. As the coins kept dropping, however, I found myself taking steps to enhance my waif image. I would carry an old ragged shirt inside my guitar case, to put on for effect. I have to admit I could look plumb pitiful. Years later, I wrote a song with my brother Floyd called "Nickels and Dimes" that was based on that experience.

Soon Uncle Bill decided I should go to Nashville. After all, that's where the real business was, and he had high hopes for me. He would buy some kind of an old junked-up car, and off we'd go. The car would probably only hold up for one or two trips to Nashville and back, but that's all we wanted. We didn't even care that much if it got us back, as long as we got there. It was all we could do to get gas money together. So we had to sleep in the car and wash up with cold water in gas-station rest rooms.

Our main objective was to get me on the Grand Ole Opry. We would go there and get as close as we could to where the action was. Uncle Bill was never shy about talking to people about me. After a while he got to know some of them pretty well.

One event that will forever be etched in my memory is meeting Johnny Cash. One night after a show at the Ryman, Bill and I waited for him in the parking lot. It was late and I was getting sleepy. I kept saying to Bill, "Come on, we can meet him some other time." Then a man stepped out the stage door and walked over to us . . . and there was no other time. There was only this moment. There was only me and Johnny Cash. I had never seen a man with such a presence—tall, lanky, and sexy, with that trademark voice that cut through me like butter. Now I knew what star quality was. He had it. It was a combination of personal charisma and intense sex appeal. The way he walked, the way he looked at you, everything about him was special. I was blown away. I was just a thirteen-year-old girl from the Smokies, but I would have gladly given it up for Mr. Cash right there in the parking lot.

Bill introduced me to him, and I didn't know if I would be able to speak. Somehow something took hold of me, and I found myself blurting out, "Oh, Mr. Cash, I've just got to sing on the Grand Ole Opry." I know he must have heard that kind of thing all the time; anybody in show business does. But he looked at me as if he was thinking, "You know, this kid is really serious."

I was serious. I had come to know Carl and Pearl Butler from having performed with them on the Cas Walker show. They were a couple from Knoxville who had moved to Nashville to further their careers. They had done quite well and had some hit records. "Don't Let Me Cross Over" was their biggest and was named song of the year in country music. They were like second parents to Uncle Billy and me. Pearl was especially sweet to me. She would buy me a new dress every now and then, and of course I liked that a lot. They put together a band to play road dates and gave Bill a job playing guitar. They were lifesavers in those days.

Carl and Pearl had come to know a lot of people in country music. Since I knew *them,* I was convinced they could help me. That's the way being a show-business squirrel works. If you don't know somebody, you try to know somebody who knows somebody. There's that one tree with all the nuts at the top, and you just keep trying to jump one limb closer. That's show business, all right. All the nuts are at the top.

I kept bugging Carl and Pearl, "I want to be on the Opry, I want to be on the Opry!" I guess they thought my chances were pretty slim and wanted to spare me a heartache, so they'd come up with answers like "You're just a kid" or "You have to be in the union" or just about anything they could think of. But I just wouldn't be denied.

You had to have a slot on the program to sing on the Opry, and there was no way I was going to get one. But finally, Jimmy C. Newman, who had a spot one Saturday night, agreed to let me go on in his place. I will always be grateful to him for that chance. He was a dark, handsome Cajun from the same area as Ed Shuler and his son Johnny. I was still carrying a torch for Johnny, and in my romantic mind I thought surely my sweet, dark-eyed lover boy had somehow sent this nice man to help me out, even if only in a spiritual sense.

Even though I got my wish, to actually sing on the Opry, the reality of it hadn't really sunk in. I took my place backstage that night, my usual cocky self, acting as if I sang on the Opry every night.

When my time came to sing, none other than Johnny Cash introduced me. "We've got a little girl here from up in East Tennessee," he said. "Her daddy's listening to the radio at home, and she's gonna be in real trouble if she doesn't sing tonight, so let's bring her out here!"

Now the reality hit me. I had that same feeling I had felt the first time on the Cas Walker show, but this time the audience was ten times as big. Not only the live audience: I knew very well that the radio broadcast was going out live all over the country. I was in the big time. If it hadn't been for that earlier experience, I don't know if I would have ever been able to make a sound come out of my throat.

I walked up to that mike with the familiar WSM call letters on the little box built around it. "This is actually it," I thought. For a split second I was a tourist as I pondered the mike, the same one I had seen in so many press photos of the stars I looked up to. I was standing on that same stage in the same place they had stood, where five seconds ago Johnny

Cash had stood welcoming me to the stage—me, little Dolly Rebecca Parton from Locust Ridge.

Someone in the audience took a flash picture, and it snapped me out of being a tourist. I wasn't sure I could sing at all. But God had brought me this far and had put something in me that would not be held back. As I heard the band play my introduction, I lifted my head and looked up toward the lights. I smiled at the people in the balcony and then let 'er rip. I sang the way I had that day in the old chapel. I sang for God and Mama and Daddy. I sang for Sawdust and Aunt Marth. I sang for everybody who had ever believed in me. Somehow, I believed in me. I guess it showed in my voice.

I was stunned by the way the crowd reacted. I don't think I had ever seen two thousand people in one place before. I know I had never heard a crowd cheer and shout and clap that way. And they were doing it all for me. I got three encores. This time I was prepared for an encore, but not three, not at the Grand Ole Opry. Someone told me later, "You looked like you were out there saying, 'Here I am, this is me.'" I was. Not just to that audience but to the whole world.

That performance did a lot for my confidence. I remember walking to Uncle Bill's old car that night after the show, still flying treetop high. I said, "Well, Uncle Bill, I'm pretty good, ain't I?"

He laughed and said, "Yes, I guess you are."

I was to see a lot of that old car in the next couple of years. I can't count the nights Bill and I slept in that old crate in the parking lot of some club or on the street in front of some record company or promoter's office. It was an old brown Ford that had been hit on the passenger side. The fender on the other side didn't match the rest of the car. I guess it had been wrecked on that side too and then repaired, after a fashion.

The door on my side had been wired shut with a coat hanger, so Bill would have to open the door on his side and I'd slide across. I'll bet a lot of people who saw that thought he was being a gentleman. In truth, Bill's manners were more suited to that car than they would have been to a new Cadillac.

Bill would sleep in the front seat, and I would sleep in the back, once we finally got to sleep, that is. Many nights we would sit up writing songs or working on arrangements or just dreaming about all the big times to come until almost daylight. There is a healthy amount of dreaming that has to be done for any project to really be worthwhile. All of those doors have to be knocked on. Some have to be slammed in your face. All of those tapes have to be sent in. Many will end up in the trash without ever having been heard. It's all a part of the process.

To an outsider the quest for stardom might seem too frustrating, too heartbreaking. The whole system might seem cruel. Front-office people might seem put there simply to keep you from getting anywhere. The fact is, they are. Trying to weed out those few people with talent from all of that sea of dreamers is quite a job. It's a lot like looking for four-leaf clovers, which would be easy to find if it weren't for all of those three-leaf ones. The problem is, every one of those three-leaf clovers thinks he's a four-leafer. He has to in order to keep going and pushing, always on the move so you can't count his leaves. It's the front-office person's job to keep me out, and it's my job to keep on trying. That's the system, and there's nothing we can do about it. Talent is a subjective thing.

That is especially true when it comes to songwriting. It's usually pretty obvious if you can sing or not, but everybody thinks he's a songwriter. You can't go through a drive-through window at a fast food stand in Nashville without getting a cassette tape of some-body's would-be hit along with your french fries.

The story goes that Johnny Cash was in church one Sunday at a big service in Nashville, and he was called upon to go to the altar and pray. He went up the aisle and got down on his knees and was about to begin praying when he became aware of someone kneeling next to him. Before Johnny could start his prayer, the man slipped a tape into his pocket and whispered rev-erently, "I've got a song for you." I have no doubt that story is true. I also have no doubt that if he had been at that service, that man could well have been my Uncle Bill.

Whatever Uncle Bill was or wasn't, there was no doubt he believed in me, or at least that something could be made of or from me. He was always on the case. He would knock on doors wearing his best smile and sell me as if I were a vacuum cleaner. He would approach people with sparkly boots getting out of Cadillacs and talk me up in every possible way.

His favorite way was to hang out at Tootsie's Orchid Lounge. This was, and is, a somewhat seedy little dive across an alley from the back door of the old Ryman Auditorium, where the Grand Ole Opry was held at that time. Many of the big performers, promoters, songwriters, and publishers would hang out there between or after shows. It was a fertile field for a squirrel like Uncle Bill to dig for acorns in.

He would con and connive and finagle his way into an audition if he could. If nothing else, he would usu-ally convince his mark to take a tape of our songs. Of course this portion of his "work" included having a few drinks with whoever he was chatting up our songs to. This was a job he relished, maybe a little too much. Most nights he would "work" himself right onto the floor. Then he would fall back into the car or the flophouse room, if we could afford one that night, to sleep it off and begin all over the next day.

We would drive around town in that old car without much of a plan of what to do. But you could bet night wouldn't fall without our trying to create some opportunity to be heard. It seemed like during this driving, the dreaming part of our "job" was shifted into high gear. We would make up songs or parts of songs and sing them at the top of our lungs. It was hard to play guitar while the car was moving, so I would usually just beat on the dashboard. Those old cars were built really well, but that dashboard finally began to buckle after fifty or so songs.

As writers we were on the same wavelength. We wrote a lot of great songs together, and we still do. We had the same kind of energy when it came to our careers. Neither of us ever gave out as long as something was happening or at least had the look of something that might happen. Nothing mattered to Billy except his work. I knew exactly where he was coming from.

That is why I understood when he stepped in front of a bus in Knoxville. His plan was to get injured just enough to get an insurance settlement (hopefully cash out of court) to get gas money to go to Nashville. He wanted to be able to buy some lights, a microphone, and a little sound system so that we could play somewhere. I was just hoping he wouldn't wind up playing in the angel band. But I understood why he did it. I'm enough like my daddy that I did not always agree with Uncle Billy's methods, but I certainly identified with the drive that made him do that kind of thing. I would sometimes cringe when he would take his wife's hard-earned waitress money and buy a tank of gas for a show or a trip. But because I shared the dream, I said nothing.

Bill had many wives, as dreamers often do. I'd like to publicly thank all of them for their contributions to my career. I know they put up with a lot from Bill and me, and I appreciate them for it, especially Chris. The wives came and went, but the quest for stardom went on.

On one particular day, our objective was to get in to see Buddy Killen at Tree Publishing. I believe Bill had met him somewhere, and Mr. Killen, as people will do, said something like, "Stop by my office sometime," never expecting the invitation to be taken seriously. He obviously didn't know Uncle Bill. We walked into the outer office, with our guitars in tow, and proudly announced ourselves. We thought we gave off an air of serious music professionals. Looking back, I'm sure everybody in that office could recognize us as a pair of backwoods doorknockers with more brass than credentials. Even if we had known that at the time, it still would not have stopped us, or even slowed us down.

We were told Mr. Killen was in a meeting, and I'm sure he was. We waited. Mr. Killen was on the phone. We waited. Mr. Killen had to go out to another meeting. That meant he had to walk right by us. He did. There were strained smiles in response to Bill's advances. There were sideways "Can't you get rid of them?" looks at secretaries. We waited.

Country people claim that if a snapping turtle gets a hold of your toe, he won't let go until it thunders. Well, it wasn't about to thunder in that office, and Bill was the stubbornest snapping turtle a music executive could ever hope not to run across. Finally, at about six o'clock, Mr. Killen came back to his office to tie up a few loose ends and found our loose ends still tying up the better part of his sofa. He gave in and said with a sigh, "Y'all come on in."

When we first walked into the outer office, I had been a little bit nervous, but by now I felt like a caged animal that had been set free. I flapped open the lid of my cardboard guitar case and whipped out my old Martin. Mr. Killen seemed a little taken aback. I think he wasn't sure whether I was going to play the guitar or brain him with it. He breathed a sigh of relief when I went into a song. Bill hustled his guitar out as fast as he could and joined in. I sang loud and strong with the security that comes with knowing that one way or another, it'll be over soon.

By this time, Bill and I had written several songs that we thought had potential. To our amazement, so did Buddy Killen. I think he admired our guts as much as anything. What really thrilled me was that he liked my voice. He even thought I had a chance at becoming a recording artist. Of course that was sheet music to my ears.

Bill and I signed a deal with Tree Publishing as songwriters. That was great, but there was something else that absolutely made my spirit soar. I was to have a demo recording session for Mercury Records. That usually meant a three-hour session that would produce four songs. Bill and I had to make two or three more trips to Nashville before the records would actually be cut. Now it seemed like our old car had wings. Maybe it wasn't the car at all. I believe I could have flown from Sevierville to Nashville on my own.

One person who was very helpful to us during our time at Tree was Jerry Crutchfield. His name might well have been "Crushfield" because I had a big one on him. He had a very distinctive voice and a way of carrying himself that really blew my skirt up. I had visions of the two of us between the sheet music. I don't know if he ever knew how I felt. I was such a moony-eyed kid, I don't see how he or anyone else could have missed it. Jerry went on to become one of the biggest record producers in Nashville, and I still think of him as a very special person.

Somehow, in between girlish sighs over Jerry Crutchfield, I made the records. The A side was a song that Uncle Bill and I had written called "It May Not Kill Me (But It's Sure Gonna Hurt)." On the other side was a song that I had written with Uncle Bill and Uncle John Henry. The title of it was "I Wasted My Tears (When I Cried Over You)." Both of the songs got airplay on the local station back in Sevierville, as did all of the "homemade" records I had made before. I will never forget hearing "It May Not Kill Me" on a Knoxville station, WIVK. There I was, actually hearing myself sing, not on a tape or studio monitor but on a real radio station that thousands of people were listening to . . . at that very moment. I was so proud I walked around for days with my chest all stuck out. Somehow, nobody noticed.

That feeling didn't last, and neither did our association with Mercury and Tree. The realities of the music business began to reveal themselves to me. It is one thing to have a record company take a chance on an unknown and finance a record. It is quite another to get radio stations to play it. The overall response to my records had given the label little reason to pursue future recordings with me. We had all tried our best, but there's just no way to guess what the public is going to go for at any given time. I will always be grateful to Buddy Killen for the faith he had in me. I hope that the success I've had since that time has at least given him the satisfaction of knowing he was right.

While it takes more than that to discourage an Owens dreamer with a Parton will, it seemed the best thing for me to do was to go back home to the hills and finish high school. This was not a thought I relished. I never liked school. I was the first one in my family to ever finish high school, and I am proud that I did. But I had known so early what I wanted to do with my life that I couldn't see the importance of my learning geography or plane geometry.

I was not well liked in school either. In fact, I was actively disliked by many—especially the other girls. I liked to dress flashy, and I had an unearned reputation for being a tramp. That reputation was fostered largely by girls who appeared to be goody-goodies all week but on Friday nights were something else altogether. When they made a car rock, it wasn't from beating out songs on the dashboard. Of course the rumors of my whoring made me very popular with the boys, which tended to make me even less popular with the girls. The irony was that the other girls' mothers all thought I was a bad influence on them.

I guess I have to admit that the way I usually looked would have made just about anybody think that. I became aware of my body at a very early age. By the time I was twelve I had sprouted what some of the boys called "headlights." I was five feet two when I was twelve, and I have never grown another fraction since. I wanted to look sexy from the time I was about ten, but it didn't go into overdrive until about thirteen. After that, nobody could stop me, not Mama or Daddy, not Grandpa Jake, nobody.

I saved what money I could keep from "The Cas Walker Show" to buy peroxide, makeup, and sexy clothes. I couldn't get my hair big enough or "yaller" enough. Couldn't get my skirt tight enough, my blouses low enough. Couldn't get my boobs to stand up high enough or squeeze them together close enough. Of course, I had to get away from home to really put on the dog. I'd go into the four-for-a-quarter picture booth at Woolworth's, unbutton my blouse, push my headlights up with my arms, and take pictures. On the next quarter, I'd pull my blouse down off my shoulder and practice my sexy look.

Believe it or not, I thought I needed falsies. To simulate those, I would sneak into the closet and cut the shoulder pads out of a woman's coat, Grandma's or somebody's. I'd do that in the middle of the summer when I knew they wouldn't be missed for a long time. When I discovered that there was actually a thing called a push-up bra, that, to me, had to be the equal of the day Einstein figured out that relativity thing. After all, it's all relative. And now my relatives would have to go around in the winter with slumpy-looking shoulders.

I tried to make the best of school. I think what helped me get through it at all was my friendship with Judy Ogle. We had met many years earlier when we were in the third grade. My family had just moved from Locust Ridge to Caton's Chapel, and I was going through the typical "new kid" shyness. In Judy I found somebody shyer than I was. She was an absolutely withdrawn little girl with ragged clothes, chapped lips, and skinned knees, with a piece of a rubber band taken from an old pair of underwear, what we used to call "bloomer rubber," in her hair.

I suppose most people wouldn't have noticed her, but I was drawn to her because of her big green cat-curious eyes. I was also fascinated by her hair, the color of a new copper penny. We had some redheaded relatives, but their hair was closer to auburn. Judy's hair was orange. I must have seemed just as strange in my own way to her. We were both fish out of water. Unlike her, my greatest defense against shyness was to be outgoing. I am very glad that I was outgoing enough to get to know Judy. It was the beginning of a friendship that has lasted a lifetime.

Everybody knew her father, Mayford, was a moonshiner who sampled his own wares and could be pretty nasty to live with when he had done a little too much "tastin'." Judy's mother was the complete opposite. Blanche, or Granny Ogle, as everybody calls her, is the dearest, sweetest woman you could ever hope to meet. She was always hauling other people's kids around, thankfully me included, to this dance or that practice or whatever else a good mother needed to be about. Every year she would play Santa Claus. She's a skinny little woman and looked more like a praying mantis in a red sock than like Santa. We got a kick out of it and loved her for it just the same. Anybody can be Santa Claus if the desire and the love are there.

Judy had to work the fields like a man as she was growing up. Her father had even hired his kids out to work for other people in addition to working on his own place. She was as tough as nails, in body and in spirit, and mostly kept to herself until it came time to play at sports. We used to call her "Booten." When it came to softball, kickball, or just about any kind of ball, I would always yell, "I want to be on Booten's team." That was partly because I liked Booten and partly because I liked winning. Whichever team had Judy on it was pretty much assured of doing that. She could knock a softball a mile, sink a basket from anywhere on the court, and run like the wind. She would always pick me for her team, and that made me feel good because most of the other girls wouldn't. Judy played hard enough for both of us.

I was not that athletic or physical. I wanted to think, dream, create, sing, write. Judy was fascinated by that part of me. I did the thinking and planning, and she played it out. We made a great pair. She always thought I was so funny. She got a big kick out of the jokes I would make to cover up my clumsiness and my feelings of inadequacy.

Judy and I were in the high school band together. I had no desire to march at football games, but at least it had something to do with music, so I gave it my all. I never learned to play a marching band instrument or read music, but I knew how to keep a beat. It was a little impractical to carry around an old Ford dashboard, so they gave me a snare drum. I used to always have a big ugly bruise on my leg from lugging that drum around.

The best part of band was that the director seemed to realize that I heard a different calling. Instead of trying to teach me band music, he would let Judy and me sit in the band room for hours, picking out songs on the piano. I would "hunt and plunk" my way through a song and make up words to it as I went along. Judy would write it down. Even today many of my songs get written that way. More often than not, the first person to put pen to paper to write down one of my songs has been Judy Ogle. She is my best friend, and the two of us have been as close as any two sisters could ever hope to be. That accounts for the confusion outsiders sometimes have when they hear me call Judy "sis" or "sissy," which I do most of the time.

School was always a strange experience for me, but one Monday I arrived to find it stranger than ever. The minute I entered the hallway, I could see and feel a change come over the other kids. People were pointing at me with their eyes from a distance and whispering to one another. It wasn't unusual for rumors to circulate about me, but suddenly I was a total outcast. This went on for several days until finally I was almost in tears. I asked one of my few girlfriends, Janice Patterson, what was going on. She said, "You mean you don't know?"

"Know what?" I asked.

"Then it's not so?" she asked, looking very puzzled and disturbed. I convinced her I had no idea what she was talking about, and finally she told me.

The story was out all over school that I had been raped by a group of men over behind A. J. King's Lumberyard. My mouth fell open. I was absolutely devastated. I couldn't say another word to Janice, though I have always been grateful to her for her honesty. I walked away from school without looking back. I didn't wait for the bus; I walked all the way home.

As I walked, I thought about the story and how twisted the minds of those who created it must have been. If it had been true, wouldn't I have been an innocent victim rather than someone to be shunned and looked down upon? And what about these fictitious men that had been so wrongly accused? In a strange way, I was almost as outraged for them as I was for myself.

By the time I got home, my outrage had turned to just plain hurt, and my tears flowed freely as I told Mama what had happened. I told her I was never going back to school. Mama and Daddy had never forced any of us to go to school. There was plenty to be done at home, helping to raise the younger kids and doing chores. But Mama knew this was about more than school.

She had a way of speaking and of holding her head up that said, "You know I'm right." And she always was. She said, "All right, you can quit if you want to and let everybody think the story is true." Her head got a little higher and her lips took on yet another degree of righteous firmness as she continued, "or you can march right back in there with your head held high, knowing the truth in your own heart, and show them you're better than they are."

That is exactly what I did. School was not something I would have fought for under ordinary circumstances. But, by God, no vicious, lying cowards were going to deprive me of it. Mama was right. It wasn't about school at all. It was about self-respect.

That was not the only story that was told about me in school, but somehow after that they lost their power to hurt me. There was a real good-looking guy named Curly Dan Bailey who worked with me on the Cas Walker show. Even though I was only fourteen at the time, the rumor spread that I had gotten pregnant by Curly Dan and that Rachel was actually my illegitimate child by him. Rachel does have a curly mop of hair, but then, so does our daddy.

I think the lie made Mama madder than anybody. Rachel had to be taken by cesarean and was the last child she would be able to have. There are those who still think Rachel is my child—sometimes, I think, even Rachel. Of course it's not above me to have a little fun with that. Even today when Rachel's hair fuzzes up from the rain or humidity I will sometimes call her "Curly Dan." The fact that I was able to laugh off stories like that felt good to me. I had really learned Mama's lesson about self-respect.

Self-respect was difficult enough to maintain at home, especially for a young girl trying to become a woman in a house half full of men and boys. People have often asked me how we girls managed any privacy in a house with so many boys and no private rooms. It was difficult. We used to bathe with a washcloth from a pan of water. We would first start with our necks and faces and wash down as far as possible. Then we would wash the road dust from our feet and wash up as far as possible. Later, when the boys were out of the room, we would wash "possible."

It was these circumstances that led to a very

embarrassing mishap that I have told very few people and would not relate here if it were not so funny. We had an outdoor bathroom, and there were times in the middle of the night when it was very inconvenient to dress and go out into the cold just to take a leak. For these times there was a little room, actually a closet, that had in it what was called a "slop jar" or "slop bucket." It was actually an enameled pot with flared sides that was made to accommodate a woman squatting over it to do her business. The closet had no door as such, just a sort of curtain hung on a tight piece of wire. After dark when the fire had died down, it could afford some kind of privacy at least.

One night when I was about sixteen or seventeen, I had been out on a date and got home fairly late. Everybody was already in bed, and I didn't want to wake them and alert Mama and Daddy to the hour of my homecoming. I was absolutely bustin' to pee, so I fumbled my way through the dark until I found the curtain to the closet and stepped inside. I dropped my panties and hiked up my skirt and assumed the position over the slop jar. I was feeling relieved in a physical sense and quite grown-up and somewhat smug that I "pulled it off," so to speak.

But suddenly, here in the middle of my little triumph, or more accurately here in the middle of my rump, came the cold nose of an unexpected intruder. A raccoon had gotten into the house, and unbeknownst to me, we were sharing the closet as well as a very intimate moment. When I felt that cold nose on my butt, I screamed bloody murder and literally peed all over myself.

Of course I woke the whole house with my unscheduled concert. Daddy grabbed the poker to fend off an intruder. Mama started praying. The little kids cried, and the big kids just ran around confused.

When everybody found out what had happened, they all had a good laugh at my expense. Except, of course, the raccoon. Once the lights were turned on, he acted like any man caught in a compromising position with a lady and bolted for the door. I often think of that moment at times when I'm feeling "too big for my britches," and it tends to have a humbling effect.

9

I continued to bide my time in school, waiting to be eighteen, waiting to be free, waiting to follow my dream. I still sang on the Cas Walker show during breaks from school. It was during one such break in 1963 that the boy I was dating at the time agreed to drive me to Knoxville to do the show. He was a good-looking boy who had always been nice to me. He had a pretty good car with a radio that worked, so I was looking forward to the trip with him.

We were riding along listening to WIVK. The country music program was interrupted for a special news bulletin. What I heard sent my heart crashing through the floorboards. Even the radio reporter's voice quivered with emotion as he announced that President John F. Kennedy had been shot and killed in Dallas.

I had loved John Kennedy. Not in the way a woman loves a man but in the way one idealist recognizes another and loves him for that place within themselves that they share. I didn't know a lot about politics, but I knew that a lot of things were wrong and unjust and that Kennedy wanted to change them. He was young. He looked at the country with fresh eyes that saw what his predecessors could not or would not. I grieved for the country. For the loss of a spirit that young people and poor people and downtrodden people could share and call their own. I was choked silent. I was numb. That turned out to be fortunate. Otherwise, I don't think my heart could have stood what happened next.

On hearing the news that had sent me into such grief, my boyfriend said, "I'm glad they shot the niggerlovin' son of a bitch!" I couldn't believe what I had heard. I couldn't believe that a young person with whom I had shared intimacy and laughter could be so ignorant, biased, and insensitive. How could he dismiss a man, any human being, with so callous and hateful a remark? I suppose in your heart you always know such people exist, but you don't want to believe those close to you could be that way. It was obvious to me that a person who thought that way could never understand or truly appreciate me or anything I believed in.

The show was canceled that night. I got the boy to drive me home. I never saw him again and never gave him an explanation. I didn't feel he deserved one. More than that, I knew he didn't have the sensitivity to understand anyway.

At times like that, I did have some real friends to turn to, especially my soul mate, Judy Ogle. We shared some other friends too. Judy's other best friend was Shirley King. She was the twin sister of Dewey King, the boy who had bought my pie at the pie supper. Then there was my other best friend, Georgia "Road Hog" Justus. She is also my cousin. But then, in those parts, who's not?

We called her Road Hog because of the way she

drove the old rattletrap of a car that her daddy had got for her. None of us knew anything about driving. I guess Georgia was afraid of running into something on the side of the road or into the ditch, because she would kind of take her half of the road out of the middle. The rest of us didn't care so much, as long as we had a ride, but other drivers used to honk at her all the time. That old car served for many a songwriting night and day, and for chasing boys.

Georgia and I were just a little wilder than most of the other girls. We were kin, after all, and wild hares did run rampant in our family. We used to cruise Gatlinburg and Sevierville, circling the Tastee-Freez, flirting with the boys, and singing. I'd always carry my guitar. Most of the girls around there were kind of shy, and I would always manage to attract the boys with my singing and joking.

Georgia listened to my dreams, like Judy did. She believed me when I talked about all the things I was going to do. She loved the songs I'd write and took pride in the fact that I wrote them in her car. I know she did, because she recently went on a segment of "Geraldo" about growing up with celebrities and said so.

Georgia was my cousin on my daddy's side. A cousin on Mama's side was a good friend to me too, Hope McMahan. Her mama was my great-aunt Exa. She and her husband, Cleo McMahan, owned a little grocery store. They were very good about allowing people to have credit during the hard winter months and then pay when times were better. They probably kept many a family up there from starving to death.

I don't think Hope necessarily believed all of my talk about being a star. At the time, she thought I was just full of myself . . . or something. She was the one who gave Judy Ogle the nickname Booten. Any time there was a game of any kind, Hope would be like a cheerleader saying, "We're all rootin' for Booten."

Judy and I had one other friend who was very dear to both of us. Her name was Colleen Reagan. She was a beautiful girl with coal-black hair and chiseled features. Her mother had died when Colleen was very young, during the birth of Colleen's baby brother, Shelby. There were five kids altogether, including Colleen's twin brother, Carl, and two sisters, Maxine and Charlotte. They had a real tough time growing up without a mother. To make things worse, their daddy was a heavy drinker.

Colleen adored Elvis. A lot of girls liked Elvis. Some girls wanted to have Elvis. Colleen wanted to *be* Elvis. She cut her hair short and swept it back like his. She even fashioned some of the front part into "sideburns" that came down in front of her ears. She had gotten a leather jacket from somewhere, and she would wiggle her hips and wobble around, shaking her leg, just like The King. She was normally a very shy girl, but when she was Elvis, she was a tiger. I guess in a way it was an escape from some pretty tough times.

When word went around that Elvis was going to be on "The Ed Sullivan Show," Colleen was just hellbent to see him. Almost nobody up there had a TV. Most of the ones who did wouldn't let any of the kids watch Elvis on it, because they said he was vile and "of the devil." Well, Colleen knew this one old lady who never missed Ed Sullivan and would no doubt have her set tuned in to the show that night.

She and her sisters decided to sneak off over there to watch Elvis, even if it meant they'd have to watch through the old lady's window. As they were walking into the yard that night, they got attacked by a pack of dogs and were bitten all over. They finally did get to see Elvis, but then Colleen was beaten up when she got home because she had sneaked off. I doubt anybody ever paid a higher price to see Elvis.

She acted it all out for those of us who didn't see him, shaking her pelvis, doing the upper lip, the whole thing. It all seemed worth it. We didn't care that she got chewed up either. To us, for that moment, she was Elvis.

Colleen's Elvis phase continued for quite a while after that. She eventually married my uncle Louis Owens, the one who gave me my first guitar and helped me out in Nashville. Colleen always had a fascination with hair, and after they were married, she went to beauty school. I volunteered to be her model. She practiced every perm, every style, every color on me. I even went with her to the state board to model for her when she got her license. She did my hair for "The Cas Walker Show" and later in Nashville. We really got into some big hair together. Friends like Colleen and the others helped make my high school years fun, although I never took my mind off my ultimate goal.

I remember New Year's Eve 1964. I was so excited that I waited up to welcome not only the New Year but the sunrise as well. This was the year I was to graduate high school, the year I would finally be free to pursue my dream full-time. It has long been a custom for graduating classes to go on a senior trip. Mine was no exception. To pay for the trip, we sold Krispy Kreme donuts, all kinds of candy, Burpee seeds, and whatever else a group of kids could sell (usually to their parents). Nineteen sixty-four was also the year of the New York World's Fair, and that was to be our adventure, with Washington, D.C., thrown in for good measure.

Try to imagine several busloads of backwoods kids riding all the way to New York, the twangy cries of "Are we there yet?", the numerous stops to pee, the questions about everything and everyplace we passed on the way. The bus drivers and I will never forget the moment we finally rolled through the Lincoln Tunnel into New York. Everywhere you looked, on buses, on billboards, on the tops of taxis were the words "Hello, Dolly!" Naturally I made jokes. "I don't know how they knew I was coming" and "I didn't know they'd make such a fuss" were the sorts of things my classmates had to put up with all day long. Of course, we found out that "Hello, Dolly!" was a new Broadway show. But to me, it was still a great welcome to the world outside the mountains, the one I had always lived for, the one where I would be a star. Years later I was in fact welcomed to New York in almost as grand a style and given the key to the city by then-mayor Ed Koch. I have always felt welcome in New York City and still get a feeling of exhilaration every time I see the skyline loom up in the distance.

Graduation day itself was almost a nonevent for me. What I was really anticipating was heading for Nashville the following day. I was proud that I had earned my diploma though (by the skin of my teeth), and Mama was very proud too. She and some of my brothers and sisters attended the ceremony. It wasn't like Daddy to leave his plow for such a thing. It was a small class, so each of us in turn got a chance to stand up and announce our plans for the future. "I'm going to junior college," one boy would say. "I'm getting married and moving to Maryville," a girl would follow.

When it came my turn, I told what I considered to be the truth: "I'm going to Nashville to become a star," I said as straightforwardly as I could. The entire place erupted in laughter. I was stunned. What were they laughing at? I remember thinking to myself, "They don't know. They just don't know." Somehow that laughter instilled in me an even greater determination to realize my dream in a kind of "I'll show them" way. It is very likely that I might have crumbled under the weight of the hardships that were to come, had it not been for the response of the crowd that day. Sometimes it's funny the way we find inspiration. Those of us who know God don't find it all that strange.

Early the next morning I boarded a Greyhound bus with my dreams, my old guitar, the songs I had written, and the rest of my belongings in a set of matching luggage—three paper bags from the same grocery store. I had asked whatever relatives could afford to give me a graduation gift to please make it cash. I didn't want any additional baggage, and I knew I would need the money for a grub stake until I became a star. I genuinely thought that would happen before my little bit of money ran out. I suppose if it weren't for naivete and fool-hearted, pigheaded stubbornness, nobody would ever see their dreams through. Except for lottery winnings, there are few things of any value that come without some trials and disappointment.

Some disappointment I was prepared for. I was not prepared for the amount I was dealt. My money disappeared in no time. I was hungry and homesick and disheartened. I had never slept in a bed by myself before. I missed things like brother and sister toenails digging into my shins. Believe it or not, I even missed being peed on. I wrote the following letter home:

June 2, 1964
Nashville, Tenn.

Dear Mama and Daddy,
I hope this letter finds you well. As for me,

I'm fine, I guess, just a little lonesome and a whole lot homesick. I got here okay and I thought I'd write to let you know because I knew you'd be worried about me. I don't want you to be worried about me because I'm going to be alright, once I get settled and used to being away from home. I didn't realize how much I loved you and them noisy kids until I left. And I didn't realize how hard it was to leave home until I started to leave and everybody started crying.

I cried nearly all the way and, in a way, I wanted to turn around and come back, but you know how I've always wanted to move to Nashville and be a singer and I believe that someday if I try long and hard enough I'll make it. Don't worry about trying to send me no money or anything because I've got a job on an early morning TV show and a couple of people that might record one of the songs I wrote, so I'll be making some money. So don't worry about me being hungry or anything. Nashville is not exactly what I thought it would be, but I think I'm going to like it here once I get used to it.

Don't worry about me getting in trouble. I'll be good, just like I promised. Well, I guess I'd better close for now. Write soon and tell everybody I said hello.

With love as always,
Dolly

I knew I had painted the picture a little brighter than it actually was for Mama and Daddy's sake. But I didn't realize how much I had lied—especially the part about not being hungry. I remembered old stories people would tell about times during the depression when down-and-out diners would go to a café and order a pine float—a glass of water and a toothpick. I had heard of people making soup out of hot water and ketchup. I can tell you personally it's not very satisfying. At a time like that, you can either dine for as long as possible on your own fingernails or learn to get by some other way. I tried both.

I would sometimes go to hotels at night and walk up and down the halls until I found a room-service tray that had been left outside the door for pickup. Sometimes those selfish hotel guests would clean their plates. Other times I would find half of a sandwich or an uneaten piece of chicken. Occasionally, I would lift a cover and find the mother lode, part of a steak. I have always hated to see food wasted in a world where so many people are hungry. In those days, that had a personal meaning for me, and I did my best to see that, at least in that hotel, no food was wasted.

It's not something I'm proud of, but I would do a little eating on the sly at grocery stores. I would get a cart and wheel it through the aisles. While I pretended to shop, I would pick up items I could easily open and eat from the package. I would eat a bag of potato chips while pretending to check the produce for ripeness. Or I'd drink a pint of milk while trying to decide which brand of coffee I wasn't going to buy. I would hurriedly gag down a handful of baloney and cheese while keeping an eye out for the store clerks. Finally, I would put my cart away and make my escape. If I had any money at all, I usually tried to buy one item, a pack of gum or something. I guess, in my mind, that somehow made it better. Even a basically honest person can do desperate things when hunger begins gnawing at them. But I shop now at all the stores I stole from, so I more than paid them back.

I lived in a little apartment on Wedgewood Avenue. There was a Laundromat downstairs called the Wishy Washy. One day, while I was waiting for my clothes to dry, I bought a Coke and sipped it as I walked around on the sidewalk out front. I remember I was wearing a red ruffled rib-tickler outfit with tight bell-bottomed pants. If someone had asked me, I would have said that looking for a man was the last thing on my mind. Now that I think back on the way I was dressed, maybe my subconscious was doing a little bit of "trolling."

A man drove by and said something like, "You're going to get a sunburn in that outfit."

"That's all right," I said, giving him a wave. I have always tried to be friendly. Besides, there's just a natural reaction a country person has when a car goes by: Your hand flies up. It never occurred to me that perhaps a young girl shouldn't be waving at strange men in cars.

I guess the man liked what he saw because he drove around the block and came by again. This time he stopped his car and began flirting with me. He was drop-dead handsome, so I wasn't bothered much. I talked with him awhile, and we made a few jokes back and forth. When I told him I had to take my clothes out of the dryer, I expected him to go on his way. I was shocked when he came inside the Laundromat with me. I didn't want this handsome man with his fine car watching me while I folded my ragged drawers.

He wasn't interested in my drawers, at least not the ones I was folding. I was surprised and delighted that while he talked to me, he looked at my face (a rare thing for me). He seemed to be genuinely interested in finding out who I was and what I was about. What I was about at that moment was of course being interested in him. He was so different from the men I had known back home. Once I had a boyfriend back in Sevierville who'd bought me a ring and put a down payment on a house, expecting me to marry him. Perhaps if he had asked me about it, he might have stood a better chance, but I doubt it. I had no plans to marry him or anyone else. I was here to become a star.

But in spite of all of that, there was something irresistible about this man. I remember looking into his eyes and getting the most wonderful feeling. I said to myself, "Well, I'll be dogged." The man's name was Carl Dean.

He came to see me every day for the next week. I was baby-sitting to earn a little money. That meant I couldn't leave the house, so a real date was out of the question. Still Carl would just come and sit with me at the bottom of the steps next to the Wishy Washy, where I could keep an eye on the little boy. I wasn't wishy-washy about keeping my eye on the big boy.

Finally, the child's mother had a day off and we could have a genuine date. Carl picked me up right on time. He has always been prompt. He has also always been mysterious. He didn't give me any kind of hint as to where we were going, so I didn't know how to dress or anything. As we drove along, I was trying to see what part of town we were heading for to get some clue as to what was up. I was surprised when we pulled into the driveway of a private home. Carl walked me to the door and opened it.

Inside, his mother was just putting supper on the table. Without any other word of introduction Carl said to his mother, "Fix this girl a plate. She's the one I'm going to marry." With a nervous laugh I tried to acknowledge that he had made a little joke. But something in his voice told me he hadn't. In all my life, I have never felt such an odd combination of emotions. First, I was shocked that he wanted to marry me, since he had never given me any indication that he cared that much for me. Second, I was astounded. I remember thinking, "Who the hell does this guy think he is?" I felt flattered, outraged, touched, turned on, scared to death, and completely confused. The boy back home who had bought the house was not even this presumptuous. At least he had said he loved me at some point.

There I was, feeling as mixed up as a road lizard in a spin dryer, and having to act sociable while trying to keep my dinner down. I somehow got through the meal and worked things out in my own mind enough to keep seeing Carl.

I soon moved to a different apartment. It was in a part of town where I didn't know anybody, and I was very lonely much of the time. I didn't have a radio or TV, and without a car I was left to just entertain myself. Of course, my favorite way to do that was to sing and play and write songs. Carl often showed up without warning, sometimes even in the middle of the night. I was glad to see him because I was becoming more and more serious about him. But some of his behavior did seem awfully odd. In fact, he seemed odd. Maybe the fact that he was so different made me that much more attracted to him. He was always a perfect gentleman, though. I guess if I had to say one thing about Carl it would be that he is not only a gentleman but a truly gentle man. We would usually sit on the porch so that the neighbors could see that we weren't doing anything improper. If we went inside, Carl would always leave the door open.

He had a little transistor radio, the kind from Japan that were so popular in the sixties. I thought it was just the greatest thing in the world. We would sit and talk and hold hands and kiss and listen to that little radio. Otis Redding was our favorite. "These Arms of Mine" and "I've Been Loving You Too Long" were our special songs.

In all this time, Carl had never said he loved me. He had never even said he liked me. He had, and has, a strange way of talking and an odd sense of humor. He was so handsome, I used to wonder if he had other girlfriends, but he never said or did anything to lead me to believe he did. Here I was falling more and more deeply in love with a man who had never given me any indication at all about his feelings for me.

That made it that much more horrifying to me the day he waltzed in and told me he was joining the army and going to Vietnam. I went berserk. If I had any doubts about my feelings for him, they were instantly washed away in a flood of tears. The lump in my throat told me in no uncertain terms I did not want to lose this man. The next thing that happened made me want to strangle him. Carl took me by the shoulders and told me it wasn't true, at least not the part about Vietnam. He was joining the National Guard and going away to boot camp. There was only a slim chance he might be sent to Vietnam. Having come to know Carl as I do now, he probably painted a worse picture for me so the real story would be easier to take. He does things like that. Sometimes I still want to strangle him, but his heart is usually in the right place. Lucky for him his throat is in the right place too, making it difficult for me to reach.

As Carl boarded the bus for boot camp, he still had not told me he loved me and had never asked, or even suggested, that I wait for him. But I did. Finally, he called and asked me if I would come to see him. He was at Fort Stewart, Georgia, near Savannah, so I

planned a trip to Jekyll Island with Judy and some of
my younger brothers and sisters so that I could be
near enough to visit him.

I took Judy and the kids to the beach and then set
out for the army camp. I remember it was one of the
first times I had ever worn a wig. It was just a short
one, relatively small compared to some of the hair
mountains I have these days. It was styled in one of
those sixties bouffants that are embarrassing when
you look at old pictures of yourself, but at the time, I
thought I really looked good. It took me a while to
find Carl. When I did I ran up and threw myself into
his arms. He is about six feet two inches tall. When I
hugged him so hard, his chin grazed the top of my
head, sending my wig flying. Carl never missed a beat.
He caught my wig in one hand while he continued to
hold me with the other. He gave me a deep, slow, passionate kiss. I felt that he was genuinely glad to see
me. Either that or the National Guard issues handguns to its new recruits. I was certainly relieved,
because I had obviously flipped my wig over him.

While Carl was away at boot camp, I threw myself
into my work. Of course my work at that time consisted
mostly of trying to find work. After a lot of knocking on
doors and singing here and there, I finally began to
become what people in the business call "hooked up." I
did live spots on "The Ralph Emery Show" and another
early-morning radio show, "The Eddie Hill Show."
Being on one of those shows meant you would be
singing at five o'clock in the morning. Anybody who
sings can tell you that your voice is not likely to be at
its best at that hour, but I did the best I could.

Uncle Bill had also been working his way up the
ladder, mainly playing guitar for Carl and Pearl
Butler, but that meant he had to spend a lot of time
on the road. Finally we got our first big break when

Fred Foster, who owned both Combine Publishing and Monument Records, signed us to a deal.

Fred invested a lot of time and effort and money in me. He bought clothes for me so that I would "look the part" and made a great effort to get me known. I thought of myself as a country singer, and that was all I had ever wanted to be. But Fred thought I should be more rockabilly. He must have had visions of making me into a female Elvis or something. He did various things to promote my career such as booking me on "American Bandstand" and at a jukebox convention in Chicago.

Going to Chicago meant I had to fly on an airplane for the first time in my life. What a first flight it was. It was stormy and the winds were gusty, and my plane was bumped and battered around the whole way to Chicago. I was miserable. I did my best at the convention, but I couldn't really enjoy any of the trip because I knew I had to get back on a plane to go home. To this day I am a white-knuckled flyer. I make a joke about it in one of my songs: "She's a sparrow when she's broken, but she's a chicken when she flies" (from "Eagle When She Flies").

Carl finally came home and would come to see me almost every night, usually staying to the wee hours. He was working with his father in his asphalt-paving business in South Nashville and I was living in Madison, Tennessee. Between that and the time he spent with me, he wasn't getting any sleep at all. Finally, one day he said, quite matter-of-factly, "You're either gonna have to move to the other side of town or we're gonna have to get married." That, to Carl, was a proposal. People always want to know how he asked me to marry him, and I always have to say, "He didn't exactly ask." Part of me was thrilled that he wanted to marry me, but another part was a little taken aback. That must have been the strongest part because that was the one that answered.

"You never have even said you loved me."

"Hell, you know I love you," was Carl's answer.

I attribute this to that same kind of unspoken communication that I explained when describing life with my daddy. It is one of the Parton/Dean rules of conduct I have become a one-woman committee to abolish. Always at holidays or other family gatherings, people would hug and say good-bye, but they would never say "I love you." Sure, I know that the love is there, but dammit, I want to hear it! I was the first one in my family, that I know of, to ever tell other family members that I loved them.

One day, after I had been living away from home for many years, I was saying good-bye to Daddy when I told him, "I love you." He responded in the usual nonverbal, look-at-the-ground Parton way, and I just couldn't stand it anymore.

I took his head between my hands and made him look me right in the eye. "You tell me you love me," I demanded.

With no small amount of embarrassment he said, "Aww, you know I love you'uns" (a mountain word meaning more than one).

"Not you'uns!" I kept on. "This has got nothing to do with Cassie or Bobby or anybody else. I want to know if you"—I emphasized the word by poking my finger into his chest—"love me," I said with an emphatic point toward myself. He tried to look to one side, but I held his face firmly. He blushed and sputtered and finally said haltingly, "I love you."

That must have been the crack in the dam. Once the top man had fallen, it was easier to teach the rest of the Partons to say "I love you." Now it is something we all do freely.

My early years were spent in a one-room school-house. One teacher taught grades 1 through 8.
(Used by permission. c. 1994 Junebug Clark)

A familiar country baptizing. I was about this age when I was baptized.
(Used by permission. c. 1994 Junebug Clark)

Aunt Martha
Williams (Marth).
(C. 1994 DOLLY PARTON
ENTERPRISES)

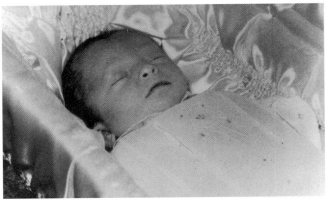

Larry, my baby brother who died.
(C. 1994 DOLLY PARTON ENTERPRISES)

The blond one in the middle is me!
(PHOTO BY DON WARDEN)

First Dolly Day parade in Sevierville.
(PHOTO BY LES LEVERETT)

My favorite school picture.
(C. 1994 DOLLY PARTON ENTERPRISES)

Me at three, already posing for the camera.
(C. 1994 DOLLY PARTON ENTERPRISES)

Picture made the day they buried Larry. My Aunt Dorothy Jo had bought us some new clothes.
(C. 1994 DOLLY PARTON ENTERPRISES)

Cas Walker, my first employer.
(PHOTO BY BOBBY DENTON)

One of my early publicity shots.
(C. 1994 DOLLY PARTON ENTERPRISES)

Senior picture '64.
(c. 1994 Dolly Parton Enterprises)

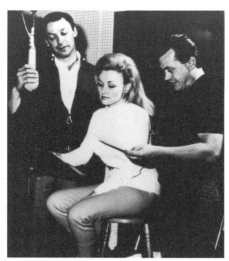

Fred Foster, me, and Uncle Bill in studio, at the first Monument recording session. (COURTESY FABRY STUDIOS)

The Parton family. Back row, left to right, Randy, David, Willadeene, Rachel, Dolly; front row, Cassie, Stella, Denver, Freida, Floyd, Bobby (not pictured here Larry—deceased). (PHOTO BY DENNIS CARNEY)

Emmylou Harris, Linda Ronstadt, and me on "The Tonight Show" with Johnny Carson.
(Courtesy NBC)

Chet Atkins and me.
(PHOTO BY KIM STANTON)

Me and my early awards.
(PHOTO BY BILL GOODMAN)

My pride and joy, a statue in the courthouse yard in Sevierville.
(PHOTO BY DON WARDEN)

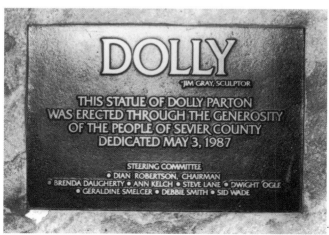

DOLLY
JIM GRAY, SCULPTOR

THIS STATUE OF DOLLY PARTON
WAS ERECTED THROUGH THE GENEROSITY
OF THE PEOPLE OF SEVIER COUNTY
DEDICATED MAY 3, 1987

STEERING COMMITTEE
• DIAN ROBERTSON, CHAIRMAN
• BRENDA DAUGHERTY • ANN KELCH • STEVE LANE • DWIGHT OGLE
• GERALDINE SMELCER • DEBBIE SMITH • SID WADE

Judy and me—back home and back to back.
(PHOTO BY JANET KNUTSEN)

Me outside my chapel, where much of this book was written.
(PHOTO BY CHRIS KELLY)

Bar mitzvah—Sandy at thirteen. One of my favorite pictures.
(C. 1994 DOLLY PARTON ENTERPRISES)

Me and Porter. Oh boy, a ring, but what I wanted was a raise.
(PHOTO BY LES LEVERETT)

My invalid Grandma Parton and my sisters. We were careful not to shake her bed.
(C. 1994 DOLLY PARTON ENTERPRISES)

Grandma Rena Owens and me. Before my prom, 1964 (she was not my date, she was going to church).
(C. 1994 DOLLY PARTON ENTERPRISES)

From left, Grandpa Walter Parton, me, Grandpa Jake Owens.
(c. 1994 DOLLY PARTON ENTERPRISES)

My Aunt
Dorothy Jo and
Uncle Lester
Owens.
(c. 1994 DOLLY
PARTON ENTERPRISES)

Me in my favorite angel dress. Designed for singing
"He's Alive" onstage.

(PHOTO BY ROBERT D'AMICO, COURTESY ABC-TV)

Dolly and Carl in front of church on their wedding day in Ringgold, Georgia.
(Photo by Avie Lee Parton)

Dolly and the "Unknown Husband."
(Photo by Dennis Carney)

Carl on the trike that cut his leg on "Downt the calley."
(Photo by Mama Dean)

Carl dressed up.
(Photo by Dennis Carney)

Grand Ole Opry cast that appeared on "The Dolly Show."
(PHOTO BY ROBERT D'AMICO, COURTESY ABC-TV)

Some Grand Ole Opry/Nashville buddies: left to right, front row, Uncle Bill Owens, Faron Young, Dolly, Bill Carlisle, Bill Phillips, Jimmy C. Newman; back row, Ralph Emery, Porter Wagoner, Fred Foster, Curly Putman, Johnny Russell, Buck Trent.
(PHOTO BY ROBERT D'AMICO, COURTESY ABC-TV)

Some of my Grand Ole Opry girlfriends: left to right, Kitty
Wells, Del Wood, Jan Howard, Skeeter Davis, Minnie Pearl,
Dolly, Jeannie Pruett, Norma Jean, Jean Shepard.
(PHOTO BY ROBERT D'AMICO, COURTESY ABC-TV)

Loretta Lynn, Dolly, and Tammy Wynette.
(COURTESY SONY MUSIC; PHOTO BY KIM STANTON)

Dolly and
Sylvester
Stallone.
(COURTESY
TWENTIETH
CENTURY FOX)

Burt Reynolds
and Dolly
pretending to
be caught by
tabloid
photographers.
(COURTESY
UNIVERSAL
PICTURES)

The picture Carl wanted
me to run in the tabloids
as "Burt Reynolds and
Dolly Parton's Baby."
(PHOTO BY DENNIS CARNEY)

Dolly, Sandy Gallin, and Barbra Streisand.
(COURTESY SANDY GALLIN)

Oprah Winfrey and Dolly.
(PHOTO BY CRAIG SJODIN, COURTESY ABC-TV)

Dolly and Miss Piggy.
(PHOTO BY CRAIG SJODIN, COURTESY ABC-TV)

Sittin' on the front porch on a summer afternoon,
in my Tennessee Mountain Home.
(PHOTO BY JOHN SEAKWOOD)

Me at a Dollywood function.
(COURTESY DOLLYWOOD; PHOTO BY J. R. RAYBOURN)

A sign I thought was funny. Wrestling was after the show, but Tom's always had a headlock on my heart.
(PHOTO BY JUDY OGLE)

Me at the Dollywood opening, with Bobby Goldsboro, Lily Tomlin, Burt Reynolds, Charles Durning, Ray Benson, other friends, and Dollywood cast.
(COURTESY DOLLYWOOD; PHOTO BY J. R. RAYBOURN)

Dr. Dolly Double D. A degree from Carson Newman College.
(COURTESY CARSON NEWMAN COLLEGE; PHOTO BY RICKE HESTER)

Frances Preston presenting me with the prestigious Robert J. Burton Award, one of my favorites.
(PHOTO BY PETER C. BORSARI)

Me and Gregg Perry on the set of *The Best Little Whorehouse in Texas*.
(COURTESY UNIVERSAL PICTURES)

Kenny and me on my first "Dolly" TV show. I turned him gray.
(PHOTO BY HOPE POWELL)

My favorite picture of Judy.
Her hair looked like a new
copper penny.
(C. 1994 DOLLY PARTON
ENTERPRISES)

Judy's been trying to get me
off her back for years.
(PHOTO BY FLATO)

One of my favorite pictures—Judy and I in
Ireland. The rocks all look like angels to me.
(PHOTO BY MARK KIRACOFE)

One of my best friends and favorite writer, Buddy Sheffield. (Courtesy ABC-TV)

Outside of my sisters, these are some of my best girlfriends: Judy Ogle, Shirlee Strahm, (me), Susie Glickman, Colleen Owens, Janet Knutsen.
(c. 1994 Dolly Parton Enterprises)

Imitation is the sincerest
form of flattery: my
littlest fans
(C. 1994 DOLLY PARTON
ENTERPRISES)

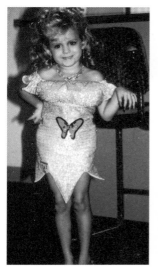

Check out these bell bottoms!!! Me on the set of the original
"Dolly Show" in the mid-seventies.

(PHOTO BY HOPE POWELL.)

Me at fifteen—a hillbilly hood ornament.
(PHOTO BY GEORGIA JUSTUS CAMPBELL)

Taking a
bath in the
mountains
in a barrel
of fun.
(PHOTO BY JOHN
SEAKWOOD)

Me clowning around in my usual amount of
makeup.
(PHOTO BY JANET KNUTSEN)

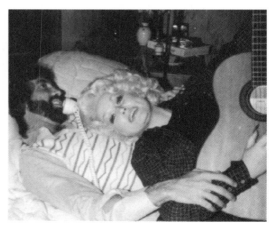

Me and Sandy, each holding our favorite
instrument.
(PHOTO BY CHUCK HAWKINS)

Porter and Wagonmaster reunion during taping of "The Dolly Show." Don Warden, Jack Little, Mac Magaha, George McCormick, Porter, Dolly, Bruce Osborn, Jerry Owens, Buck Trent, Speck Rhodes.
(PHOTO BY ROBERT D'AMICO, COURTESY ABC-TV)

Uncle Dot, me, and Aunt Estelle Watson.
(C. 1994 DOLLY PARTON ENTERPRISES)

The whole family at Dollywood for the Thanksgiving "Dolly Show."
(PHOTO BY JOHN SEAKWOOD)

Me with my nieces and nephews: Heidi, Hannah, Rebecca, (me), Donna, Dena, Chris, Jennifer, Tever, Jada, Danielle, Bryan, Tim, Clint, Mitchell. Not in the picture: Janet, Sabin, Nora Jane.
(PHOTO BY DENNIS CARNEY)

Mama and Daddy now.
(PHOTO BY OLAN MILLS)

It is still not something Carl does on a regular basis. But now and then, in a kind of sidewinding way, he will say it.

Carl's mother was ecstatic that we planned to marry. Her only daughter had eloped, and she never got to throw a big wedding for her. So she was very excited about giving one for Carl and me. I told Fred Foster I wanted to get married, and he asked me to wait a while, until my career was on firmer footing. He felt that having a husband would take away some of my appeal to men in the record-buying public. I told him I would, and then broke the bad news to Carl. He didn't want to wait. And since he was still the perfect gentleman, and I was getting pretty horny, I wasn't too keen on waiting either.

We told everybody that we had postponed the wedding. Then we secretly made plans to get married in another state so that it would not be recorded in the Tennessee newspapers. We decided on Ringgold, Georgia, which, as its name implies, has a whole industry built around hasty weddings. You could literally get a blood test at a roadside stand. And getting a marriage license was as easy as a drive-through.

I wanted to have my mother at my wedding, so we took Mama and headed off to Ringgold. Mama made me a wisp of a veil to go with a white eyelet dress she had also made. She had also wrapped a little white Bible in lace and tied it up with field flowers for me to carry.

It was a Friday when we got to Ringgold. We got our license without effort at the city hall. The judge, or justice of the peace or whatever title the man had, spit his tobacco against the wall and started in on the marriage rites. "Wait," I said. "I want to get married in a church."

Well, between spits the judge explained that we

could only be married right away if we did it there at the courthouse. If we wanted to be married elsewhere, we would have to wait until Monday. I'm sure that rule was to enable the city to make a few extra dollars, if not by the fees charged at the courthouse, then from the motel taxes. A motel was way beyond our budget, but I was determined to be married in a church. We decided to go back to Tennessee and return on Monday.

So here I was trying to get married to a man who hadn't really asked me, with a boss that didn't want me to and a town that wouldn't let me do it when I wanted. Yet I knew in my heart it was right. I couldn't wait till Monday to pick where I was going to be married, so we drove around town until we found Ringgold Baptist Church. We went in and had a chat with the minister. He didn't ask a lot of questions. He just seemed to sense by looking at Carl and me that we were sincere about being together for life. The minister, Don Duvall, shook our hands and said he'd be pleased to marry us on Monday. Finally here was somebody, other than Carl, who wanted me to get married. I couldn't help grabbing him and giving him a big hug. Unfortunately, there was nothing he could do about the Monday rule either. So off we went back to Nashville.

That weekend seemed about a decade long. I came to understand that saying that goes, "When you've found the one you want to spend the rest of your life with, you want to start the rest of your life right away."

Mama stayed with me that Saturday and Sunday. Now, I love Mama, but she wasn't exactly the companion I had hoped to have those two nights. There's a funny thing about time and how long or short a piece of it can seem. It depends on what you're doing and, more importantly, who you're doing it with. It may be discovered someday that an orgasm actually lasts for hours and only seems like a few seconds.

Monday came on the back of a snail. We put our things back in the car and drove some 150 miles to Ringgold once again.

On Memorial Day, May 30, 1966, Carl and I had a sweet little wedding service with Mama and the preacher's wife as witnesses. Mama had brought her camera and snapped a few pictures. Because of the Monday rule, we were now pressed for time. Carl had to be at work the next morning, and I had agreed to do the Ralph Emery show, which was done live at that ungodly hour. I would have to get up at three o'clock the next morning to prepare. Our plan was to drive Mama to Chattanooga, where she would catch a bus back to Sevierville. Then we would head to Nashville to spend whatever time we could as man and wife before the alarm went off.

We got almost to Chattanooga when Mama threw a monkey wrench into our plans. She realized with horror that she had left her handbag at the church. It was obvious there was nothing we could do but go back to Ringgold to get it. I'm afraid Carl was a lot more generous with his new mother-in-law than I felt like being at that moment. We drove all the way back and got the purse, then retraced our tire tracks and finally delivered Mama to Chattanooga.

By the time we got to Nashville and our bed(!!!), there was only a little while left before I was due on "The Ralph Emery Show." I guess you could say our honeymoon was about two hours long. We made the most of those two hours, though, and to his credit I will say that for a man who had had trouble telling me he loved me, he left no doubt about it that night. We never got to have a real honeymoon until a year later.

That year gave me a little time to learn more about this odd man that I had married after an even odder courtship. I am still learning about him to this day. I think that's the way a relationship should be. It's wonderful to have the feeling of comfort and security that comes from believing you completely know a person, inside and out. But it's also exciting to know in the back of your mind you actually don't. I guess I will always keep learning about Carl, but it seems only fair that I make an effort to bring you up to speed.

Carl Thomas Dean was named for one of his dad's army buddies—the Carl part. The Thomas comes from Saint Thomas Hospital in Nashville, where he was born on July 20, 1942. His mother's name is Virginia Bates Dean, and his father is Edgar Henry Dean, although they're known as Ginny and Ed. They are both from Dickson, Tennessee, and have two other children, Sandra and Donnie. They are a small family compared to mine. I have come to love them all very much. Donnie and his wife, Karen, have two wonderful children, Elliot and Carson. Sandra is married to Neil Chaffin, and they have a lovely family, Dea, Chad, and Joshua. In the next generation, Dea and her husband, Andy Cunningham, have a beautiful daughter named Christian, and Chad and his wife, Cindy, have two sweet kids, Chase and Brooke.

Carl's mother, Mama Dean to me, was always one of my best friends. She was the rock of that family and had a great influence on Carl, who has always been a mama's boy. We lost her to liver cancer a few years back. I still think of her every day. She was pregnant with Carl when Ed had to go away to the war. During his early life, Carl and his mother lived with his grandmother and grandfather, Minnie and Con Bates. He was very attached to those two women. He still loves to cook, sew, and do housework, although he's a very rugged outdoorsman. Still, he's got that sweet, gentle streak that I love so much.

Carl is not easy to know. He has his favorites, and it's not hard to tell who they are. He has favorites among my sisters and among my nieces and friends. He has other favorite women scattered in various places, whether it be the girl at the bank, the insurance company, or whatever. He communicates well with women, and he loves to brag on them, as long as it's okay with me, which it always is. He always checks women out, whether it's okay with me or not. He only looks and talks. I believe with all my heart that I am the only woman Carl has ever been intimate with.

He is a true and devoted husband, friend, and son. He never misses his weekly visits to spend the day with his dad. I love Ed. We have a special kind of communication. He's a lot like Carl. The two of them have become much closer since Mama Dean's death. They go to the races and ball games and things like that together often.

I guess you could say that my husband is a wonderful combination of men. He's a great mechanic who will work all day on a truck or tractor and then come in and sew up the pocket on his old work shirt. He loves to buy an old junk car and fix it up. He'll work and sweat until he absolutely falls over. He can fix anything. Like they say, "It's nice to have a man around the house." Well, it's especially nice to have all of these men around the house and all in the body of Carl.

He studied art in high school, and he likes to paint. I wish he would paint more, but he won't get out from under the car long enough to do much of it. Every once in a while he'll write a sweet verse or two, but you can bet he won't stick around to watch you while you read it.

Carl would rather have his body hair painfully pulled out than spend money. I call him Scrooge. He's so tight he squeaks when he walks. In great contrast, I can't get rid of the stuff quickly enough. He's always said to me, "I could take the money you waste and have more than Donald Trump." He has great investment ideas, especially in real estate. Carl is one of those people with a knack for buying property at a cheap price, in some unlikely location, and then having the interstate go through there a few months later. I thought he was nuts when he bought property a few years back that seemed like it was in the middle of nowhere. That nowhere is now where the Saturn plant in Tennessee is located. He makes his own money, but our money is our money.

He loves to horse trade, not with real horses but tractors, trucks, or whatever, and come out with something better than he started with. I sometimes feel lucky that nobody ever came along with a trashy-looking blond country singer with fewer miles on her and lower maintenance.

Here is this man with all of the money and material things he could ever want or need, and he still loves to dig around in dumps for what he calls "treasures." I don't mind. I'll sit in the camper for hours and read or write while he's roaming around. Carl's mother told me that he always loved the dirt, and he still does. He used to sit for hours on an ash pile, digging around. She said she'd have to literally run him down to feed him or change his diaper. She once told me that she felt if it hadn't been for me, Carl would never have married.

He's very much a loner, and of course that suits my lifestyle perfectly. We see each other often, but we are not in each other's face all the time. I often sit up late at night writing, as I am with this book, while he's snoozing away. Then he'll be up and gone before I get up.

Carl's favorite place when he was little was an alley that he called "the calley." His mother would call for him, "Carl Thomas Dean, where are you?" And he'd say, "Down't the calley." I had a sign made by some of the craftsmen at Dollywood, my theme park, that says DOWN'T THE CALLEY and put it up over his barn/workshop. Nothing could be more appropriate. I always know if he's not in the house, he's "down't the calley."

I love to smell Carl's clothes. When we were first married I would smell that odor of grease and smoke (yes, he does smoke cigarettes, trying to quit). He leaves his work clothes hanging in the mudroom, and sometimes I'll just smell them, especially if he's not around, I'm going out of town, or I'm just missing him. Don't that sound silly? He does the same thing, though. I wear a lot of perfume, and sometimes I'll see him just walk into my closet and pull the frilly things up to his nose and get a good whiff. He always says that nobody smells like me.

I have often wondered, if something happened to one of us, whether we could stand to smell each other's clothes. My prayer is that we will die at the same time, so I won't have to worry about such things. We'd sure lose a lot if we lost each other. All of this might seem strange to people who know that Carl and I are not physically together much of the time. What must be understood is that we are always together emotionally and spiritually. An audience member at my TV show once asked me, "Do you believe in living together before you're married?" I joked back, "Hell, I don't believe in living together *after* you're married."

People who don't know Carl would think that he's shy and bashful. That's not really true. He loves to have a great time and was voted wittiest in his high school class. It's just that he's comfortable with his own surroundings, with people he knows.

Carl's very devoted to his family and friends. He's the first one to the hospital, the funeral home, taking food to the bereaved, whatever. He's also readily available to give the bride away if some redneck father in the family is too embarrassed (or, if the truth were known, too afraid of crying in public). Carl looks great dressed up, and the bride never seems to mind the substitution.

Carl loves to play characters. He will spends hours or even days working one up and putting together an outfit to try out a new one. He started out doing this kind of goober character with blacked-out teeth and red underwear and a pillow for a stomach. Then once he became what he called the "L.A. doper." He was this odd guy wearing Mickey Mouse ears and smoking a tampon as a big joint. He goes to any length. Once, when I was having dinner guests, he came downstairs wearing a Styrofoam wig head on his shoulder. He spent the whole evening as "the two-headed monster," just as if that were the normal thing to do. One day he taped a big head of cauliflower to the side of his head and said he had "cauliflower ear." Well, a lot of comic types might have held the vegetable up to the ear for a second to make the joke, but only Carl would wear it for the rest of the day.

Once I was in the kitchen having a manicure done by my friend Lois Baker. Well, in comes Carl from the barn with ten big nails taped to the ends of his fingers. "Can you do anything with these nails?" he asked Lois. She happens to think Carl is the funniest thing in the world, so she nearly busted a gut laughing. The funny thing is, I don't think he cares if anybody else laughs or not. It's more for his own amusement than anything.

Now that you know Carl, you'll understand better his reaction to an event in my career not long after we were married. Uncle Billy and I finally got our first big break. It came from the publishing side of our deal with Fred Foster. Bill Phillips wanted to record a song we had written called "Put It Off Until Tomorrow" (no, it was not about my wedding night). Not only that, but he had asked if the girl singer on the demo tape could sing harmony with him on the record. Naturally, that girl singer was me.

The record was a big hit, and although I was not credited as a backup singer, disc jockeys all over America began to ask, "Who is that girl singing harmony?" That gave Bill and me ammunition to go to Fred Foster and convince him I should be singing country. He agreed, and I began to make records like "Dumb Blonde," which had been written by Curly Putman but seemed tailor-made for me, and a song I wrote called "Something Fishy."

"Dumb Blonde" made it into the top ten on the country charts. Fred Foster must have felt that my career had found a pretty solid footing. He called me into his office one day and said, "If you and Carl still want to get married, I think it would be all right now." I couldn't help laughing. "Do you remember a year ago when you asked me not to get married? Well, I did anyway." Fred laughed too. Carl and I had managed to keep our marriage secret from the entire Nashville community. I didn't like deceiving people, but I'm glad I put my marriage first. The only one I really felt badly for was poor Mama Dean, who never did get to have her big wedding.

"Put It Off Until Tomorrow" was named the BMI Song of the Year in 1966. Uncle Bill and I were so excited about going to the big ceremony to accept our awards. After all, this was the first of our songs to be recorded by a major artist. To have it recognized in that way by all of those established songwriters was a huge confidence builder for both of us.

I asked Carl to go to the event with me, and he agreed. We rented him a tuxedo, and he looked very handsome in it, if a little uncomfortable. The tuxedo was only the beginning of a miserable evening for Carl. Everywhere we went there were crowds of people, including photographers, and everybody made a big fuss over us.

Carl sat through the ceremony and patiently waited afterward while I shook hands and accepted congratulations from a throng of music-industry people. I thought he was really handsome in his tux, but you could tell by the look on his face it suited him like a sock on a rooster. He didn't say much all evening long, but on the way home, he took off his tuxedo jacket and tie and then even his shirt. I'll never forget the way he looked sitting there in the car with his suspenders across his bare chest.

Finally, he turned to me and said calmly, "Honey, I love you and I will support you in your career any way that I can. I know it's a big part of you and you wouldn't be the same person if you didn't do it. But the limelight's just not for me. I'll be there at home waiting for you, but I am not going to any more of these wingdings." He has been a wingdingless man of his word ever since.

It was at that moment that I first began to realize that a performer has to give up certain things in her personal relationships in order to have a "bigger" relationship with the public. By "bigger" I don't necessarily mean better. Carl will always be my husband when the lights die down; I will always go home to him. He loves me for what I am, and he knows that my singing is a big part of me. It was about to become a much bigger part.

10

One day I walked into the office at monument records and was surprised to find a message for me from Porter Wagoner. It was a request to come to Porter's office at a specified time with my guitar. I had sent songs to people all over Nashville, including Porter. He had the number-one syndicated television show in the country at the time, and I was well aware of his importance in country music.

I was also familiar with the female singer on his show, Norma Jean Beasler, the one Porter always called "Pretty Miss Norma Jean." Everybody loved her, myself included. She had done some fun songs that I relate to, like "Don't Let That Doorknob Hit You Going Out." I had some songs I thought might be right for her so I had submitted them to Porter for consideration. I assumed that was the reason my guitar and I were being summoned to Porter's office. Never in my wildest dreams could I have imagined what was about to take place.

I sang a song I had brought with me from the

Smokies. It's called "Everything Is Beautiful in Its Own Way." It was not the Ray Stevens hit, but a song of mine that I had recorded for Monument Records in 1965. My version of the song was never released. The producer for that session was none other than Ray Stevens. That gives some idea what a young girl trying to break into the music business at that time could expect. I had no idea what to expect from Porter Wagoner.

I finished my song and looked to Porter for a reaction. He was never a man to let on much about what he was thinking. The way he just sat there for a minute or two with his hand on his chin made me more than a little nervous. Then, like a bolt from the blue, he blurted out, "Norma Jean's getting married and moving to Oklahoma. I want you to be my new girl singer."

He went on to say that he had heard "Dumb Blonde" and "Something Fishy" and had seen me on local TV shows. He said he had seen "something magical" in me. I just stood there with my mouth open. Now Porter became the businessman. His brow furrowed up a little bit as he said with conviction, "All I can offer you is sixty thousand a year."

I was almost completely dumbfounded by the offer and the dollar amount, but I tried to act cool. Everything I had ever heard from my daddy about horse trading and everything I had ever learned from Uncle Bill about the music business quickly flashed through my mind. Porter looked a little puzzled and prodded me with "Will you accept that?" I said with the best poker face I could put on, "I'll have to think about it. . . . Yes I will." So much for horse trading. I had just made a big commitment and taken an even bigger step into the big time of country music in the blink of an eye.

We immediately began talking about my place on the show, how I was to dress, the kinds of songs I would be doing, et cetera. Porter mentioned a few things about costumes and then went on to talking about songs. When he asked me, "Do you know many hymns?" I was still thinking costumes. I thought he had said, "Do you know Minnie hems?" "Why no," I answered, "does she sew here in town?" We both got a good laugh out of that, but it would not be the last misunderstanding in our relationship . . . or the last time I would be talking about one thing and Porter another.

Any relationship is like a house with an upstairs: it's got two stories. I know that everybody who knows anything about me and Porter would like to have the true story of what happened to us. Nobody would like to know that any more than Porter Wagoner and me. I could bad-mouth and say all manner of bad things about Porter, as he has about me through the years. I choose instead to tell it from my own standpoint and try to see it through the spiritual, rather than the natural, eye. I truly believe that all things and all people are brought into our lives for good (God) reason. No matter how hard things may be, or appear to be, at the time, God never gives us more than we can handle. "That which does not kill us, makes us stronger," as they say.

I have analyzed my relationship with Porter, over the years, and come to understand that even though it was the hardest and worst period of my life, those seven years were the most prosperous, productive, and growth-filled ones as well. When I think back on it all now, it is the good I remember. After all, good memories enrich and sustain us through a bad present or an uncertain future. God meant for it to be that way, just as he meant for us to forget the bad. Otherwise, a woman would never have a second child, a soldier would never report for the second day's battle, and a heart would never sail more than once into the treacherous waters of love.

Looking back at the sentence I have just written, it seems to fit my relationship with Porter even better than I had thought. It was in many ways like giving birth, it sure as hell was a battle, and there was definitely love involved, if not the kind the tabloids would have you think.

First of all, I want to say that I will forever be grateful to Porter for the chance he gave me to display my God-given talent in such a big way. I sometimes wonder if Porter doesn't take more credit than he deserves. On the other hand, I often wonder if he gets enough credit. Porter did not discover me, as my Uncle Bill had spent many years heading me in the right direction. Bill had brought me to the attention of Fred Foster, Monument Records, and Combine Publishing. I had three chart records of my own and had cowritten a "country song of the year" with Uncle Bill. I had a band and had traveled around the country by then. I had appeared on national television shows, including "American Bandstand."

Porter had seen and heard about the "new girl on the scene," and that is why he brought me in to audition. It was rumored that Porter had a reputation for sleeping with all of the girls he worked with, and he probably thought I would fill that bill nicely too (I may be flattering myself here). As Porter has always adamantly denied having a romantic relationship with me, I am "not about to admit nothing he ain't."

We did, however, have a very passionate, stormy, and (at the start) very loving relationship. As the years went by and we began to disagree strongly, we lost much of the warmth and affection and respect for each other, during that time and for many years after the split.

At the beginning, I was like a kid in school . . . one of those accelerated schools where you have to learn a lot in a hurry. There was a lot Porter could teach me, and he was generous with that information. I could sing when I met Porter. After knowing him, I knew how to perform. Even now, that training helps me out of difficult spots onstage. When a drunk is creating his own show or I have completely forgotten what the next number is, I find myself using a Porter line or move to smooth over the situation.

Porter knew his audience. He loved them. They loved him. Every night after performing on the road, no matter how small the town or seemingly insignificant the venue, Porter would stay and sign autographs until the last fan who wanted one had been satisfied.

It was at one of these autograph sessions that I met Jolene. She was not the fiery-haired vamp who tried to steal my husband, although that makes a much better song. She was actually a beautiful little girl of about nine or ten. She came up to the edge of the stage for an autograph, and right away I was taken with her long auburn hair. "You sure are pretty," I said. "What's your name?" "Jolene," she said as she shyly held out her scrap of paper. I had never heard that name before and it made an impression on me. I remembered it a year or so later and got the idea for the song. I don't think that little girl ever knew she was my inspiration. Maybe she will read this and know it at last.

I will never forget my first appearance on the TV show. I was confident enough in my singing, but had no idea how to behave in front of a camera. Years later, when I had my own series on ABC, I did one special show from Nashville. As part of their research material, my writers watched a tape of that first Porter show. They laughed because at the end of the show, in the middle of my second number, Porter came in and interrupted me to say good night. That was not out of rudeness. It was simply the way the show was done back then. It was impossible to tell in advance how long the various segments of the show were going to be, so when the time was up Porter would just say good night. Nowadays everything is timed out to the fraction of a second. I guess that's good for the people who buy the commercial time. To me there was a certain charm about those old "anything can happen" days.

People in general, and country people especially, are slow to accept change. For the first year or so that I appeared with Porter, the words I heard most often were "Where's Norma Jean?" I don't think they meant it out of disrespect for me. They had come to know and love Norma Jean and were genuinely interested in her welfare. She had been around a long time and had several hits. I could understand their loyalty to her, but I could have done without their yelling for her in the middle of my number. In a subtle way, it was one more of those little inspirations for me. Whether or not I ever voiced it, the words "I'll make them forget Norma Jean" were in my thoughts back then.

I would have gladly stepped aside to make way for Norma Jean's temporary return when it came to the live commercials. Some of them weren't so bad. I didn't mind telling folks about "the flowery towels in boxes of Breeze" (in my mountain dialect it came out "flardy tals"). After all, I had hawked Blue Band Coffee on "The Cas Walker Show." I could also smile with some degree of believability while pushing Soltice, a cold remedy or "croup salve" as we called it.

What used to almost kill me with humiliation was

to have to do commercials for Cardui. I know the Chattanooga Medicine Company was a loyal sponsor of the show and its support ultimately paid me, but that did not make it any easier for a young woman to go on TV and talk about "menstrual cramps" and "water bloat." My face must have turned colors, even in black and white.

As if that weren't enough, I had to join with Porter in singing the praises (literally) of Black Draught. This was a laxative that made you "Smile from the inside out" according to the song. I hope my colon was smiling sincerely because the smile on my lips was phony as all get out.

The jingles were sung, the smiles were faked, and the checks were cashed. Try to imagine what sixty thousand dollars represented to a young woman who had grown up in poverty in the Smoky Mountains. It was a world of money. It was probably more than my daddy had earned in his lifetime. I did act kind of silly with it at first. The joke is that the hick who strikes it rich always goes out first thing and buys a Cadillac. So did this hick. I still like Cadillacs. I guess I'm just a Cadillac kind of girl. I went up home in my new car and told everybody how much I was making and they were in awe.

I always told myself, and I suppose I made a secret promise to God, that when I made it big, I would make things better for Mama and Daddy. That first Christmas I took steps to keep that promise. I don't remember what story we told my parents to get them out of the house for the day. Whatever it was, they fell for it. That left the way open for me, with the help of brothers and sisters, to work a minor miracle in the house while they were out. I had bought all new furniture, carpet, and curtains for the house, and we completely redid the place that day.

It wasn't all for Mama and Daddy. I wanted the younger kids to have the nice things I never did, especially the girls. I wanted them to have a pretty, frilly, feminine room. I joked that I wanted them to have a bed with a "canopy" over it instead of a "cano' pee" under it. I now saw to it that they did.

Then there was Dolly Parton Day back home in Sevierville in 1970, which Porter helped to make a success. He insisted that the event be produced as a live album, and he arranged for many well-known Nashville musicians to be a part of it. The album was a success and it made me very proud.

I can remember, though, how uneasy many of my relatives felt at having to dress up and attend the festivities. This was especially true of Daddy. He was, and is, a shy and very private man. I could tell how out of place he felt wearing a suit and standing next to the mayor and other dignitaries. Of course, none of my family felt especially comfortable around the show business types. I have often felt sympathy with my family for having to try to live up to my image. It's as though everyone expects all of Dolly Parton's relatives to live in big houses and drive fine cars. That is simply not the case. I have tried to help them in every way I can, but nobody makes that much money.

It was not so much a matter of money or what he had to wear with Daddy. He is a proud man and would have thought nothing of standing there in his overalls as long as they were clean. It had more to do with his shyness. I know him also to be a very sentimental man. If someone gets to bragging on one of his children, he is likely to get misty-eyed. He would rather fight a bear in the town square than have that side of himself revealed in public. I understand that. It comes from the deepest, most private part of him that every person should have the right to keep to himself.

Becoming a star seems to mean we have to give up that right. Even with all that stardom has to offer, that still sometimes seems unfair, much more so for those who are simply the relatives of stars. It has often seemed to me that my relatives have been sunburned by the spotlight that always follows me around.

As the years have gone by, Daddy has come out of his shell somewhat. He is very proud of me and what I have accomplished, and he loves to ride in the Dollywood parade and wave to the crowd. He would not want to have to speak in public, but he's real good at riding and waving. Ironically, my mother was always the outgoing one in the beginning, but the years have made her more reserved. It's as though she and Daddy gradually traded places.

It is undeniable that my time with Porter Wagoner had a lot to do with my becoming a star. I remember, long before I had any dream of being on his TV show, when my whole family used to watch it back in the Smokies. We could all relate to his sense of humor and his "good ol' boy" ways. I could relate to his shiny bright costumes, his flashy smile, and his blond helmet. Someday I still hope to get my hair as high as his was then. He was a Missouri boy with a dream. He had started from humble beginnings, much like I had. I admired him for having made so much of himself. So, even before I went to work for Porter, I knew many of the wonderful things about him. As I said, I don't want to dwell on the bad.

The early seventies were some of the best songwriting years of my life. "Joshua" and "Old Time Preacher Man" won BMI awards in 1971. I have since won many awards and honors, but those still stand out as special. Porter and I made many duet albums together. It's frightening to look back at some of those old album covers with the two of us dressed in almost the same clothes, wearing almost the same hair styles, and smiling identical cheesy smiles. It's funny how your tastes change.

It was also during the Porter era that I signed with RCA Records. I hated leaving Monument, because it meant hurting my friend Fred Foster. Porter wanted me to be on RCA, and what Porter wanted usually got done. He is telling the truth when he says that he made RCA a guarantee to get them to sign me. Porter told them he would pay them every cent they ever lost on me out of his own pocket. He never had to pay a dime.

I guess the real problems that arose between Porter and me were all about dueling dreams. Porter dreamed of me staying with his show forever, and I dreamed of having my own show. I had only promised to stay with his show for five years. Porter knew that and felt that that was fair and fine—at the time.

Time went by and I wrote more and more songs, and dreamed bigger and bigger dreams. Porter became very competitive and possessive, and very intimidated. I'm not sure Porter realized what a serious (and I'd like to think, talented) person I would turn out to be. Maybe I'm flattering myself here, too. I know he had no idea how stubborn and strong-willed I was. Nothing and nobody has ever been able to stand in the way of me and my dreams.

Even when Porter thought he was doing something nice for me, it would somehow turn out wrong. I once caught a fish, a smallmouth bass, about three pounds. That's not a huge fish, but it's not bad for a small-mouth. Porter said he would have the fish mounted for me, and I thought that was very thoughtful, until it came back. It was not my fish. It was a ten-pound largemouth bass. Porter thought my other one wasn't impressive enough. I didn't care. I wanted *my* fish, the one I had actually caught. The bigger one didn't mean anything to me.

I started playing golf with Porter, and I got to where I wasn't half bad. I actually shot a birdie one day on a par three hole. I wanted to have the ball mounted, and Porter, once again, offered to take care of it. The ball I had scored the birdie with was a Titleist. The ball I got back on a plaque was an Arnold Palmer, so that didn't mean anything either. I never had the balls to ask Porter where my ball was, and my fish. I just let it go.

Don't get me wrong. Porter did believe in me and put himself on the line many times on my behalf. We just didn't always agree (seldom agreed) on how to handle my career and how I fit into the overall scheme of things. In all fairness to Porter, it was his show. He was the boss, and I was nothing (big deal, the boss of nothing, joke, joke). Seriously though, I guess I should have been more willing to go by Porter's rules, but they just went against every cell in my body after a point. That was not unique to Porter. I had seldom agreed with parents, teachers, anybody who tried to exercise control over me, my talents, and my beliefs.

Porter was just as stubborn as I was, and I had not planned on that. Even though we were both at fault, I will claim any and all blame and responsibility. I'm sure Porter will be pleased to hear that, and be in total agreement. I think it all had less to do with me or Porter than either of us might like to believe. I think it was God's will for a higher purpose for both of us. I can't speak for Porter, but I truly believe I have become a wiser and better person for the growth I accomplished during those difficult years.

It was a great lesson in patience, tolerance, acceptance, love, and especially forgiveness as we dealt with greed, spite, possessiveness, jealousy, fear—even hate at times. The former being angels, and the latter being demons, I think of Porter as one of the most important angels in my life, even with all of his demons. I have enough of my own demons to wrestle with, as we all do. We certainly were not shy about turning our demons loose on each other at any given moment. It was not uncommon for us to argue and holler loud enough to be heard a block away, or at the back of the bus.

I usually try not to argue and fight. It's truly not my nature, and it makes me very nervous. Even as a kid, I would cry at being scolded, or even when given a sour look. Porter liked to quarrel and argue and shout. He did with most people. I don't think he really meant any harm by it. It was just his way. He especially seemed to enjoy fighting with me, though, and after a while I started to get into it myself. It seemed to be the only way we could communicate and was a relationship we both understood, stupid as that may sound. I have known other relationships in which fighting seemed to be the only excitement. It made me tough and strong, though.

If you could win an argument with Porter (which I seldom did), you had really done something. I would usually find another way to win . . . like leaving! We were way past the point of no return after three or four years, but we kept "Holding On to Nothing," as one of our biggest hits says. I wanted to go. He wanted me to stay. I resented the fact that Porter pushed Fred Foster, my Uncle Bill, and Uncle Louis as far out of my life as he possibly could. That may be just my opinion. Some say my relatives don't know "their butt from a biscuit" about business. I disagree, since they were no less educated, less qualified, or more rednecked than Porter or me. It's all in how you look at it.

At any rate, we couldn't agree on what I should do, what I should sing, what I should write, if I could write, or who would publish the songs I did write. We were on a dead-end street. They say, "All good things must come to an end." I say, "All things must come to new beginnings." So I left. As hard as it was to go, and as long as it took, we finally arrived at a place where I think Porter was actually relieved to get me out of his face, his hair, his ear, his show, and his life. I know I felt that way about him at that time.

I had already stayed two years longer than the five I had planned. Looking back, it seems appropriate. After all, the indentured servants who came to the New World had to work seven years for their freedom. Seven years is traditional. Jacob worked seven years for the right to marry Rachel, then was tricked into marrying Leah and had to work another seven. I worked seven years to pay my way into the new world of stardom. I guess I still came out seven better than Jacob.

Making the decision to leave was much easier than the actual leaving. It happened while we were on the road. I can still see the taxi waiting there in front of the hotel with its door open, welcoming me to my new beginning. As I walked toward it, it seemed like a mile. It was almost more than I could do. My knees nearly buckled, my heart nearly stopped, but I walked on. I knew what I was doing was right. I knew I was saving whatever love and respect Porter and I had left for each other. That's what kept me going. That's what moved one foot in front of the other until I was inside that cab. When that car door closed, I knew it was the end of an era. One Dolly Parton had walked so painfully to the car and climbed inside; another stronger one had closed the door.

Of course Porter was not about to just disappear. He would be coming back to Nashville, and there were things to be settled. After all, we had been in business together for seven years, and we had started many ventures together. A few weeks after I left, I went to Porter's office and we tried to work out as many business details as we could without fighting. He really made very little effort to get me to change my mind. I think he realized it was over.

As I left his office and began to drive toward my home out on Crockett Road, it began to rain. So did I. I cried, not so much out of a sense of loss, but from the pain that almost always comes with change. It was a sad kind of freedom. Then I began to sing a song to myself, "It's been a long dark night and I been waitin' for the morning. It's been a long hard fight, but I see a brand-new day a-dawnin'. I've been looking for the sunshine, ain't seen it in so long. Everything's gonna work out just fine. Everything's gonna be all right that's been all wrong. And I can see the light of a clear blue morning." And I swear to you on my life, the sky cleared up, it stopped raining, the sun came out, and before I got home, I had written the song "Light of a Clear Blue Morning." It was my song of deliverance. It was my song of freedom, and I knew that God was in it. I knew that I was free. And when the Lord has set you free "Ye are free indeed."

And so the Porter Wagoner era, at least that part of it that didn't involve a court of law, had come to an end. Many people think that the song "I Will Always Love You" was written about breaking up with some lover, but in fact I wrote it about Porter and the special, although painfully heart-wrenching, time we spent together.

The rumors about a romantic link between the two of us have lasted to this day. There had been the same kind of stories going around about Norma Jean and even Tammy Wynette, who had filled in for her at times. One day I was talking to Tammy and she asked me, "What if Porter claims we all slept with him?" "Don't worry, Tammy," I said. "Half of the people will think he's lying and the other half will just think we had bad taste."

Whatever Porter did to me, I will always be grateful for what he did for me. He gave me my first big break in show business. Who knows, I might have made it some other way, but he was the only person who could have given me that opportunity at that time and in that place.

Of course, this has all been my side of the story. If you would like to have Porter's, I suggest you read the book he wrote with Steve Eng, called *A Satisfied Mind*, which was published in 1992 by Rutledge Hill Press of Nashville.

Porter and I have outlived a lot of the hurt and bitterness we both felt and can once again share a stage from time to time when we work together. There is no question he did a great deal for me and for country music. So, thank you, Porter Wagoner, for all the good that you have brought to me and forgive me for the bad, as I have forgiven you. It's like the old saying, "As good as you are and as bad as I am, I'm as good as you are, as bad as I am."

II

As I began to move out on my own, Don Warden came to work with me. He still does. As this book is being written, we are celebrating twenty-five years together. Throughout that time, Don has been as solid as a rock, loyal, trustworthy, and constant. I call him "Mr. Everything." I can always depend on him, and I like to think he can on me as well. If I were hanging from the edge of a cliff, Don Warden is the one person on this earth I would want to be holding on to my hand. Actually, let me amend that. My husband Carl is the person I would want holding on to my hand. Don Warden is the person I would want on the phone calling for backup.

Don is not a big man in stature, but he is the tallest man I know. Anybody who knows him—and he knows everybody—looks up to him. At one time there was even a T-shirt being sold around Nashville that read I KNOW DON WARDEN. People are still calling me and asking, "How can I get one of those Don Warden

T-shirts?" Sometimes it feels like people are only using me to get to Don.

Don, like Porter, is from Missouri and had started with him way back in the early days. He played steel guitar as one of the Wagonmasters and sang the high part on "Satisfied Mind" and songs like that. He knows absolutely everything about the business. A much rarer thing than that is that he's willing to share what he knows. I always get a kick out of seeing young people come to "sit at the feet of the master" and learn from Don.

Another great angel that God has brought into my life is Don's wife, Ann. I truly believe I would have met her somewhere else if she had never known Don. I know Don is awfully glad she does. She's a beautiful Missouri girl who used to be a model, but she's even more beautiful inside. She loves to draw and paint and has a real gift for decorating. She did a lot of the decorating at Dollywood, and she and my brother Bobby have done wonders with my Tennessee Mountain Home. She even designed the "Dolly Doll" that came out in about '75. Ann and Don are such treasures to me, and I thank God for them every day.

I would have to say that what I am most thankful for in this world are the wonderful, friendly angels God has blessed me with in every part of my business and personal life. Another person who is a Rock of Gibraltar to me is Mark Kiracofe, one of my dearest friends, my production manager and personal assistant. He also serves in a production capacity anytime I do TV. I can't imagine life without him. There's Teresa Hughes, who runs my Nashville office and my publishing company, Velvet Apple Music, and Larry Seaver, who is operations manager and my security supervisor.

One big question in my mind in the early days after

the Porter split was my relationship with RCA. Porter had insinuated that the label would not be interested in me without him. Since I had burned my bridges with Monument to some extent, this was a big concern to me. I asked for a conference with RCA in New York and flew up to meet with Ken Glancy and Mel Ilberman. I went in loaded for bear. I was prepared to do a big sell job. "I know I'm not the same without Porter," I started in, "but I'll be something really special by myself."

I had barely begun my sales pitch when I could tell by the faces in the room that what I was saying was taking them by surprise. One of the executives finally spoke up and said, "We're somewhat interested in maintaining a relationship with Porter Wagoner, but we think you are the real star."

"Then you still want me?" I beamed.

"Yes, we still want you!" was the answer. It may have been the biggest relief I had experienced since I found the cow that took me home that night back in the mountains. It wasn't just this group of people or this particular record company. To me it was a confirmation that the world had accepted Dolly Parton as a free and independent entity.

I will never forget my first day recording for RCA, back when I was still with Porter. I had just bought a new car, and was running a little late for my session. I had driven very little in my life and was not that secure about my ability behind the wheel. The man at the driver's license bureau in Nashville had given me my license without even a road test, presumably because he thought I was cute. I guess I did too and somehow felt that made me qualified to drive a car.

In my rush to get to the studio that day, I forgot one basic element of driving—braking. I arrived at the old RCA studio on Music Row and plowed right into the side of the building. Bricks were still falling onto the hood of my car as I walked nonchalantly into the recording session as if nothing had happened. When we took a break a little later, the men went outside to have a cigarette and noticed my car stuck in the wall. They commented on it, but I never did say anything or confess that it was my car.

That old studio is now a historic site in Nashville. If you visit there, you can still see where the bricks are a little different in that one particular spot. The way Chet Atkins reacted, I think he knew whose car it was. Chet, if you did, I thank you for never letting on.

Chet Atkins has always been a special friend of mine. If you were to come to my house for dinner, it would not be unusual for Chet and his family to be at my table. Like Roy Acuff, Stringbean, and Minnie Pearl, Chet is just "good people." We come from the same neck of the woods (literally), and we understand each other.

I first met Chet when I was very young. I remember meeting him at Shoney's restaurant with Uncle Bill and a group of other music-industry people. I had strawberry pie, something Shoney's was known for. There was another restaurant in downtown Nashville called Leinbaugh's (pronounced "Line Baw's"). It was a place where I spent a good bit of time while Uncle Bill was working the room (and his elbow) at Tootsie's Orchid Lounge—the latter was not a place for a little girl to hang out. I sometimes had the strawberry pie at Leinbaugh's and had always marveled at the size of the strawberries.

This day at the table with Chet and the others, the waitress brought my strawberry pie and I said excitedly, "Just look at these strawberries! They're as big as Leinbaugh's!" Well, everybody at the table broke into hysterical laughter because they thought I had said "lion balls."

If my embarrassment had ended there, it would have been bad enough. It didn't. I was trying to tell the story of the family we were having the feud with back home. They lived down the hill from us. Mountain folk always say, "I'm going down to so-and-so's" or "I'm going up to so-and-so's." I was telling the part where Daddy had gone to the other family's house. Quite innocently, I said, "Daddy finally got tired of them pickin' on us, so he went down on 'em." The table erupted in shrieks of laughter again.

I didn't understand and looked to Uncle Bill for an explanation. He shrugged it off and said under his breath, "I'll tell you later." Of course when he told me that to "go down" on somebody meant to give them a blow job, I was mortified. Chet Atkins never let me live that down, in a jovial way. For years after that he would ask me, "Has your daddy gone down on anybody lately?"

Chet is always ready with a joke. So are a lot of people, but one big difference about Chet is that he laughs just as hard if the joke is on him as he does when it's on you. Chet is very ticklish and I always grab every opportunity to grab him in a sensitive spot or gouge him in the ribs. As this book is being written, we are carrying on a fun joke through the mail. He is suing me for the last time I grabbed his butt. He goes to a lot of trouble to make it look all official and legal, so I do the same thing back. In my last "brief," I commented that his suit for sexual harassment should actually be "his-assment."

I had survived the Porter ordeal and had secured my place as a recording artist on my own. I had gathered wonderful, helpful friends about me. I felt great. I felt like my dream was on course. I put together a new band made up mostly of family members and called it the Traveling Family Band. It included brothers and sisters and a few cousins. I had a great musician and friend named Bill Rehrig who served as the band's leader and had found a very talented young man, Richard Dennison, to lead the background singers.

The unfortunate part was that I took on the "mother" role. They played and sang fine, but I stayed in a constant frenzy trying to keep up with my brood. What time did Randy get to bed last night? Whose room was that Rachel was going into? Are Freida and Floyd drinking in the back of the bus? It just got ridiculous.

I don't mean to take anything away from any of my family. They are all talented, and I love each of them dearly. They are not at all at fault for what happened. I had made a huge mistake. Here I was trying to listen to another voice, trying to move in a new direction, and my falling back into my family was grounding me in my past. Their music is wonderful and pure and does reflect the truest, deepest part of me, but I was hearing a different drummer.

Maybe that was the part that was the mistake, I don't know. I only know that my dear, sweet family members were not the people that this particular incarnation of Dolly Parton needed to be on the road with. Perhaps I had drawn them around me for security, for the realness of their love. That is what made it so painful when I had to tell them the Traveling Family Band was to disband. It was crushing to me too. I have always had dreams of all of us working together in big-time show business that not even watching the Jacksons could dim. It may happen one day yet. The talent is certainly there.

One positive thing that came out of that experience was the relationship between two of my backup singers, my youngest sister, Rachel, and Richard Dennison. They were young people with very active hormones at the time we were traveling together. I tried to stay on top of things, like keeping them off the top of each other. Little did I know it was the real thing. They are now happily married and are the parents of my beloved niece Hannah. Richard is still with my band. He is a talented performer and a fine person, and I'm proud to have him in my family.

At the time of the family-band experiment, my career was in an odd state of affairs. Just when I needed him, an old friend came to my rescue. It was Mac Davis. I had known Mac for some time. Mike Post, a record producer, had once arranged for me to appear on Mac's TV show, and we had kept in touch. He was in Nashville working on a record and was staying at this great little hotel downtown, called the Spence Manor. He had heard I had left Porter and invited me down to have breakfast with him. I did, and we talked and talked. I was still going through a lot of heartbreak, and Mac was a really good listener.

He was also the one who suggested that I meet with Sandy Gallin. "I don't know if he's the right manager for you," Mac said, "but if he's not, he'll know it right away and he'll steer you to someone who is." Mac also booked me and my new band, Gypsy Fever, to open for his shows all that summer. That was a great boost to my solo career. Mac was very big at that time. Appearing with him gave me a lot of credibility and exposure. We did some writing together.

Mac is one of the best songwriters of all time, bar none. I love his poetry and his sensitivity. You can just tell by talking to him, looking into his eyes, or even listening to one of his songs that he's a person who feels things very deeply. I can relate to that. He was very kind to me at a time when I really needed it. Mac has remained a friend and I still love to write songs with him.

My solo career was building. I was learning more about business. I was also learning more about who I was and what I had that would sell. I was having a pretty good old time being Dolly Parton. What happened next hit me like a pan of cold dishwater thrown in my face.

Porter Wagoner filed suit against me for approximately three million dollars, claiming he had made me a star and was entitled to a percentage of my career for life. I could have probably won the case in court, but to spare Carl and my family the heartache a long bitter court fight would have caused, I agreed to settle out of court for around one million dollars. I should note that as a part of the settlement, we both agreed not to make the amount of the suit or settlement public. But since Porter has already done that in his book, I suppose it's okay for me to mention it here.

Although I appeared to be a star in the eyes of the public, I did not have a million dollars or anything even close to it. Even a millionaire would be hard-pressed to put his hands on a million dollars in liquid assets under such circumstances.

It is fitting that this is chapter 11. If I had been a shrewder person, perhaps I would have gone bankrupt and Porter's judgment against me would have been worthless. I have always been a person who paid her debts. Even if I didn't feel it was justified, our settlement was binding and legal, and that, to me, made it almost sacred. My ego and self-respect also came into play. If I was going to prove I could be a star on my own, my pride wouldn't let me admit how crushing a blow this was.

I paid the debt. It took everything I had, everything Carl had, everything I could make for years to come, but I paid it. I made up my mind that if he could live with it, I could live without it. I have done all right without it. I suppose Porter has done all right with it. I am neither his conscience nor his accountant.

The major player in my crossover success was Sandy Gallin. When I met Sandy, we hit it off instantly. From the time I was a kid singing to chickens over a tin-can mike, he was the only person I ever met other than Uncle Bill who wanted me to be a star even more than I did. I'm not saying that is the basis for our friendship, but it certainly gave us a good place to start. The way our relationship started, it's a wonder we gave each other more than a hello and good-bye.

I flew to L.A. for the express purpose of meeting Sandy and checked into the Beverly Hilton. I had spoken with Sandy by phone, and he said we would have dinner. I assumed that meant we would go out to dinner. I had no idea what a wealthy man Sandy was. How was I to know he had such a grand home with his own personal chefs and what have you? In my own way (which was even more tasteless then than it is now) I got dressed up for the occasion. I put on a white outfit with sparkles and spangles and fringe on the sleeves—and of course the biggest hair I could afford up to that point.

I had no idea what Sandy looked like, and I wasn't sure he knew what to expect from me. The time came for him to pick me up, and I walked across the lobby to the front door of the hotel. I must have looked like a Cadillac some hillbilly had fixed up with mud flaps and spinners and pimp wheels. In my own mind, I was dressed to kill or at least seriously injure. That self-image was deflated a little bit when I noticed a man sitting in a Mercedes convertible, laughing hysterically.

"Are you Sandy?" I asked, halfway hoping he wasn't.

He nodded and said, "You've got to be Dolly."

"I guess if one of us has to be, it might as well be me," I said as I got into the car.

Sandy was dressed very casually in the corduroy pants and penny loafers that were his trademark at the time. There we were, him as L.A. as a person could get and me twice as Nashville as the neon sign at Twitty City. In spite of that, we hit it off like magic. He called me "White Diamond" because he said that was what I looked like. I suspect if he had been truthful, he would have gone ahead and called me "Cubic Zirconium."

When we got to Sandy's house, he loaned me a pair of his pants and a shirt, which I wore for the rest of the night and took back to the hotel with me. I still have them as a memento of our first meeting. No, I didn't leave my spangly outfit at his house. He would have enjoyed that too much. I started right in telling him that I wanted to be a star, a big star. I told him that with the right help there was no end to what I could do. I knew that he managed big stars like Cher and Joan Rivers, and I gave him my best sales pitch. "I'm going to be a superstar, and whoever helps me will also be rich and famous," I said, dead serious.

Sandy began laughing uncontrollably again. "Why in the hell are you laughing?" I demanded to know. "I'm serious."

"I'm not laughing at you," said Sandy, still chuckling, "I'm laughing with you." I could see that there were tears in his eyes. He was laughing for joy at having found me. I instantly felt as if all my life I had been waiting for Sandy. In that one moment, I realized I had found someone who understood me completely. That made me want to cry.

Once the door had been opened, we went on talking and planning and dreaming all night. I proceeded to tell him that I didn't think he should try to change me too much. I thought I should keep my hair the way it was and so on. I thought I should grow at a rate I was comfortable with and only do the things I felt confident doing.

That rapport has continued to this day with Sandy. I can be totally myself with him. We are both high-energy people and both very spiritual, me in my way and Sandy in his. We both love a challenge. Sometimes a project will seem like too much to hope for, even to us. We'll look at each other, and if Sandy notices a hint of doubt in my face, he'll say, "Well, they can kill us, but they won't eat us."

Sandy set to work right away to clean up that mess in Nashville, all the legal stuff with Porter and the lawsuit. At the time he was partners with Ray Katz and Dan Cleary. The firm did a terrific job of freeing me from all of the ugliness. Next, Sandy started to work with RCA Records to make the big Dolly crossover. He found the song "Here You Come Again" through Charles Kopelman. Sandy was determined that it should be my first crossover release.

I resisted it, saying, "I don't want to scare my audience to death." I wanted to put out "Two Doors Down" first. Sandy said, "We'll do it later. This is your first song. It's going to be a giant hit. You've got to trust me sooner or later." I trusted him. I am very glad. He was right about all of it. "Here You Come Again" was a huge hit, my first million seller. I will always be indebted to Sandy for his vision as well as to Barry Mann and Cynthia Weil for such a great song. Gary Klein did a first-class job of producing the record, and the Scotti brothers did an equally top-notch job promoting it. I had a big hit. I thanked God, my lucky stars, and the wonderful people I had to work with.

I had a lot of trouble dealing with the resistance to

my crossover from the old-timers in Nashville. To me it was simple arithmetic. "Jolene" had been a number-one song in the country market and had only sold sixty thousand records. A hit on the pop charts could sell millions. I'm not saying that it was all about money. To me it was all about building a bigger audience. I would hear some of the old-timers complain that I was "leaving country music." I would always reply, "I'm not leaving it, I'm taking it with me to new places." Abraham Lincoln was great not because he was born in a cabin but because he got out of it.

There is always resistance to change. For a long time, drums were not allowed on the stage of the Grand Ole Opry. Before that it was electric guitars, and before that it was black people, or women, or anything or anybody else that somebody thought was a threat to tradition. I love to hear Bill Monroe sing "Mule Skinner Blues" as much as anybody, but I also love to hear Garth Brooks or Alan Jackson or Trisha Yearwood. Change is not always bad. Nor is it always good. But one thing is certain: Change is inevitable.

When "Here You Come Again" was a big hit with country audiences too, I felt completely vindicated. Not only had I proved I was right about the arithmetic, I helped to make a whole segment of society change the way they thought about country music and country singers. Now Nashville began to respond a little differently to me. When I was nominated by the CMA as Entertainer of the Year, it was a sure sign that Nashville had finally gotten over my crossover.

These days, of course, country music is the most successful part of the recording industry. Hopefully, in some way, I can take credit for some of that change. Like I said, change is not always bad and not always good. The "nationalization" of country music and the Top 40 kind of thinking that goes with it have made it hard for an over-forty hillbilly to get radio airplay anymore. (Hey, DJs, I'm forever thirty-nine, so please play my records!)

As Sandy Gallin took over the reins of my career, I began to grow, by necessity, as a performer and businesswoman. One of the first ventures was "Dolly!," my syndicated television show, produced out of Nashville by a man named Bill Graham. He loved show business, and he admired my spunk. He had big plans to do big-time television with me. He was a wonderful man with the best of intentions. But the difference between the kind of show he wanted to do and the kind that could actually be produced in Nashville at that time sometimes made for funny situations.

I used to open the show on a swing with ivy and flowers twined around the ropes. Me and my big hair and flashy clothes and the too cute scenery gave the whole thing the look of a cartoon. I had some really odd guests: dog acts, monkeys, Captain Kangaroo—not exactly the perfect chemistry for my personality.

I did manage to do one show, however, that I will always be proud of. It is probably the best half-hour of television I ever did. My guests were Emmylou Harris and Linda Ronstadt. The three of us really got comfortable with just us, our voices and guitars. The result was some of the most unspoiled, pure country music I have ever been a part of. It was a forerunner of our *Trio* album, something else I will always be proud of.

Kenny Rogers was also a guest on that early show. That began the chemistry that would make such a hit with the public in our future projects together. There was something about the combination that just worked. I think it was because Kenny has a kind of cool energy that is a perfect complement to my hot energy. Whatever it was, people just instantly began to think of us as a couple.

"Islands in the Stream" was our first duet, and it was a huge crossover hit. We never really worked that much together, but for a long time people insisted on thinking of us as a duo. I would be out on a tour by myself, and people would yell, "Where's Kenny?" The same would happen to him (although obviously they would yell, "Where's Dolly?"). Even now, when I'm in Pigeon Forge, Tennessee, where Dollywood is located, I sometimes see a couple that impersonates Kenny and me. I guess that goes to show how people still think of us—sort of like Mickey and Minnie (and I don't mean Mickey Gilley and Minnie Pearl). I still work with Kenny from time to time, and the chemistry is still there.

My little TV show didn't last very long, but I did it long enough to know that TV was something I wanted to do. I know I will do it successfully one day yet.

The way that Emmylou Harris, Linda Ronstadt, and I had blended so beautifully on that little local show made it seem obvious to me that the three of us should do an album together. We all thought so and tried to coordinate everything to do just that, several years before the *Trio* album actually happened, but it didn't work out at that time. One thing good, one very special person who came into my life through that attempt, though, was Bob Hunka. He was working with Emmylou at the time and was an old friend of her husband, Brian Ahern. Bob, like Brian, is from Canada, and he is one of the classiest men I have ever known.

Bob is a world-class chef, a connoisseur and collector of fine wines and fine art. He loves the theater, good books, candlelight dinners, and brilliant conversation. You would think the two of us would be like oil and water and that those two things don't mix. Well, somehow, we made the damnedest batch of watered-down oil you ever saw. We just took to each other. We had the same views on God, religion, and life. Odd as it may seem, we are soul mates, not lovers, but just warm, wonderful friends. Some of the most rewarding spiritual journeys I have ever been on were taken with Bob.

One of the strangest I took with Bob as well. Bob had a girlfriend, a beautiful actress from Texas named Frannie Parish. He had explained to her at the start that his very best friend just happened to be a woman. She did her best to accept that, and I did my best to make her comfortable with it. There was one time, though, when I pushed my luck. Bob told me that he and Frannie were getting married. While I was happy for them, I desperately wanted one last trip with Bob. I had always wanted to see Paris, and so had Bob. I decided I would take him to Europe for two weeks in April as a wedding present.

Well, there were Carl and Bob's fiancée, waving good-bye as Bob and I took off on an incredibly romantic adventure. Carl would never do anything like that with me. He's not into candlelit dinners and fine wine. He's not about to eat anything he can't see, and he doesn't drink at all. He wouldn't deprive me of it, though. He'd rather that I be with a man, because he feels like I'm more protected from a safety standpoint than I would be with another woman. Whatever baggage Bob and I took with us, guilt was no part of it.

We had the best time two people could have had. We spent time at the great Churchill Hotel in London, with a limousine at our beck and call. We took trains to the country. We saw Stonehenge and had a fantastically spiritual picnic there. The sights, the food, the companionship—it was the trip of a lifetime.

One night we went to the grand opera. I mean to tell you, it was grand. The opera house, those highfalutin' people in all of their finery, it was almost overwhelming to me. I know Bob must have been a little embarrassed to take me there in my gaudy, tasteless outfit, but if he was, he didn't say anything. It was grand opera meets the Grand Ole Opry.

I don't remember what the opera was. I do remember that I had had quite a snootful of the best red wine I ever tasted during our fabulous dinner before the show. That huge curtain went up, and those people came out and began singing in those big dramatic voices in what I referred to as "strange tongues." For some reason, it struck me funny. I started in snickering. Just a little at first, but enough to be heard by the people around us. It was like being in school and having something strike you funny. No matter what you do, there's no way you can stop.

I decided I'd better go to the bathroom and snickered my way like a hillbilly fool all the way up the aisle. I finally got to a stall and just fell on the floor laughing. I was having a good time and enjoying the opera in my own way. Bob found me at half-time, and we left. We rode around for a while, went to another fine restaurant for dessert, and laughed ourselves numb. Then we went to bed—not together. I'm sure we could have slept together and nothing would have happened. That has happened with me many times. Friends are friends to me, male or female. If you're going to screw, you're going to screw. You're going to find your time to do what you want to do.

Every time I think of that story, it makes me laugh. I never said I was cultured. You know, money don't make you smart. Money don't make you happy. But it can make you comfortable if you're smart enough to be happy. That's as happy as I need to be. I guess what I'm saying is that if you feel like having a good time, laugh, have it at any cost. "A merry heart doeth good like medicine," the Bible says. Don't ever miss a chance to have fun. Life's too serious most of the time. Just find the humor and laugh, and laugh at yourself, mostly.

Sandy Gallin and I decided it would be fun to do a big Las Vegas show. Sandy was a genius at negotiating the deal. At the time it was the biggest deal in Las Vegas history. It called for two shows a night for two weeks at the Riviera for a multimillion-dollar figure. The deal was big, and that was a good thing. The show was big, and that was a disaster.

Although I look like a drag queen's Christmas tree on the outside, I am at heart a simple country woman. I am at my best in simple situations where my true personality can flow naturally. This show was an extravaganza, with big flashy sets and costumes. I felt as out of place as Gomer Pyle at Harvard. I think it's because my persona is oversized and flashy. That makes me a kind of a fish out of water in normal surroundings, but when I am surrounded by things that are just as flashy, I become a fish in water and tend to get lost in the shuffle.

The ill-fitting show would have been bad enough without the personal problems I was having at the time. I was very unhappy with my weight. I was experiencing "female problems." I had trouble with my band, trouble with my family, and trouble with my voice. I was taking cortisone for the vocal nodes that had continued to plague me. That tended to make me puffy and bitchy. On top of all of that, I had been betrayed by certain people very close to me. All of that together was just too much.

I had always been a trouper who believed as strongly as anyone that "the show must go on," but this situation got the best of me. I stopped the show and pulled out of Las Vegas. I did not go back for many years. When Elvis first played Vegas, he had an equally miserable experience that soured him on it for a long time. Years later, he returned in triumph. I also returned later and had a wonderful experience working for Steve Wynn, first at the Golden Nugget and later at the Mirage.

One of the most gratifying things that ever happened to me was the reception I got when I appeared in Europe, especially England. We did a special for HBO from the Old Dominion Theatre in London. At first it looked as if the entire event would turn out to be a disaster. I knew that the British people had heard my songs on the radio and on records but didn't really know what I looked like. I always thought of England as very proper and conservative. I didn't know how they would react to the big, overblown, oversequined cartoon of a woman who was about to stand before them.

I wasn't even sure a crowd would show up, but to my surprise the place was packed. I was also amazed at the wide diversity of people who came to see me. The boxes were filled with royalty in fine gowns and evening wear. I was a little surprised that nobody ever said, "I say, isn't that the hillbilly who laughed at the opera?" In the cheap seats were teenage punks with lime-green hair and safety pins through their noses. By "punks," I don't mean to put the kids down. This was at a time when the punk movement was at its height, or depth, depending how you felt about it. I couldn't believe that kids who were into Sid Vicious could want to hear a country singer from East Tennessee. I began to wonder if they had come to heckle me or perhaps try to disrupt the show in some way.

The next thing that happened looked as if it would

kill the entire project. A bomb threat was phoned in to Scotland Yard. Well, everybody was forced to evacuate the building, including me and my entourage and the television crew. Sandy and I sat in a tea shop across the street and wondered, "What the hell have we done this time?" But before long, a polite English policeman came to announce, "The unpleasantness is over, and you may return to the theater."

We went back in, fully expecting to be the only ones there. To our delight and surprise, the entire audience had returned. They had all waited outside until the bomb squad and its dogs had done their search and then filed back in as if nothing had happened.

When the show finally began, I was barely able to sing because of the lump in my throat. These people didn't just accept me and my songs, they embraced both of us with warm, open hearts. When I sang "Coat of Many Colors," I could feel the tears welling up in the eyes of audience members. What's more, I could see tears in the eyes of the punks in the front rows. What was it that touched them and me so much?

After thinking about it, it made perfect sense. My songs, and the old mountain songs that they were influenced by, come directly from the English, Irish, and Scottish folk songs of old. A phrase like "Come all ye fair and tender maidens" rolls as easily off the tongue of an ironworker in a Liverpool pub as it does off that of a sharecropper in the Smokies. A bow being pulled across the strings of an Appalachian fiddle makes the same kind of baleful moan as bagpipes wafting through the highlands. Our roots and the deepest parts of our very souls are tied to the music. Even the young kids, who would outwardly scoff at the music of their ancestors, could not help responding to it inside. There might be a safety pin in the nose, but there's a hillbilly in the heart.

Sandy had always said he wanted to broaden my appeal. He booked me on "The Tonight Show" on my birthday in 1977. That was when I first became aware of the power of big-time television and what it could do for a person's career. It doesn't hurt your record sales any either. Johnny got a huge laugh when he pretended to be fixated by my bosoms for a while and finally said, "I'd give a week's pay to look under that shirt."

I always had a great relationship with Johnny Carson, although I never saw him except on the panel during the show. It became something of a tradition. He would always come to my dressing room and knock on the door before the show, but I would never come out. After a while, he knew I wasn't coming out, but he played along with the custom as if we were a bride and groom before a wedding. When we were on the set, we always talked and laughed and had a great time. People would think we had been friends forever, and in our own special way, we have been. I never did "The Tonight Show" with any other host until after Johnny had left.

I have a similar relationship with David Letterman. I have never seen him off the set either. We talk during the commercials and whatever, but I think the fact that we don't see each other anywhere else makes our conversation more real and interesting. I communicate with David in a special way because something about his demeanor, the way he acts, and reacts, reminds me of Carl.

When I decided to do my first Barbara Walters special, a lot of people warned, "Oh, you're crazy to do that! She'll chew you up and spit you out." Nothing could have been further from the truth. Barbara is a very insightful person. Once she realized I was real, that my insides weren't as phony as my outsides, she got completely into it. I even had her singing a little bit at one point. I'll bet that surprised her more than anybody. She took the TV audience on a tour of my customized "Dolly" bus and showed everybody my wigs and shoes and all of the trappings of being me.

Before that special I think a lot of people were curious about me but didn't quite know what to think. Just like Barbara, they found out I was real and took me into their hearts. That special did incredible things for me, and I have gone back to do others. Barbara and I have always had a mutual respect and admiration, and I'm sure that will continue.

I told Barbara Walters during that first special that I wanted to be a superstar. I'm sure a lot of people thought I was full of it. I think Barbara was even humoring me a little bit. But when I look back at it, everything that I told her came true. I never doubted any of it myself, from the time I was a dreamy little kid. I guess that is the definition of faith.

When I was in the third grade, the Gideons came to our school. There were two men, but I don't remember anything about one of them because I spent all my time staring at the other. He was a wiry little man in a blue seersucker suit. He reminded me of an insect we used to call a walking stick. What fascinated me so much, though, was that his hair was snow-white, his skin was pink, and so were his eyes. He had Coke-bottle glasses that magnified them as they darted about the room like frantic pink searchlights. I know now that the man was an albino and it wasn't right for me to stare, but then I was just a curious kid who couldn't help it.

The thing I will never forget was the talk he gave about faith. While the forgettable man handed out little red leatherette-bound New Testaments, "Searchlight" passed out key chains. They were not just any key chains. Each one had a little plastic ball on the end with a single mustard seed inside. The plastic globe magnified it, much like the odd man's eyes. If you looked closely, you could read a Bible verse on a shred of paper next to the mustard seed. It said, "If ye have faith, even as much as a single seed of mustard, ye shall be able to move mountains." I took that to heart. In my particular case it might have said, "Ye shall move from the mountains" or even "Ye shall grow mountains and parlay them into a huge career."

Even at that age, I could tell that the walking-stick man had faith. He spoke with such conviction. I know it took courage for him to go to schools every day, knowing the kids would probably stare. If this unusual man could have both courage and faith, why couldn't I?

He told a story about a man who had read that same verse from the mustard-seed key chain. The man decided to put it to the test. He stayed up all night praying that the mountain to the east of his house would be in the west when he went out the next morning. When he looked out and saw the mountain still in the same place, he said, "See there. I knew it!" That is a case of faith working in the negative. I knew my dreams would come true. He knew his wouldn't. And that, as they say, has made all the difference.

I2

Forty years of friendship, Judy and me. A true friend is one of the greatest gifts a person can ever have. They say that in order to have a friend, you have to be one. No truer words were ever spoken. Judy and I have given a lot, and we have taken a lot. We have had our problems, our ups and downs, but the love has always been great enough to overcome. One thing we've had to overcome is the constant rumor that Judy and I are lesbian lovers. It is understandable. Most people can't understand two women being so close and devoted to each other.

The fact that Judy has never married probably fans that flame. That's not to say that she hasn't been around, hasn't been asked, hasn't broken a few good ol' boys' hearts by saying no. She loves her work and she loves traveling. I know if she ever found somebody she loved enough, she'd give it up. I also know that I love her enough to let her go. Judy is one of my most special angels.

I'm sure many a maid in many a hotel has wondered

why Judy and I will leave a double room with only one bed slept in. We have always slept together since we were kids, class trips, whatever, and it has always been honest and innocent. We sit up in bed, watch TV, read. We lie in the darkness and talk just like any old couple would. Why scream across the room when you don't have to? I don't like to sleep alone, never did. I try not to whenever I can help it.

Tabloid headline: AFTER ALL THESE YEARS, DOLLY ADMITS, "I SLEEP WITH JUDY OGLE." Maybe that'll help sell this book. I could titillate you by telling you that Judy and I make love, but then I'd have to disappoint you with the truth. We've made a lot of love through the years, for ourselves and other people, but we've never been lovers, just good old pure, sweet, fun-loving friends. I will admit we talk a lot about sex. We always did growing up. We, like all kids, were very curious, playing doctor and nurse, very healthy, exploring.

Our relationship is wholesome, but exciting and fun. Thelma and Louise ain't got nothing on us. Judy went to the Air Force right out of high school at the same time I went to Nashville. We kept in touch and saw each other when she was on leave and decided she would come to live with me as soon as she got out. By the time that happened, I was already married to Carl and had worked with Porter and done pretty well for myself. Judy came to work with me as my assistant, my valet, hairdresser, makeup artist, everything she needed to be. She still is.

Well, life was pretty good, and it seemed like the time was right for my old friend and me to go on an adventure. I thought we should go to New York City and shoot the moon. Porter's show was not seen there, and the two of us could go unnoticed. It seemed perfect. At that time, Judy and I both carried

.38-caliber handguns in our purses for protection. Judy had been an expert markswoman in the service. I felt comfortable enough around a gun, and at that time I thought carrying one was the thing to do. So Thelma and I put our "shootin' arns" into our checked baggage to be put into our purses after we arrived in New York.

We checked into a nice hotel, one room, a big bed. We got ourselves all decked out in our gaudiest hillbilly glamour clothes. Of course, I had always dressed like a trash queen, with my big hair, gaudy jewelry, and clothes too tight. Judy had been much more plain until her days in the service. Now she had her hair teased up, painted her eyebrows nearly up to her hairline, and wore tight skirts. She had even taken to smoking and drinking.

So off we went to party. We weren't looking for men. We just wanted to do the city and let the chips fall where they may. One thing I had always been curious about was porno movies. There was nothing like that back in Tennessee at that time, at least not out in the open. We wanted to check one out, just out of curiosity. It wasn't hard to find one in New York. We waited around outside the theater for a few minutes. I guess even with all of our sense of freedom, our upbringing still made us feel like we had to sneak into a place like that.

Outside, the theater with its flashy marquee and provocative movie titles seemed sexy and alluring. Inside it seemed kind of sad and twisted. There was an awful smell in the place, and everything felt gummy and sleazy. I think we must have been the only women in there. There weren't all that many men even. The ones who were there were the raincoat type.

The movie started. What we thought would be exciting and sexy was gross, filthy, and insulting. My

spirituality turned my guilt meter up to high. I looked
at Judy and could tell she felt the same way. Without
a word, we bolted for the door and right out the front
of the theater. I wanted to just keep running until the
night air had cleansed us, until we were well away
from anybody who had seen us come out of that
place.

We got a few blocks up the street and stopped and
leaned against a wall to catch our breath. When we
were able, we started laughing at how stupid we had
been. So, there we were in that part of town, dressed
the way we were, leaning against a building. A man
came up and started talking to me. He said, "Come
on, baby, what's it going to cost me?"

I was too rattled to understand what he was talking
about at first. I said, "Go on, now. Leave us alone.
We're just visiting. We don't need no company."

The man had been drinking. He kept pulling at me.
"Come on, baby," he pressed, "you know you want
it. Just tell me what it costs." By this time, Judy is
laughing her butt off. She had been to nightclubs
when she was in the service and was more accustomed
to this kind of thing. I was getting really upset. That
made Judy laugh harder. She gets a real kick out of
seeing me get myself into stupid situations. I got more
and more frustrated. By now, the man was grabbing
at me in places I reserve for grabbers of my own
choosing. I became irate. I pulled out my gun and
said, "You touch me one more time, you son of a
bitch, and I'm gonna blow your nuts off!" There is a
line like that in *Nine to Five* about "turning a rooster
into a hen." At that moment, I was in no mood to
soften my language like that.

The man didn't want to argue with Smith &
Wesson and me, so he turned tail and left, although I
could hear him calling me a bitch as he walked away.

I breathed a sigh of relief. Then I breathed a sigh of disbelief as I turned to see Judy, smoking a cigarette, still laughing. I turned on her: "Look, you laugh one more time, and I'll shoot your nuts off too!" I couldn't believe she had the balls to laugh at me at a time like that. She must have believed me enough to take on a much more serious demeanor.

The next man who came along was a businessman, probably cruising Forty-second Street for the same reason as the first one, but being from out of town, he recognized me from the Porter Wagoner show. "You girls are lost, ain't you?" he said. I was so glad to hear a familiar, southern-sounding voice, I would have almost given him what the other man had been willing to pay for. We admitted that we were lost, and he offered to walk us to our hotel.

On the way, he explained to us that prostitutes in that part of town work in pairs for safety's sake. That, coupled with the way we were dressed, would naturally lead men to make assumptions. I was grateful for the information but a little puzzled. By my own standards, I thought we were at the height of fashion.

When we got to our hotel, we were shocked to find our luggage out in the hall. Apparently, the hotel management had assumed we were "working girls" as well. After all, we only had one room. We put our things directly into a taxi. We had somebody put our luggage in there too. We waited almost all night at the airport to get a flight back to Nashville and vowed that we hated New York and would never return. It struck me as a contrast to our high school trip when the whole city had been plastered with "Hello, Dolly." Now it seemed to be saying "Goodbye, Dolly."

Of course, I love New York now. I have an apartment there, which I share with Sandy Gallin, and Judy and I often go there. We're a little more sophisticated now and pretty much know what's what when we go out to the movies—real ones, not porno. After all, we can see that on TV now . . . joke, joke. I might add here, Judy no longer smokes or drinks.

I know that Judy is always there for me. I'm likely to wake up in the middle of the night with an urge to write and feel like driving out to my Tennessee Mountain Home, two hundred miles away. I'll call Judy and ask, "How long would it take you to get ready to go? I'm on a writing binge." She'll be at my door within an hour. Free to go, free to stay, as long as we want or need to. It's a wonderful feeling of freedom to know that you can do a thing like that, with a person who's as excited about it as you are.

Judy will get into my head, waiting eagerly for whatever comes out next. I sit with my guitar, and she writes everything down. Sometimes I'll ask her, "Put down all the words you can think of that rhyme with this or that," or whatever. I tend to forget to eat (if you can believe that) when I'm writing, and Judy always keeps me from hurting myself. Just about the time my blood sugar gets low, she'll be there with a bowl of Jell-O. Writing is an intensely personal thing, best done alone. Being with Judy is better. It's like being alone but with somebody, if that makes any sense.

The two of us often go on what we call "spiritual journeys," to the mountains, to the sea, to meditate and to pray. Judy doesn't read the Bible or study religion the way I do, but she loves to hear me discuss it. She knows how I hunger and thirst after righteousness. We do affirmations and make lists. I guess I'm her guru in a way. If she has a problem, I can usually find a scripture that will be of some help. By the same token, her strength and her natural goodness are just as supportive to me.

Judy is very protective of me. She knows when I'm in a bad way emotionally or have PMS or whatever, and she'll screen calls and keep pressure away from me at those times. My family is especially grateful for her devotion to me. Carl knows that when I'm with Judy, I'm well taken care of. Everybody thinks of her as a part of the family.

People I work with sometimes hear me call her "Sissy," and they think that's her name, like Sissy Spacek. Before long, somebody else will refer to her as Sissy, and she'll say, "My name is Judy. Ain't nobody calls me Sissy but Dolly."

Once I got a good laugh on Judy. She was home on leave from the service. She knew I had gotten married, but she had never met Carl. I was visiting her at her folks' place back in the mountains. Carl had come with me, but being the junkyard dog he is, he was out combing through the considerable junk-car collection Judy's dad kept around as a part-time parts business. Judy noticed Carl out the window and just about flipped. She was practically climbing the cabinets trying to get a better look at him and asking her mama, "Who's that good-looking man in the yard?" I wanted to keep her going for a while and enjoy the moment, but her mama put her out of her misery with "That's Dolly's husband." Her "damn your hide" competitive-woman look quickly melted into the "I'm so happy for you" smile of a true friend.

Judy still thinks Carl is a hot number. They have a mutual love and respect, although it is largely unspoken. They look out for each other in little ways. Carl will change the oil or rotate the tires on Judy's car. She'll make sure he has enough milk in the fridge or pick up the latest copy of *Wheels and Deals* for Carl before driving out to our place. The main reason the three of us have managed so well for so long is that we all respect each other's privacy. It is a wonderful and necessary part of any relationship to know that you can depend on someone to be there. It is just as essential to know that, at times, you can depend on them not to be.

Carl and I were aware of that when we bought the property our house would eventually stand on. I had not yet achieved anything that could be considered stardom. Still, I said to Carl, "We'd better buy a big-enough lot so that we can have privacy when the tour buses come by trying to look in." He accepted that notion without question, showing that he had faith in my dream too. This made me love him even more. They say that love isn't about two people gazing into each other's eyes, it's about two people gazing outward in the same direction. I believe that with all my heart.

Although it was hard for us to afford at the time, we bought seventy-five acres in Brentwood, Tennessee, to build our dream house on. Nowadays that would be impossible at any price. Brentwood has become quite a popular place to live, but back then there were hardly any homes out there.

When I had first come to Nashville, I lived in the most awful places you can imagine. I occupied cellars, tiny little trailers, and anything that was cheap. When Carl and I got married we first lived at the Glengarry apartments on Murphreesboro Road. The first house we bought together was a two-story brick home in Antioch, and it was nice enough but not our dream house. The house we built in Brentwood was, and still is.

Our home is special to me for many reasons. My Uncle Dot Watson was the primary builder. It gave the house a special feel to know that Uncle Dot helped to create it. In appreciation, I let him talk a new generation of Parton children into planting horse turds on the grounds outside.

Carl also put his blood and sweat into the house—literally. He busted his fingers many a time and left his blood on the rafters here and there. My brothers Denver and Randy also helped build. It was very much a family affair. Denver was a much more serious carpenter than Randy, who only worked on the house when he couldn't get a gig playing music somewhere. I remember one day Carl needed power for a saw and yelled to Randy, "Give me a cord." Randy asked, "What kind of cord?" to which Carl jokingly replied, "Well, not a damn guitar chord."

Our house is in what they call the Confederate style, with twenty-three rooms. A lot of people call it "Tara," but Carl and I never have. To us it will always be Willow Lake Plantation. True to my dreams, the tour buses do come by now, and fans can see the house. But it is set back far enough from the road that they don't actually see us.

Maybe it was because I grew up in such a small cabin with so many people that I found ways to fill the rooms. Some of my younger brothers and sisters were still living with us. People often asked me why I took them to raise. I always answer that they "took me to raise them." I don't mean to imply that my mama and daddy were not capable of raising them or that they were unwilling to. It was just that some of the kids wanted to get out of the hills and have a better chance at life, and I wanted to help them do that.

First, my sister Cassie came to live with us, then my sister Freida and my brother Floyd, the twins. Finally Rachel became a part of our extended family. Randy sort of came and went. When she got out of the service in 1969, Judy came to live in our house as well and was a great help in taking care of all of the kids.

Carl was good enough to let them all stay. I guess, to be honest, I should say he was good enough to let *me* stay after taking in so many kids.

We were like parents to them in every way. We fed and clothed them and saw that they got to school and back. We couldn't help worrying about them. I did everything I could to worry the hell out of them in return. At least now we have a house big enough for everybody.

I guess it has always been my way to draw my family and those I love to me, into my home, my business, and my life. My Uncle Louis Owens had come to Nashville to help me run my publishing company. Of course, his wife, my dear friend Colleen, came with him. They lived close enough that we could walk together and play together. There was a great hill for sledding behind Colleen's house, and on snowy days, when you couldn't drive anyway, we'd get together over there and have a bang-up time going down the hill. It was as though our childhoods had just been continued.

A group of us created a club we called "Hell's Belles," jokingly patterned after the Hell's Angels. It was just a bunch of overgrown girls with mopeds, but we thought we were every bit as bad as the originals. The charter members were Judy, me, Colleen, Cassie, and Colleen's friend Margaret Hickle, who had come down from Knoxville to help Colleen with her children and do my housecleaning.

Colleen sewed really well, so she made outfits for all of us. I bought the mopeds in all colors, and we were off to terrorize the back streets of Nashville. One day we were out on the streets, in a competitive mood, and decided to race to see who could be the first one back to my driveway. Each "Belle" took off on what she thought was the fastest way back to my house. I went down one street and Colleen took another. We got to the house at the same time but from different directions. I tore across the front yard, trying to get the jump on Colleen. She took a different angle toward the same destination. With our eyes more on our goal than each other, we crashed together, then into the same tree.

We were both bruised, burned from the exhaust pipes, scratched and scraped, but laughing to beat the band. Judy and Margaret came along and picked up what was left of us. Colleen had sprained her wrist. Since she was a hairdresser, that was an unfortunate injury for her. I had scratched my face, and since I was on TV, that was about the worst thing I could have done. That was the end of the gang, at least as far as the mopeds were concerned. We turned them over to my "adopted kids" and to Colleen's two real ones, Richie and Jeff. Of course, we were awfully picky about how carefully the kids rode them, after having been so harebrained ourselves.

I think the reason the moped idea had appealed to me in the first place is that I was so strictly controlled as a kid. I longed to just do something wild, even dangerous. I love my mama dearly, but she will still try to control me today in certain ways if I let her. Carl thinks that Mama is a lot like me—and she is . . . or I am. Well, we are.

Mama and I aren't alike when it comes to decorating, though. I wanted my big house in Nashville to be done real special. So my favorite decorator, Bill Lane, came in from Los Angeles. I told him to give it a good cross between L.A. and Nashville, with different things from all over the world. He mixed in a few Oriental pieces and included several religious statues. And he added one big fat Buddha that sat in my music room.

Well, Mama came to visit. I came home one day to find all my Buddha statues sitting out in the yard. Without asking, she had taken all the pieces that were against her religion and got them out of the house. She said, "I ain't having no young'un of mine worshiping no idol god." I didn't know what to say, as I'd paid a lot of money for them and thought they looked good in the house.

Carl has a special love relationship with my mother. He just said, "Well, if they're bothering your mama, I'll get rid of them."

So he took them all up to the storage barn. Of course, after Mama had left, we brought them all back into the house again. Except for the big fat one, which I gave to a friend, because I didn't want to go completely against Mama. Mama was very pleased that Carl had taken her side.

I believe, however, that Carl may have simply been setting her up in his own mischievous way. See, Mama had this groundhog's foot on a little gold chain that she wore around her neck as a good-luck charm. It was a superstition, like a lucky rabbit's foot. And it was as offensive to me as the Buddha had been to Mama. But that was different, 'cause it was about Mama. She said, "Your daddy killed this groundhog, and I fixed it for him with sweet potatoes. And he said it was the best that he'd ever had. Well, we had such a good time after supper that night that I thought I'd have a little charm made out of that groundhog's foot. And now I wear it for good luck and memories." Well, that was all she had to say.

Later that day, Mama and I were in the kitchen cooking supper when Carl came meandering back in from the barn. Around his neck was a huge, and I do mean huge, log chain that hung down to his knees. And on that swung a big, old, bleached cow skull, with the chain threaded through its eye sockets. He didn't speak, he just clanked as he walked over to the sink to wash his hands. Nobody said a word as he milled about the kitchen. All through dinner, he sat with that giant lucky skull hanging down to the floor, but we talked as if nothing were unusual. I was dying of laughter inside, though, because this was his way of getting on her about her lucky foot and my Buddha. And I know she must have been dying too, but she just couldn't ever admit it.

So, in a way, Carl was getting revenge on my behalf. There's something kind of sweet and almost romantic about that. Carl is not romantic in the way that some men are. Actually, he's cheap. He's the kind who'll go to a drugstore on Valentine's Day and get two boxes of candy. He'll give one to me without a card and say, "Well, here." The other one he'll put in the freezer for next year, just in case he might forget.

I used to take this personally. But I don't anymore. Carl is also the same person who will pick the first spring flowers and put them in a jar and place them in my music room with a little poem written just for me. And sometimes he'll write a song or even paint me a picture now and then. These things can make up for anything.

One year a magazine came out with what they thought was a scandalous story. They reported how the unromantic Carl had given me a stove for Christmas. They assumed my husband would give me some jewelry or a car. I don't know why people thought that was such a funny thing. Do they think stars don't eat? Just because they don't use the bathroom! Well, they don't know this star. But Carl does. He knows how I love to cook for everybody. I seem to cook for everybody but Carl. He cooks for himself. He doesn't like my food because it's too rich and fattening. But he is supportive of this passion of mine. On holidays, Carl will go to the dollar store to buy me plastic containers and baskets to hold the treats I've fixed. This way I can give it away to the homeless, or to friends and family who like my cooking for the same reasons Carl doesn't.

Carl is always good about backing me up. But there was one time when it came as quite a surprise to me. I was doing a show at a rodeo in Louisville, Kentucky. I was lost in a crowd of thousands who packed a giant barnlike arena. At that time I was opening my show with a classic song, called "Higher and Higher." Carl always loved that song. He was there that night, and I caught a glimpse of him just as I went out onstage. As I began singing, I heard a strange voice. I glanced around at my backup singers, only to find Carl at the microphone just letting it go.

Carl has a real pretty voice, and I love hearing him sing around the house. And he'd always threatened that he'd get up onstage one day, but I thought he was kidding. He loved both of my background singers, Anita Ball and Richard Dennison, Rachel's husband. So he felt completely comfortable walking straight up there to finally get his chance for fun.

But I just couldn't let him get one on me without some kind of retaliation. What kind of fun-loving wife would I be? I casually walked over to a cop who was right at the front of the stage. I leaned down to him and said, "That man back there in the white shirt is not a part of our group. Somebody has been stalking me, and it might be him. Would you take him offstage and put him in jail until the show is over? Then I'll come and we can take care of it." Well, they did come up and were about to haul him off when Don Warden stopped them. Afterward, Carl never even mentioned a thing about it and still hasn't to this day. And I've never said a word to him about it either. That's just the way we are. We do these things for the fun. Carl likes it better when nothing is said and it's just funny inside. Maybe it stays funny longer that way.

Carl keeps a lot inside, but he's very opinionated. He loves to talk politics, sports, and especially religion. He would have made a great minister, if you could get him to go to church on a more regular basis. He's more religious than I am. I guess I'm more spiritual. I don't argue religion like Carl can. And I don't talk politics either. So Carl has to do most of his opinionating with his family and friends.

I try not to argue with Carl at all. We've never had a full-blown, screaming fight. That may be because I always say I'm sorry, whether it's my fault or not. Carl would go to the grave before he would apologize, and he'd give me the cold shoulder until then. I'd rather say I'm sorry and get it all over with. So I guess to me love means having to say you're sorry. I just know I don't want to say things to hurt him. Carl is a very stubborn yet sensitive person.

Carl shows the true depth of his sensitivity when it comes to his dogs. When he was a boy he had a little brindle-and-white puppy named Toodelum. They were buddies. Toodelum was part bulldog, so he was small but feisty. He fought all the other dogs down at the "calley," and Carl would proudly egg him on. Carl would bet money that his dog was the toughest.

Then, one day, Toodelum went up against a whole pack of fierce dogs, and they killed him. Well, Carl's sister said this just crushed him. He didn't get over that little dog for years. This story made me think I had to get him a dog someday.

When we were building our house, Uncle Dot Watson and Aunt Estelle moved into a trailer on the property during the construction. Well, Dot also brought a couple of his hunting dogs with him, and one of them was named Blue. Blue liked it here on the farm, and he soon began to follow Carl everywhere he went. Carl began to get real attached to Blue.

When the house was finished, Dot and Estelle moved back home. But Uncle Dot gave old Blue to Carl. And that's saying a lot, when a man gives away his favorite hunting dog. Blue was old when we got him, but he was around for many years. Then one day he just went to the barn and lay down and died.

I could see how sad Carl was, so I came up with this idea to get a new dog. I hunted far and wide to find a brindle-and-white Boston terrier, the same colors as Toodelum. I was on the road at the time, so my brother Randy and his wife, Deb, drove down to pick it up at the breeder's in Brownsville, Tennessee. They put the puppy in a basket by the kitchen door, with a ribbon and tag around his neck that said, "Old Blue sent me." Well, Carl found him just as planned. He must have had an idea that it was me, but I never admitted to anything. I believe to this day that Carl thinks Blue had something to do with it.

I came home a few days later and denied any knowledge of the wriggling, panting surprise. I asked what the puppy's name was, and Carl said, "I don't know yet. He'll name himself when the right time comes." So one night at supper, we were both looking at his big old eyes when Carl yelled, "Popeye! That's his name. Hell, he's pop-eyed."

Well, we had always kept our dogs outside up to this point, but Popeye was different. He was like a new kid in the house. But then, I've never seen a kid chew a couch like Popeye. He was a tough little handful. Carl had never trained a dog before, so many a chair was torn up, carpets stained, and drapes peed on. But it didn't matter. Carl loved him. He would cuddle him and hold him just like a baby—a baby with a flat, wet nose, who snored like an old man under the covers.

Carl and Popeye ate together, slept together, and traveled all over the country together. In most places we stayed, like the Bel Air Hotel, where I lived during the filming of *Nine to Five*, you aren't allowed to have dogs. But Carl had a special suitcase with a breathing hole at the end of it. He could covertly carry his pal in and out of any fancy hotel without raising a bellhop's eyebrow. Popeye didn't move or make a sound until Carl opened it up and gave him the okay. He even stashed him in the suitcase behind the couch when the maids came. Popeye loved that suitcase, because he loved going. Every time he heard the zipper on that suitcase, he'd come running.

The years went by, and our special little friend became ill with a disease called Krypto. It's a disease usually found in large animals, like cattle, that is picked up from fowl manure. They didn't think he was going to make it. But they were testing a new drug at Auburn University, and we decided to let them try it on Popeye. He was just the saddest, weakest, most pitiful little thing you ever saw. With his hair falling out, he looked like a rat. And his eyes were so big in his head.

Carl stayed with him every moment. He'd carry him around on a pillow and lay him on the table while he cooked. He even slept with him on the floor. Anyone who loves an animal like that knows there isn't even a question when the animal gets sick: You do whatever you have to do. And that's what Carl did.

The treatment worked, and Popeye lived several more years. His hair came back but just a little more gray. His struggle for life had made him old. He was blind and couldn't hear well. He spent most of the rest of his life just lying around snoring. But, what the heck, that's not so different from some of my relatives. Unfortunately, because of all of the drugs and illness, Popeye developed heart trouble. And one day Carl came in from the barn to find Popeye had gone to sleep in his chair in the den, never to wake up again.

I've never seen a man more grief-stricken. Carl built a tiny coffin in his woodshop and wrapped Popeye in my old purple robe that he loved to lie on. Carl put some of Popeye's toys beside him and buried him out in the front yard, right below our bedroom window. He then made a small wooden marker and carved "Popeye" into it. He placed this on the grave, then grieved uncontrollably for a year. He couldn't stand to see photos of Popeye or any of his toys. I had to put everything away until he was able to deal with it. It took almost three years for Carl to really get back to normal.

I eventually built a tiny fence surrounding Popeye's grave in the flower garden. I got him a real marker too. It's a precious little statue of a Boston terrier, carved in stone that's just about as tough as Popeye was. And now we've added a memorial for old Blue and our other dogs too. We can talk about Popeye a lot now. But Carl doesn't want another dog. And I know better than to push my luck trying to get him one. So now Carl has to put up with just me, and my lack of a little, flat, wet nose.

Carl was wonderful when Popeye got sick, but he doesn't handle it well when I'm ill. He gives me lectures and says things I don't want to hear, like, "Well, hell. You wouldn't be sick if you'd slow down long enough." Maybe he's right. I think maybe he just gets scared. So I try to keep most serious things from him.

Carl doesn't get involved with my business decisions. He trusts my judgment and knows that I've surrounded myself with good people. This doesn't mean he doesn't have an opinion, though. He's always telling me that this or that song would be great for me or for somebody else. In fact, he loved the song "Here You Come Again." When he heard it, he said, "That's a damn million-selling record you've got there." So when it did become a hit, I had them make a gold record with his own name on it. And he's even given me a few ideas for some songs to write that turned out really well. But however talented and opinionated Carl may be, he still doesn't want the responsibility of making high-powered business decisions. So that's up to me.

Carl has put up with a lot from my being in show business. But from most standpoints, he's just about got it made. He has anything he wants. And he has his own time. He doesn't have to work if he doesn't want to. But he loves to work, so he does. He's pretty much retired now, but he never stops working around the house and on his cars. Carl sticks fiercely to the same daily routine, so I always know where he'll be if I call him from the road. I, on the other hand, just love spontaneity. To me, any change is good, except when it comes to Carl. If he gets thrown off schedule, it wrecks his whole day.

It works out well between me and Carl. We both get what we really want. We both have the freedom to come and go and do as we please. Carl doesn't really mind my being gone, unless I'm gone for more than two weeks at a time. Two weeks is just about my limit as well. After that we both get a little nuts and a little testy.

And when I'm gone, Carl's not threatened at all. He's not jealous about me, and I'm not jealous about him. I've been a lot more jealous about other people than I've ever been about Carl. And he feels the same toward me. I guess that's just what comes from being sure of each other and our relationship. We trust the strength of the foundation that we have. And that's what has helped Carl survive through all the rumors, truths, and lies that go along with my celebrity. And he's had to endure quite a heap.

Carl has had various people and even family members approach him to say I was having an affair with this or that person. Carl would simply say, "Well, I would think less of any man that didn't fall in love with her." And he means it. He seems to have an understanding of how I am and how people are toward me. He seems to know that I'll be back, and that love affairs and relationships are just part of my dealings with people. He knows that I will always come home. And as long as I live, we'll always be together. That's all that matters to him. And he's right.

Carl is not as affectionate as I am. He's not a big cuddler like me. So I force him to let me baby him, and I make him baby me. He loves it—eventually. I pinch him or grab him in unusual places, geographically and otherwise. If it embarrasses him, well, it's just that much more fun for me. But there was a time that the tables were turned.

Carl and I were roaming around a drugstore, and I wandered off to pick up some things to take on the road with me. After a while, I spotted Carl with his face buried in one of his favorite magazines. So I just sashayed up behind him, whispered affectionately into his ear, and proceeded to feel up his balls. Well, I'm proud to tell you, he was just climbing that magazine rack! And when I glanced around to see if anybody was watching, to my great horror, I discovered Carl behind me. He was watching the whole fiasco and quietly going nuts with laughter. And there I had grabbed a whole handful of somebody else's.

Well, my poor victim turned around in alarm. I just went running to Carl, pleading, "You gotta go apologize to this guy!" I was burning with embarrassment. So Carl did tell the man that he was sorry that I mistook his identity. But I don't think Carl was sorry at all, with all the entertainment he got out of it. I was never more embarrassed. But I can laugh about it now, when I picture this guy telling the incredible tale of the time Dolly Parton played grab-ass with him. I guess this has taught me to pay a little more attention.

Carl is still one of the most handsome men I've ever met (including the one in the drugstore). He has wonderful brown eyes, dark skin, and a big, long— smile. And I'm extremely lucky because to Carl, I will always be young and beautiful. He thinks I'm the most beautiful woman in the whole world. He still sees me just like he did the day we met in Nashville, when I was eighteen and had on my little red rib-tickler outfit. He says the reason he thinks I'm pretty is because I'm "just this much from being damn ugly." And he's not joking. He doesn't like perfect beauty as much as he likes flaws, and scars, and freckles, and little crooked smiles. So Carl certainly got his blessing in me. And I know for certain that I've been blessed with him.

Our relationship has not always been so perfect. A year or so after we were married, Carl decided to ask me if he was the first man I'd ever been with. I'm not sure why he asked me at that particular point. I thought that maybe because I was getting so involved and actually enjoying sex so much, possibly Carl felt I knew more than I should. Maybe he figured I'd either been around, was getting around, or wanted to start

getting around. Whatever the reason, I didn't understand why he was asking me then. But I didn't even
think about lying, because our relationship had been
so good, open, and honest. So when Carl asked me if
he was the first, I told him no, and it just about shat-
tered him.

But he got over the hurt and confusion and never
mentioned it again. He became an even better husband and friend after that. In fact, he's been the best
husband a girl could ever have. And I grew up in a
way. I got over it too. In the end, our marriage
evolved into a very strong and understanding relationship. Maybe this is partly due to what we went
through.

It was still a painful experience. I often wonder
what I would say if Carl asked me that same question
today. What would I answer? If I knew then what I
know now, I probably would have said yes. I don't
think you should have to admit things that you don't
want to, if it can cause you great trouble down the
road. Even though that was a painful learning experience, it did inspire me to write a song called "Just
Because I'm a Woman."

13

Even after our so-called adopted kids, my brothers and sisters, began to have kids of their own (except for Floyd, who has never been married, and me, the Partons are a fertile bunch), Carl and I continued our roles as surrogate parents of sorts. The question arose as to what the so-called grandchildren would call us. Of course they have legitimate grandparents on both sides, and I didn't want to take anything away from those relationships. I came up with the names "Uncle Pee Paw and Aunt Granny" for Carl and me . . . respectively. I love my little nieces and nephews just as if they were my grandchildren. Sometimes people ask, "Why do you let them call you Aunt Granny?" "Let them?" I say. "I make them."

I have never been pregnant. I don't know what that feeling is like. I think God has different purposes for different people. Some women are meant to be mothers and grandmothers. I was meant to be Aunt Granny.

Outsiders will still try to create drama (or guilt)

where none exists. They will ask, "Why didn't you adopt?" They don't know how special and fulfilling my relationships with my brothers and sisters and their kids are. The kids see me as I really am. The new generation grew up with my stardom and think of it as completely normal. I can be totally comfortable with them, let them see me without my makeup or whatever. They love Aunt Granny. They know the star, Dolly Parton, too. To them, it's almost as if we are two separate people. They are proud that their Aunt Granny gets to put on all that glitzy stuff and play Dolly Parton.

I was doing a better job of playing Dolly Parton these days. I had new management, new producers, and I had found a brilliant new bandleader in Gregg Perry. He had been a child prodigy from Wisconsin and had played and conducted at Carnegie Hall when he was just a teenager. He was good-looking and educated and capable—of anything. Not only did he play keyboards better than anybody in the world, he was a masterful arranger and producer. He really knew his music, and he could make mine sound pretty good too.

Gregg was a fascinating man, into computers long before everybody else had one, great on the phone and at getting things organized. On top of everything else, he was an expert wood-carver. It was as if he had a real need to fix anything and everything in my life, and there was plenty that needed fixing. He wanted to do everything for me, and I had never found so much in one person, so I let him.

Gregg and I became very close. I had never spent so much time with such a well-educated and knowledgeable man. He knew all about history, great art and literature; he was a storehouse of information and great conversation. I let myself get completely wrapped up in him.

Judy began to feel unnecessary and unwanted. I didn't mean for it to be that way, but I guess I had neglected my relationship with her somewhat. And I did depend on Gregg for many of the things Judy had always done for me. One day she came to me and said, "Sissy, I wish you well. I love you, but I feel like a fifth wheel around here. I'm going back to the military. I'm not really skilled at a trade. The benefits are good. So just wish me well."

I did and she left. She joined the service, the army this time. Life went along. I missed her, but I was happy. For the first time, I felt like my music was being handled in the right and best way. Gregg loved my music and my writing. I became to him as much as he was to me, but in different ways, for different reasons. He had found an outlet for all of his capabilities, a doorway to his dreams. Gregg had a kind of shy little-boy quality, and I was more than willing to be his mother, his mouthpiece, whatever he wanted or needed. I even had his name put on the Vegas billboard: THE DOLLY PARTON SHOW, GREGG PERRY—MUSICAL DIRECTOR, a well-deserved title.

In the meantime, Judy was unhappy in the army. Her father was desperately ill, and her folks were having a hard time financially. I could pay her more than the army ever would. I wanted to help her, but what could I do? Turn to Don Warden, that's what, as usual. He was able to get Judy a hardship discharge. Of course, she deserved and needed one, but you can't depend on the military to do something just because it makes sense. If it had taken an act of Congress, Don would have had both houses voting on it by noon the next day.

Judy had fallen in love with somebody she met in the army. Now that she had somebody, Gregg didn't seem to pose as much of a threat to her. They became friends and were able to work together quite well.

With my new management, under Sandy Gallin, hitting on all cylinders, my career was really coming into focus. They had me on the cover of every magazine in the country. I began to receive a lot of movie scripts, but most of them didn't seem right for me. I didn't consider myself an actress (and still don't), so I didn't want to do a film where I had to carry the weight of the entire project. Then Jane Fonda sent me the script for *Nine to Five*.

Jane and Lily Tomlin were already set to play their parts, and Jane thought I would add the perfect ingredient to the mix. She is a smart businesswoman and was very up-front about the fact that she thought I would help the film do well in the South.

I was still reluctant. Sandy had no hesitation whatsoever and simply said, "Do it."

"But I'm not an actress," I argued, not at all sure.

"Then don't be an actress," said Sandy, "be yourself. This part is exactly like you. Just be yourself."

I took his advice. I'm very glad I did. As it turned out, it was the perfect role for me to break into the movies.

I had no idea how films were made. I assumed it was done like a play, at least what I knew of how a play was done. I assumed we would start at the beginning and shoot it in order. I wanted to be prepared, so I took the script that had been sent to me and memorized it, not just my parts, the whole thing. I wanted to know everybody else's part too so that I knew exactly what was going on and how I fit into it. Of course, when I arrived for the first day on the set, I immediately learned that the entire script had been rewritten and that it would not be shot in order. Lily and Jane had a good laugh at my expense when they found out I had committed the script to memory. So I didn't tell them I did the same thing with the new version I was given.

The whole experience of doing *Nine to Five* was as much fun as I have ever had with two women. It made me wonder what had taken me so long to get into the movies. It whetted my appetite to do more. The director, Colin Higgins, was an absolute pleasure to work with and taught me so much. Of course, I was rather like a blank slate where the movie business was concerned. I couldn't have had a more caring and knowledgeable hand to be the first to write on it.

Jane Fonda and Lily Tomlin are two consummate professionals. Our personalities seemed to work very well on the screen, but it is a wonder they worked in real life at all. We are three very different women, but we worked wonderfully together and had the greatest time, partly by learning about how different we were.

Lily is not a morning person. In order to make the most of the daylight, movie-shooting schedules begin very early in the morning, and Lily would show up looking like something the cat dragged in and acting like something he was sorry he did. Jane is a morning person but would often do her now-famous workout before coming to the set and would show up in workout clothes and basically looking shabby and sweaty. She is, after all, an actress. If she arrived wearing street makeup, the movie makeup artist would only have to remove it to apply the screen variety. It really isn't a practical thing to do. That didn't matter to me. I don't care what time of the morning I have to be somewhere, I would not leave the house at gunpoint without my makeup and hair being done.

When I first went to California to do the ABC TV show, there was an earthquake very early one morning. Judy panicked and yelled to me, "We'd better get out of the house!" I got as far as the front hallway and saw myself in a mirror. "If this house is coming down," I told Judy, "it'll just have to fall on my ass, because I'm not going outside looking like this." That is in part, I admit, out of vanity and in part because I feel that if you are a star, you owe it to your fans to look like one. I can remember being very disappointed at meeting celebrities I had always admired and finding them looking like unmade beds.

So I would arrive at the set at 5:00 A.M. completely made up and coiffured, wearing my heels, my bangles, and my best country-girl smile. That is what prompted Lily Tomlin to remark on the third morning, "You know, you make it really hard for a person to be a hateful old grouch around you. Could you at least hold back on the perkiness, say, till around at least ten or so, and could you lighten up on the makeup until at least eight o'clock?"

There was one day when I got a laugh that made just about my whole year. Jane and I had been looking, as girls do, at the different men on the set, saying who we thought was cute. Jane sort of sighed and said, "I haven't seen what I consider a really good-looking man in a long time." Then her eyes lit up. "Wait a minute," she grinned. "Here comes one now." Then she added in a kind of "I'm joking but will scratch your eyes out if you test me" way, "And I saw him first."

I looked up at the man and said, "Oh, you did, did you?" I was laughing my butt off inside, but biting my lip. The man was my husband, Carl. He is very handsome, a tall Marlboro-man kind of guy, and he looked especially good that day. He had mentioned to me that he might come by the set. He made out like it was to visit me, but I knew he had had a crush on Jane since he saw her in *Barefoot in the Park* many years earlier. I knew that he just wanted to see her. He didn't necessarily want to meet her, because he doesn't like to bother anybody.

Naturally he walked over by us, and Jane started right in chatting him up. I let her go on until I couldn't stand it and then said, "Jane, I'd like you to meet Carl Dean."

She shook hands with him, not really grasping what I had said. "Do you two know each other?" she asked, hoping I would say no.

"Oh, we've just been married since nineteen sixty-six," I said, trying to be as cool as I could. Jane nearly died laughing from embarrassment. Carl, of course, was flattered. He got to talk to Jane. He still carries a little torch for her to this day.

There are a lot of people back home who don't share his admiration for her. It seems they never forgave her for speaking out against the Vietnam War. Once, onstage, I was talking about *Nine to Five* and said something like, "And Jane is such a veteran." The crowd began booing, and I tried to pretend it had been a joke. "I guess *veteran* is not a good choice of words for Jane Fonda," I said.

She was scheduled to appear at Dollywood a couple of years ago as a celebrity guest. That's when I realized how prejudiced people still are about her. I understand how these people feel, but I also know Jane as a sincere person, a very professional woman, and a special, special girl. She gave me a great break on *Nine to Five*, and she was also very good to my sister Rachel when she gave her the part of Dora Lee in the TV series. Jane will always be special to both of us.

That day on the set, after talking to Carl, she came over to me and asked, "What did Carl mean when he said that you're an angel?" I didn't know what he had said, but I was naturally dying to hear more. Jane went on, "I was telling him how sweet you are and how easy you are to work with, and he said, 'Well, she's an angel.' I kinda laughed and said, 'Yeah, she is.' But he looked me right in the eye and said, 'No, you don't get it. She's a real angel.'"

I was flattered and honored that Carl thought that. It's just like him to say it to somebody else, figuring I'll never hear about it. He sees me go through a lot, and I think he admires the way I handle it. I do depend on my angels and the angel spirits. We have to try to see through the eyes of God and find that part in people that is God. I don't always succeed.

People ask me, "Do you ever run out of patience? Are you ever rude to people?" Sometimes I am. I hate when it happens, but it seems like some people just try to get on your nerves. There are times when I feel like saying something like, "Why don't you get out of my face, you ugly woman. And take those bratty kids with you!" But at times like that I usually get all flustered. I get confused and say stupid stuff like, "Kiss my ass, that's what you are. And don't think I can't do it!"

When I said earlier that the whole experience of Nine to Five was a joy, I should have excluded one particular aspect of my involvement in the film. I wrote the theme song, also called "Nine to Five," on the set while shooting the movie. I remember writing the song on the back of my script and using my fingernails to create a rhythm as I sang it. I would get inspirations for different parts of the song at different times. Any time I started working on it, the women on the set would just naturally gather around to listen. My hairdresser would start clacking her brushes together in time to the rhythm I had set up. The script supervisor would chime in, slapping her clipboard in time. Before long, I had created a whole section of backup singers made up of all of the working women around me. Because of what the song had to say, I thought that was especially appropriate. It was also a heap of fun. That helped inspire me in writing the lyrics and made the song as special as it is.

After the movie and the song had both been huge hits, it nearly stopped my heart to learn that I was being sued by some people who claimed I had stolen the song from them. I thought the whole thing would blow over because it all seemed to me to be so ludicrous. I had never met these people or heard their song. They had once appeared at a Jane Fonda/Tom Hayden event where they did a song called "Money" or something like that, and it had something in it about working nine to five. The song had never been recorded on a regular label, although they claimed to have sold tapes that included the song through health-food stores around parts of California.

The people were, for want of a better term, "hippie types." Her name was Cosmic Dancer, and I don't remember his, although I think it was something equally cosmic. Apparently her mother had money and lawyers, and that was the genesis of the lawsuit. At first I treated it as a joke, but before I knew it, I found myself in a real court of law answering very serious charges. This kind of allegation is about the most humiliating thing a songwriter can endure. Even if you know you are innocent, there are always going to be a few people out there who will think, "Well, Dolly stole those poor people's song and made a fortune out of it."

They never claimed that I stole the song directly. Their contention was that Jane Fonda had taken the song and given it to me to rewrite for the movie. That is preposterous, for a number of reasons. Jane Fonda would never approach a professional songwriter such as myself with a tape and say, "Here, do something with this." She would have more respect for my talent and integrity. When all was said and done, there were only five notes that they claimed I had copied from their song. Naturally those five notes had been used in a million other songs. There are a limited number of notes, after all, and they do tend to get reused.

Even after I had definitely been cleared of any wrongdoing, they still tried to appeal the case. They claimed that the court had been "starstruck" because I had used a guitar and sang on the witness stand. After all of the embarrassment of that nerve-wracking experience, the people who sued me had the brass to try to get me to record some of their other songs. I have never understood that kind of gall.

Gregg Perry had produced the hit single "Nine to Five," but Mike Post often got credited for it. Mike had produced the album, *Nine to Five (and Other Odd Jobs)*. Gregg, as my musical director, naturally worked with Mike Post on the album, but the two of them did not gel musically. Mike is a dear friend as well and a wonderfully talented man. He only wanted to help. Gregg was disappointed that he was not able to do the whole album, but Mike Post was a big name and the label wanted him on it. It was their money. Such is the nature of the business. Still, my relationship with Gregg left me caught in the middle, as it would often.

Gregg was doing so much that he needed a secretary. We were able to find someone extremely capable, Susie Glickman. She still works for my organization today. Susie is a whiz at organization and attention to detail. She and Gregg both play tennis, so they hit it off quite well and soon became great partners and friends. Judy and I had more time for each other now with Gregg and Susie managing things so smoothly. We were able to take our trips together and felt good again. We were all spending a lot of time in L.A. now. After all, we were in the big time, the movies. Susie had grown up in Los Angeles and knew all of the good places to go and things to do. Life was good.

I was spending so much time in L.A., it was obvious I needed a place there. I was tired of hotels, and they were really running into money. I had met two wonderful ladies, costumers on *Nine to Five*, named Shirlee Strahm and Thelma Pofahl. They heard I was looking for a place and said, "Why, shoot! We own a small apartment building right off the Sunset Strip. Come live with us, it'll be fun." I did rent a place from them. It was fun. They really made me feel at home, and we all had some funny crazy times together. They were like my L.A. family and helped me to feel secure in the big city.

Judy's lover had gotten out of the army by now, and they moved in together in an apartment next to mine. It seemed all really cozy and familylike. It was, for a while. Judy began having problems with her live-in. Because I felt so protective of her, that was a problem for me. I felt the way Judy must have felt during the worst parts of my Porter Wagoner period. I thought that she deserved a whole lot better than the way she was being treated. She paid dearly for our friendship. Her lover was jealous of the time she spent with me, her devotion to me and my career.

Now I was the one who had to pull back. Gregg and Susie were tight, and he was also dating one of my backup singers, Anita Ball, another wonderful and special friend. Everything was going well for them. Judy was a wreck but apparently determined to make a go of her relationship. For the first time in many years, I felt alone. I didn't want to whine to Sandy about what seemed like such petty things.

I started to grieve a lot and eat a lot. I gained weight. I started to have female problems, nerves and stress mostly. I gained weight. I had been taking birth control pills for years and was having some long-range side effects. I gained more weight.

Along came *The Best Little Whorehouse in Texas*. The wonderful time I had on *Nine to Five* had whetted my appetite for another movie. *Whorehouse* was a completely opposite experience. It was as if *Nine to Five* had been my first lover, sweetly seductive before and gentle and caring during our lovemaking. *Whorehouse*, then, was a rapist. I was still relatively green in the movie business and didn't know that by the time I got involved, there was already what they call "a lot of blood on the project." The people who created the original Broadway show had been weeded out of the mix by the movie studio, and other principals had been fired.

Burt Reynolds had become involved, and since he was in the middle of a devastating breakup with Sally Field, he was not in a particularly good mood. On top of that, people were being fired right and left. In fact, at one point there was a bumper sticker circulating around Hollywood that read, HONK IF YOU'VE BEEN FIRED FROM "BEST LITTLE WHOREHOUSE."

Burt was in pretty bad shape, emotionally and physically. Sometimes he would just walk off the set, unable to deal with things, and I would be called upon to go to his dressing room and try to cheer him up. That was a little like the blind leading the blind, since I was in an emotional and physical turmoil of my own. We had come to love each other dearly, but neither of us was able to give the other much real support. Usually he'd begin blubbering about his woes, and I'd just join in. We'd sit and bitch and moan and sling snot until we each felt so sorry for the other that our own troubles didn't seem so bad. Then we'd go back to the set and have our red eyes retouched and try to get through another scene or two before the cycle would start all over again.

Burt and I got along about as well as two people in our situations could have. There were the inevitable rumors that Burt and I were romantically involved, and one day, in an interview, somebody asked me if it was true. "Shoot, no!" I said, "Burt and I are too much alike to be involved. We both wear wigs and high heels, and we both have a roll around the middle." Well, Burt got wind of this quote and proceeded to give me a few of his own. "You're destroying the magic!" he said to me. "How are people going to think of us as an item for the sake of this movie if we go around bad-mouthing each other?" Well, I hadn't thought of it as bad-mouthing, and I told him so. I was just trying to make a joke.

I know that Burt is a good sport, and looking back on it, I'm sure he was just a little extra sensitive at the time. He must have gotten over it because a year or so later on a talk show I heard him use the same joke. Burt was always good to me. He took me to his dinner theater in Jupiter, Florida, and he had a fabulous painting done for me that now hangs over the fireplace in my music room. He has also been a doll about helping me out at Dollywood.

There was a scene at the end of the movie where Burt, as Sheriff Ed Earl, had to pick me up and carry me. They waited to shoot that scene last, and it was a good thing they did. The cameras rolled, Burt picked me up, and I could hear him groan. I was a real porker at the time, probably the heaviest I have ever been. Naturally, being the movies, they had to shoot the scene a few times, and each time Burt groaned a little louder. The week after the shooting ended, Burt was checked into a hospital to undergo a double hernia operation. I am told he had been having problems prior to that, but I still couldn't help feeling a little responsible. So if anybody ever asks me if I broke Burt Reynolds's heart, I have to say honestly that the damage was a little further south. Forgive me, Burt. I hope they're still working.

Without meaning to, I added to the hurt feelings and confusion surrounding *Best Little Whorehouse*. Gregg Perry wanted to do a movie. I felt guilty about not having been able to get him the *Nine to Five* album and wanted to do anything I could to help him. When I asked if I could do some music for the film, I also asked if Gregg could work with me. I knew that there was to be additional music anyway (not by the original composer and lyricist of the Broadway show), and I figured I might as well be the one to write it. I had great respect for the original music and thought I stood as good a chance as anybody to add to it without the new songs sticking out like a cow patty in a pie contest. The next thing I knew, the musical supervisor of the film, Richard Baskin, had been fired and replaced by Gregg Perry. I certainly didn't mean to cost the man his job. I had hoped that we could all work together.

We were all ultimately losers in one way or another. It was not a fun project for anybody involved. Not for Burt, not for me, certainly not for Richard Baskin or Gregg Perry. I still feel responsible for that situation and the pain it caused. Dear, sweet Colin Higgins, the director, died of AIDS not long after the project was finished. We all died a little when he went. I'd like to publicly apologize to everyone on that film for any ill will and hurt feelings I might have caused.

Gregg quit altogether. He told me he couldn't take the pressure and the B.S. of the business anymore. The joy had gone out of it for him, and I'm sure I was no picnic to live with at that time. I felt responsible and betrayed at the same time. I felt I had done all I could for him. He was put through hell on that project, though. Everybody was. I was devastated when Gregg told me he was going to quit the business for good, go to medical school and become a doctor. His grandfather had been a doctor. I think it was always his second choice, but he has since become a fine doctor. I was crushed when he left, and it inspired me to write one of my favorite songs, "What a Heartache You Turned Out to Be."

Emotionally, my heart was bleeding. I was bleeding physically as well. I had to have a couple of D & C's to control hemorrhaging. I was all nerves. I even started to drink some to ease my pain. I finally asked my doctor to tie my tubes so that I could get off the birth control pills. He did. Carl and I had never really wanted to have kids. I love kids. I'm crazy about them, as long as they're somebody else's. People had often asked me about having children, and I always felt guilty and selfish if I said I didn't want them. So sometimes I would just say I couldn't have them, and that lie made me feel even more guilty. That guilt added to the other pain I was going through. In my mind, it was almost as if I had had an abortion, having my tubes tied and not even consulting Carl about it.

I was also having problems concerning my family. Some of my family members wanted to be stars in their own right, and I felt like they resented me, either for having done it first or for not doing more to advance their careers. They seemed to feel that they were just as talented and smart, and that I was just lucky. And I agree. I tried to help them, and I've always felt a certain amount of guilt connected to my success, and now it loomed larger than ever. It's hard when you want the best for everybody but you also want it for yourself. When you care so much for people, you feel a sense of responsibility. It can drain the life right out of you.

I had come to depend so much on Gregg for support, and now he was not there. I had come to depend on Judy, and now she was completely caught up in her own heartache. I collapsed. It seemed that all my support systems had disappeared. The very foundation of all of my beliefs had been shaken. The dreamy little kid from the mountains had become a fat, disillusioned, hopeless woman.

Carl, as always, was loyal to me, but he is not strong when it comes to my having problems. He would cheerfully cut his own arm off with a dull knife if he thought it would benefit me. But when I am ill or distressed in other ways, he doesn't handle it well. He knew I was physically sick, and that was enough of a burden on him without knowing the rest of my despair. For that reason, although I needed his love and support greatly, I didn't feel I could lay all of my problems at his feet. This was something I was going to have to survive (if indeed I was to survive) by myself. I had never, ever felt so completely by myself. And for the first time I felt that being by myself didn't put me in such good company.

I had never felt alone before. I had always had God. After all, I had searched for him and finally found him that day in the old church at Caton's Chapel. I had always thought of him as a friend, my constant fortress, my loving father. I had always heard the voice of God guiding me along my way through life. Now pain and anguish ripped at my heart, fear and doubt clouded my mind. I could not hear him. I wondered if even he had forsaken me. I questioned God. I argued with him.

I remembered a story I had always liked about footprints in the sand. In it, a man asks God why he sees two sets of footprints in the sand behind himself. God replies that the second set belongs to him, and says, "I am always with you." The man then asks God why, at the times when his life is the most difficult, there is only one set of footprints. God answers, "That's when I'm carrying you."

"I don't feel you carrying me!" I railed at God. "It feels like the one set of footprints is mine, and they are stained with blood from the sharp rocks and glass I can't see beneath the sand!" I prayed, but I could hear no answer. I asked questions and didn't even feel they were heard. I cried out in pain from that place deep within us that makes us human. In order to get in touch with that place, I felt I had to make myself so vulnerable that I might just die for no reason. I thought about giving myself a reason.

For the first time in my life, I understood how people could let themselves become dependent on drugs and alcohol. I understood how a person could consider suicide. I yelled and screamed at God in ways that would curdle some people's blood. "All right, this is it!" I screamed, "I'm going to blow my damn brains out if you don't give me some kind of help!" But I had always believed that the commandment "Thou shalt not kill" applied to killing myself as well as someone else. I did not want that sin on my hands, nor on my head! I had always been taught that "sin against the Holy Spirit is not forgiven in this world or the next." What was that sin? Was it suicide? Was I in danger of having a sin marked against me that would follow me even beyond the grave? I demanded answers. "What is that sin?" I asked. "Is it blasphemy? I've got to have some answers here. And what is this 'I am?' When you say, 'Say that "I Am" hath sent me,' what does that mean?"

I began to feel that there was a real chance I would die before any of this was resolved. I decided that if I were to die, I wanted to have read the entire Bible from cover to cover. So I began to do just that. I sat down and started with Genesis and read straight through to the end of Revelations. It must have opened my lines of communication with God again, because somehow I began to get answers. Then, one night, somehow I found peace in my sleep . . . and when I woke up, it looked like a regular day. The clouds that had been there, mostly in my mind, had cleared up. It became apparent to me that life goes on whether you feel like being a part of it or not. I said to myself, "Get off your big fat ass and get on with your life."

Suddenly it all made sense. The "sin against the Holy Spirit" was to sin against myself, against my true personality. Here I had been given a gift, and I wasn't using it. I had been greatly blessed and was angry because the blessing hadn't come without difficulty. To sin against the Holy Spirit was to sin against the holy self. I found great peace and comfort in that. I saw two sets of footprints once more. During the times in our lives when God is carrying us, I suppose it's natural for us to be too screwed up to realize it. I'm just glad he's more up to carrying me than Burt Reynolds was.

"I Am" also took on a new meaning for me. The I.A.M. came to stand for Individual Awareness Method, which I speak of often in this book in one way or another. It will have great meaning to me and I hope many others before my work on this earth is over.

The fog had lifted. The night had passed. The crisis had been handled, and I had grown from it. It takes a lot of strength to let yourself be truly vulnerable. And that is when you gain the most. I emerged from an eighteen-month ordeal as a stronger person, a better Christian, a better talent. I was a human being who had been melted down in the forge of torment and reshaped once again in the image of God. I became rededicated to his service and to that of mankind (myself being a member of that body as well).

You truly have to experience death to appreciate life. By the grace of God, I had done that without experiencing it in the actual physical sense. I remembered an old song that Buddy Killen had written with somebody that went, "When I've learned enough to truly live, I'll be old enough to die."

One doesn't have an experience like that without changing in some way. I will always be a little more fragile after that. It would be a long time before I would be able to love and to trust as I had before my nightmare began. But now I could love even more deeply. I also had a wagonload of forgiving to work on. And I had to start with myself.

Meanwhile, I had let my band go. I had not worked in many months. I had not sung. I had not written. I had not played a guitar. Many people had given up on me. They thought I had lost my drive. It's okay to think that about Dolly Parton, but you better not stand in the road in front of her. I was about to come roaring back.

14

I had made peace with God again. Now it was time for one of my "Earth angels" to carry on the work of pulling me back together in a big way. Sandy Gallin came to my rescue like a knight in corduroy armor (he leaves the shining to me). Everything we had talked about had come true. Everything he had promised me or I had promised him, we had done. I was a superstar before I had let myself go. My concerts were sellouts. I had made it in the movies. I had been Country Music Entertainer of the Year. My albums went platinum. My face was everywhere. My boobs were everywhere. My name was a household word. I had nearly thrown it all away.

Early in the crash, Sandy had taken me to New York, to a bevy of doctors, for my voice, my weight, my head. Now he planned a vacation to help me "get away from it all." He made arrangements for us to go to Australia. We were on a flight to Sydney without realizing that a country-music festival happened to be going on there at that time. I think the pilot mentioned that I was on the plane when he talked to the tower. At any rate, there were literally thousands of people waiting for us at the airport when we arrived.

They followed us to the hotel where we had planned to stay. We couldn't even find a place to eat without causing a near-riot—some getaway! The hotel manager was very understanding. He led us through a basement into the back entrance of one of the hotel's restaurants and said that we could be served privately there. Well, before our salads arrived, a reporter did. He walked up and put a tape recorder down on the table and began asking questions. That was the last straw for Sandy. He began trying to put together an alternate trip. We learned of a little island that was very remote. Surely we would be left alone there.

Remote it was. We had to take two different small planes and a boat to get there. When we arrived, we were amazed to see reporters and photographers from the tabloids waiting for us. Of course they were out for the big story: DOLLY WHISKED AWAY TO ROMANTIC GETAWAY BY MYSTERY MAN. Anyone who knows Sandy would know that the notion of the two of us being romantically involved is ridiculous. I am most assuredly not his type, and I don't think I am breaking any big news to say so. Sandy doesn't mind if I say that he's gay. But he would also like for me to say that he's gorgeous and available, which he is.

Sometimes I think that his not wanting me as a woman has allowed us to be much closer than if we had been drawn to each other sexually. I've always had that problem with men, them liking me too much or vice versa. I'm like Will Rogers in that respect: "I never met a man I didn't like." Men are my weakness . . . men and food, you could say.

The reporters were a bother he didn't want me to

have to deal with. So he chartered what we thought was a yacht to take us out to sea and away from prying eyes and tape recorders. The closest thing to a yacht on that remote island turned out to be a little houseboat like I would have at my house on the lake back in Tennessee. I don't know exactly how big it was, only that it doesn't seem right to use the word *big* when describing it. It had a small cabin that barely had sleeping accommodations and was advertised as having a chef. The word *chef* fit the man preparing the food about as well as the word *yacht* fit the boat. The food was literally sardines and Velveeta cheese on Ritz crackers, the kind of stuff I would have had at a hillbilly picnic back home. That was fine with me, but Sandy is used to fine cuisine. Still, he was game enough to try to make the best of it.

The couple who owned and operated the boat were nice people, and they did the best they could to make us comfortable. It seemed to me, though, that we were heading a long way offshore for such a little boat. As it turned out, my fears were justified. There I was trying to enjoy my potted meat on a cracker when a storm began to blow up out of nowhere. The man running the boat told us that this kind of thing was common for those waters and that the best thing to do was to ride it out where we were. Sandy and I are no sailors, so we decided to trust the man's judgment.

The storm turned out to be much worse even than our captain had imagined. Winds that must have been near hurricane force whipped the seas into a frenzy. The couple busied themselves with trying to handle the boat and keep it afloat, and I'm glad they did. But that left Sandy and me to fend for ourselves. Of the two of us, Sandy is the bigger sissy (he's always more afraid he's going to break a nail than I am). He had no idea what to do.

Soon it became clear to both of us what to do: hold on for dear life! Waves began washing over the rear deck, and I started to get really scared. It takes a lot for me to take my shoes off, but this is one time I decided I could forego the five-inch heels. I took them off, and it wasn't long before "my little slings," as I always called them, got slung. They went overboard with a wave, and all I could do was watch them go.

The next wave almost got me. A wall of water came crashing over the boat, slapping it around like a toy. I slid across the deck, completely out of control. I felt a rush of cold water surround me as the sea swept me in. I managed to grab a railing and stay with the boat, but my whole body was dangling overboard. I could think of nothing but the shark stories the captain had told us earlier.

Just as I began to lose my grip, I became aware of Sandy making his way across the pitching deck, reaching his hand out for me. He somehow got a hold of me and dragged me back onto the boat and into the little cabin. It felt good to be out of the water, but by all appearances, the sharks' dinner had only been delayed. There seemed to be no way our little boat could ride out this storm. You never know how you're going to respond to a situation like that until you're actually in it. The way Sandy and I chose to deal with it is still a source of wonder to me.

We held a brief high-level discussion and unanimously decided that we were doomed. Sandy's gutsy "They can kill us, but they won't eat us" didn't apply to sharks. Then we simply and calmly lay down on the little bunk, held hands, and waited to die. I thought to myself, "If this don't beat all." Here I am, a country girl from East Tennessee, about to die somewhere off the coast of Australia, side by side with a gay man from New York.

We lay there and prayed silently, Sandy in his way and I in mine. But God must have decided he wasn't through with us. The storm broke, the sea calmed, and the sun even began to peek out of little holes in the clouds. We had to stay anchored that night to keep from going through the same storm on the way in. But we were safe.

I think that experience created in both of us the feeling that if we can survive that, we can survive anything. As I look back at it, it is altogether fitting that Sandy was the one I shared it with. I know we will always be there to pull each other out of any storm in life, and that gives me great comfort. Carl is not the least bit threatened by my relationship with Sandy; in fact he is very grateful for it because he knows I am loved and taken care of when I am not with him.

Judy had bounced back too. She had dumped the dude that was causing her pain and was back at my side, her old self again. That felt good. Of course I always had the steadfast Don Warden, so my business family was healthy and together and I was itching to get back to work.

Sandy and I both thought I should do another movie right away. *Nine to Five* had been a pleasurable, enchanted experience. *Best Little Whorehouse* had been a miserable, spirit-numbing ordeal. I guess in my mind the two sort of canceled each other out. This left me feeling that movies were definitely something I wanted to do, if I could control enough elements of the film to prevent the *Whorehouse* thing from repeating itself.

While I seem to be down on the whole experience, I should point out, as Burt always did to me, that *Whorehouse* was a financial success. Also, while I had been a kind of unspoiled curiosity in *Nine to Five*, *Whorehouse* had elevated me, at least temporarily, to the status of full-fledged movie star. To anyone who keeps up with the ins and outs of the movie business, it is probably not necessary to point out that my star status was temporary. Today's ins are tomorrow's outs. The film industry might not have written "What have you done lately?" but they're darn sure the ones that cut the hit single.

There I was with this newly acquired movie stardom I didn't even know I had. Maybe that's why I was willing to gamble it (and a lot of money) on a new venture. Even if I had been fully aware of the seriousness of that dice roll, I probably would have done it anyway. I have always believed in myself, and that is something no fickle movie business could ever change. Hindsight, as we all know, is twenty-twenty, and if I had it all to do over again, I would not wager so heavily on *Rhinestone*. You would have thought with a "hind" as big as mine, it would have been easier to see.

I guess the public didn't want to see Sylvester Stallone do comedy. Or maybe they didn't want to see me do Sylvester Stallone. One thing is certain: They didn't want to see *Rhinestone*.

No matter how big a financial disaster *Rhinestone* was, it was not all bad for me. Sylvester Stallone made me laugh at a time when I really needed it. I have found no therapy more effective than laughing, although in this case there were probably less expensive ways to get it. I should point out that Sly Stallone is certifiably crazy. But he was a good kind of crazy, the kind I needed at that point in my life. After all, movies may come and go, but life is something we buy a ticket to every day—and it doesn't come with popcorn. To me, Stallone was better than popcorn. He was full of life and very healthy for me to be around (Lord, I've made him sound like a laxative).

One other good thing about *Rhinestone* was the music I wrote for it, which I will always be proud of. I still think that those songs are some of the best country songs nobody ever heard.

I suppose overall it was a humbling experience. I take nothing for granted. I'm humbled every day by one thing or another. If you get too big for your britches, you're in for a fall. The Bible says, "He who exalts himself shall be humbled, but he who humbles himself shall be exalted."

One night during the making of the film, we were shooting in an alley. There was garbage everywhere and big rats running around. We were working all night, and it was that New York kind of damp cold. I noticed a man lying there next to some garbage, and he was shivering. We had a big heater and blankets on the set. So I thought I'd go back there and get warm and put a heavy shawl I was wearing around this poor man. I didn't realize anybody was watching. Just as I wrapped the shawl around the man, Stallone walked up and jerked it away. "Don't you put that good shawl over that scum!" he said. "He could have made something of himself. We did."

Well, you could have knocked me over with an angel feather. I couldn't believe what a man I considered a friend was saying. I grabbed the shawl back from him and wrapped it back around the man. Then I stood up right in Sly's face and said, "Hey, look! That could have been you, you ungrateful son of a bitch! Except by the grace of God. Who knows. It could be an angel sent to show you what an ass you really are. At least he's one of God's creatures, and that's good enough for me."

Some of the people on the crew just stood back in amazement. They had never seen anybody talk to Stallone that way. He apparently had never heard anybody talk to him like that either. He looked at me, kind of hurt and embarrassed, and said, "You're right." The next morning I found my shawl back in my trailer. Someone told me that Sly had taken what I said to heart and had gone back that night and given the man a blanket and some money. I know that Sylvester is a good person down deep, and he's still a dear friend of mine. I don't take all the credit for setting him straight about that one instance. It was a feisty little hillbilly woman he saw in his face that night, but God was the one who really spoke to him.

Perhaps the most significant thing about the movie, or the Dolly who was involved in the making of the movie, was that it finally made me get my weight down. I guess you could say I lost my ass in two ways.

The image of poor Burt Reynolds having to carry me across the screen was still fresh in my mind. As I am fond of saying, "If I tried to haul ass, I would have to make two trips." It seemed clear to me that unless we planned to sell billboard advertising on my voluminous butt, perhaps I should try to whittle away at it. The thought of sharing the screen with someone as body-conscious as Sylvester Stallone made me really determined to get my weight down.

I tried every diet in the book. I tried some that weren't in the book. I tried eating the book. It tasted better than most of the diets. I tried the Scarsdale diet and the Stillman water diet (you remember that one, where you run weight off trying to get to the bathroom). I tried Optifast, Juicefast, and Waterfast. I even took those shots that I think were made from cow pee. I endured every form of torture anybody with a white coat and a clipboard could devise for a fat girl who really liked fried pork chops.

One night while I was on some kind of liquid-protein diet made from bone marrow, or something equally appetizing, I was with a group of friends at a Howard Johnson's and some of them were having fried clams. I'll never forget sitting there with all of that glorious fried fat filling my nostrils and feeling completely left out. I went home and wrote one of my biggest hits, "Two Doors Down." I also went off my diet and had some fried clams.

There were times when I thought of chucking it all in. "Damn the movie," I would say. "I'm just gonna eat everything and go ahead and weigh five hundred pounds and have to be buried in a piano case." Luckily, a few doughnuts later, that thought would pass and I would be back to the goal at hand. I remember something in a book I read called *Gentle Eating*. The author said you should pretend the angels are eating with you and that you want to save some for them. I loved that idea, because I love angels. I have to admit, though, there were times I would slap those angels out of the way and have their part too. A true hog will do that.

Finally, I arrived at the Dolly Diet. The concept was so simple I don't know how it took me so long to think of it. Here's how it works: I go ahead and eat all of those things I have a craving for. (I had thought of that part before; it was the next part that made it different.) The trick is, I eat them in very small quantities. The only good diet is one that works for you personally and one that you can stay with. This was the compromise movie star Dolly was able to make with pig Dolly that has kept them both reasonably satisfied.

People who go out to dinner with me on a regular basis have learned not to order for themselves because they know I am likely to order two or three entrees and then just have a bite or two of each one, leaving the rest up for grabs. None of this is to say that I would recommend the Dolly Diet to anybody else. To the contrary, I recommend that you go on the (your name here) diet. Find one that works for you, even if you have to make it up. As long as it's not nutritionally detrimental to your health and you can afford it, I say go for it.

The inescapable truth about any diet is: If you're going to lose weight, you're going to have to eat less food. I hear people all the time complaining that "I have a slow metabolism" or "I'm just big-boned." If you could see some of the people these complaints come from, you'd know that nobody's bones are that big. I have never known a fat person who didn't eat a lot. They may do it when nobody's looking, but somehow, somewhere, they are putting away some groceries. Of course, exercise is the other necessary element in this equation, but the hardest exercise for most of us is that one where we push our chair back from the dinner table.

One other hint I'd like to pass on has to do with chewing. Our taste buds are only in our mouths, after all, and we don't really taste the food when we swallow it. You can get a lot of the satisfaction from the taste of things you love by just chew, chew, chew, chew, Chattanooga chew-chewing and then not swallowing. "Wait a minute," you're thinking. "If I don't swallow, won't I have to spit the food out?" You're right. "That's disgusting," you say. That may be, but what's more disgusting? Spitting out food or being a lardass? I'm not suggesting for a moment that you spit up food. That's very dangerous, but it doesn't hurt to spit it out. I know for a fact that a lot of stars and models chew and spit. The first time somebody told me that, I was so shocked I dropped a whole Styrofoam cup of chewed doughnuts.

And so, with the success of my diet, I was not "as

big a star" after *Rhinestone,* physically or financially. All in all, while the making of the film was not unpleasant for me, it would be some time before I would make another one.

One side effect of my having lost weight and my being associated with Sylvester Stallone was that the tabloids took an even greater interest in me than ever. Of course there were rumors of my romantic involvement with Sly, and the incredible stories of how I had lost the weight. But I was not really prepared for the fascination some people had with almost every aspect of my private life.

When you are the subject of some kind of outlandish story, you first read it with amusement. You find yourself wondering how the writers (if you can call them that) could make up such a tale and who they expect to believe it. Then reality hits you in the face, and you stop laughing. No matter how crazy a story is, there are people who will believe it.

I will say that most of the stories in the tabloids, at least the ones I have any knowledge of, have some thread of truth to them, no matter how frayed that thread might be. I have sometimes been called the "Queen of the Tabloids," which is a title I don't particularly mind having. I have to admit there's a part of me that likes the idea of being the queen of just about anything. I have come to accept most of the outrageous crap with a sense of humor. I also have the business sense to know that it is not necessarily a bad thing to have my face plastered all over the supermarket checkout when I have a new album coming out. It is only when the stories hurt my family or others close to me that I get upset.

There was a time when I learned with both amusement and mild horror that some of the stories were, in fact, coming from within my family. "Within my family" is not exactly accurate. The stories were coming from an aunt I hardly know and hadn't seen since she left the Smokies when I was very young. I can't say that I was very aware of her until the stories she was selling to the tabloids began to make me take notice. Family members who actually knew her had told me, "Everybody knows she's crazy." Apparently tabloid editors are not a part of "everybody."

Although she might have been crazy, she was aware enough to know that her relationship to me could be turned into money. She simply made up stories about me. For one thing, she went to one of the scandal sheets and professed to know "the true story of Jolene, the redhead who almost took Dolly's man." That whole story, as you know by now, was something I had made up for the sake of the song. She told it as if she had been there and witnessed the whole sordid affair. The only thing truly sordid was that there was some loony woman who didn't know me telling her side of things that never happened.

I do not profess to be a perfect person. Nobody is. The family members who are actually close to me could tell much better stories if they were inclined to do so. This stuff was just crap. For a while she had a pretty lucrative career making up stories about me that she had absolutely no way of knowing about. The complete absence of the truth didn't stop her or the tabloids. The bogus stories kept on coming for a while.

This misguided woman, whom I will simply refer to as "the Squealer," was not satisfied with money. She wanted to be a star in her own right. Or should I say wrong? She tried to get on TV and wrote letters to Joan Rivers, Oprah, and Phil Donahue. Fortunately, I know those people, so they would call or write me or simply have the Squealer's letters forwarded to me. I often thought about confronting her myself but was advised against it by other family members.

Through little bits of information, I finally began to put together a picture of this woman and what she had against me, at least in her mind (a word I use with some reservation). During the filming of *Rhinestone* I had a big to-do at my house and invited some of the people from "up home" to meet the Hollywood types and vice versa. Apparently the Squealer was hurt that she was not invited to rub elbows with Stallone and the like, and she undertook her smear campaign out of spite.

Maybe I should have dealt with the Squealer more harshly. I have difficulty doing things like that. Having scratched and clawed my way to fame and fortune, I can understand that drive. Unlike some people though, I always wanted to do it on my own. I can imagine the frustration of being on the edge of something big. It's as if you are dying for lack of sunlight and then have the sun come just up to the edge of your toes, leaving you in the shadows.

As bizarre as the story of the Squealer is, it is still easier to laugh at her shenanigans than at the efforts of some other people to cash in on their proximity to the "Queen of the Tabloids." There was one time when I was deeply hurt, not by the stories that came out but by betrayal. I had become friends with certain people (at a time when I really needed friends) and had taken them into my confidence. They were obviously in need as well, and I did everything I could to help them, really opened my heart (and my pocketbook) to them. That's why it was so devastating when they tried to blackmail me.

Yes, I said blackmail. I know that is a serious word, but, believe me, these people were serious. After they had gotten close enough to me to feel they had something to sell, they approached Sandy Gallin and demanded money for "pictures, videos, and tapes" containing damaging information concerning me. Without telling me, he agreed to meet them and did in fact give them money. The big dangerous videos and pictures turned out to be nothing more than me visiting and having dinner at their house and the tapes were of me talking on their answering machine.

There's always somebody with a story or a scheme once you become famous.

Sometimes it's a burden to be a star or even be related to one. People might assume that my having become a star would open doors for the rest of my family, but I am not sure it works that way. No matter how much talent they have in their own right, people are bound to say, "Of course they got that part or that record deal, she's Dolly's sister or he's Dolly's brother." My sister Stella has her own style of singing that is very special to her and has nothing to do with me. She has had a lot of well-deserved success and deserves to be known as Stella Parton—period, end of sentence. The second man to walk on the moon left footprints every bit as deep as Neil Armstrong's, and yet how many of us know his name?

Sometimes I get to thinking about my success and the imprint that it's had on my family. It's been a blessing and a curse to them. They've had to live "in the shadow of a song," as my sister Willadeene's book title suggests. I am certainly not the first or the most talented person in my family. I just happened to be the first to become famous. Just like I was the first to graduate high school, but I'm not the only one with a diploma.

Music and writing are a big part of my family. This tradition goes way back through several generations. Within my immediate family, my sister Willadeene is a wonderful poet. She's had several of her works published, such as "Denim, Lace, and Bandanas." And, in my completely unbiased opinion, I recommend all of it highly. Willadeene writes some of the sweetest and purest things I've ever read. She has been writing stories since we were very young and probably would have been a popular, well-established writer by now, had I not gotten in the way. She loves to write fiction, but when the publishers discovered that she was my sister, they insisted that her first story be about us. The Dolly Parton name would help sell her book.

Well, I'm sure that *In the Shadow of a Song* was a hard book for Willadeene to write. She tried to be as true as possible in her presentation of the family. And she wanted to present me properly and truthfully too. It was a hard job, and she did it very well. It's definitely first on the list of suggested reading material. She did a lot of historical research that I was too lazy to do for this book. So I'm not only proud of her, but I'm grateful too. We refer to many of the same things, but of course differ in a place or two. This is only because our memory serves us differently. It's a wonder we have a memory at all. Sometimes I think I have CRN disease—I think that stands for "Can't Remember Nothing," but I forget.

I believe Willadeene has the potential to be successful at anything she writes. She could write best-selling books, plays, movies, or even a hit TV series if she were so inclined. And I hope some day to be able to produce some of her work. Willadeene has been like a second mother to all of us. She's the dearest friend a person could have. And she is always there for us. Thank you, Willadeene. We all love you.

Next, in order of arrival, is my brother David. He's a lot like my dad in his demeanor. He is a very quiet, intelligent man. He joins in on our sing-alongs, but of all the boys, he is the least interested in music. David is great with numbers and organization. He has played an important part with a major construction firm for many years. He's wonderful with people, but he's good with roosters too. His passion is raising and selling game cocks, and he can't wait to retire to do more of it. My brother David is well liked and respected by everybody. Especially by me. And, in turn, he has always been supportive of my dreams. He loves the songs I write and sing. And it warms my heart to know his pickup is full of my cassettes.

Then there's Denver. Denver and I have a very unusual but special relationship. We were very close in age when we were growing up (of course, now he's a lot older than I am—just kidding, Denver). As you know, we were a troublesome pair, but I believe that's what has made us even closer now that we're adults. Denver probably has the best voice of all the boys, but he's just too shy to play his guitar or sing in front of anybody, even family. A few beers seem to help him tremendously, though. He does his best singing up on the old mountain road, hanging out with my brothers and cousins, drinking a little moonshine. He'll start singing gospel songs (and probably preaching again), and it seems he just won't quit till the seas dry up—or till he does.

Don't get me wrong: Denver is a hard worker. He sings hard but works even harder running a farm. He also carves beautiful things out of wood. It's almost a shame we don't fight anymore, because now I could probably whip his butt.

My brother Bobby is not that interested in music, but he's one of the most creative members of the family. He's a talented developer, contractor, and builder. He's done wonderful work for me at the old Tennessee Mountain Home and at Dollywood. He may not be musical, but he has certainly been instrumental in many of my business affairs. He also works on the producing end of a lot of my TV specials and other events that we do in East Tennessee.

My sister Stella also has business smarts, along with exceptional talent. She's one of the hardest-working women I've ever met. She's been in show business just about as long as I have. She started out in gospel music but has done everything from country music to Broadway shows. She's made some hit records and now has a very large following worldwide.

Stella is always going on the road somewhere and making a good living at it. She's starred in *Pump Boys and Dinettes*, *Best Little Whorehouse in Texas*, *Gentlemen Prefer Blondes*, *Seven Brides for Seven Brothers*, and a lot of other traveling stage shows. She's a wonderful entertainer, and they especially seem to love her abroad. And I'm one broad who especially loves her.

Stella has always been helpful to me. She is also a wonderful songwriter. She uses her brilliant business sense to help organize and run my publishing company. And she has also been involved in many of the productions we do in Nashville and at Dollywood. And Stella has her own business in Pigeon Forge called Stella Parton's Best Little Hat House in the Smokies. It has wonderful coffees and teas and it's a great place to find country music and Smoky Mountain memorabilia. And if that's not enough, she's also published her own cookbook called *Really Cooking*. I told you Stella works hard.

Unfortunately, I sometimes feel like I've only been a hindrance to her. When someone else is hogging the spotlight, it's hard to get people to notice you long enough to give you a chance, even if you deserve it. And nobody deserves it like Stella.

Cassie is the only one of us girls who is not at all interested in writing, singing, or performing. She never even liked singing in church. She's a good singer, but she's painfully shy. We nearly had to hog-tie her to get her to sing in our *pig-Latin* group. And she gets especially nervous in front of a camera. She has to take a Valium to sing on a TV special with us.

Cassie has a great sense of humor that I take to the bone. We have always been very close. She was the first one of the kids to come to live with Carl and me. She's more like a daughter than a sister, and I feel like the fairy grandmother to her kids. Cassie manages all my properties in the South and keeps my personal and domestic life in great order. She is very smart and a hard worker. I call her Cat, her crew calls her Sarge. If I could ever change places with anyone, I would want to be Cassie.

Larry, who, you'll recall, was to be "my baby" but died after only a few hours of life, remains very strongly in all of our minds. And I think of him every year on July 5, his birthday.

Then comes Randy, yet another talented singer and songwriter. And I'm not the only one who thinks so. Randy has received many awards for his work. He has a great ear for songs, and I've been lucky to have him help me pick out music for my albums. He's also got a good nose for business and has become an established publisher. He has published his own songs as well as those written by other family members. And he couldn't get away with not performing at Dollywood. In my completely objective opinion, he has the best show at the park. Randy was on RCA records for a while and now is recording with a new group that he organized. I think they have a great shot at the big time, and Randy has all the talent to make it happen and keep it going. And above all this, he's a fine man.

Floyd is one half of the twins who arrived next. Even if he is my brother, I happen to think Floyd is one of the greatest writers and singers today. He wrote "Rockin' Years," which became a number-one hit for Ricky Van Shelton and me. I've always believed that he could be a star also. Floyd is the baby boy, and he's special to all of us in many ways—especially to Mama.

Freida is the other half of the twin arrangement. You will never meet anyone so gifted in your life. I marvel at the songs she writes. They are filled with fire and passion. My writing pales in comparison to hers. She's got the best voice of all of us and has a magical charisma onstage. She performed for years before a back injury sidelined her for a while. She's still on the mend, but I know she's got what it takes. She knows that I'm her biggest fan.

In the tradition of saving the best for last, now comes Rachel. You've never seen such beauty and sweetness and warmth. Hers is an angelic voice, too beautiful to believe. And her lyrics are true poetry. She's now recording with the group that Randy is a part of. Rachel loves everybody, and everybody loves Rachel. And when other family members don't get along, Rachel is the one to fix it. She's our baby, the one we all hold sacred and special.

I've been closer to Rachel and Cassie than I have the other kids because they live near me in Nashville. We stay more involved with their families. Their husbands, Larry Seaver and Richard Dennison, are like my sons-in-law and their kids, Rebecca, Bryan, and Hannah, are like real grandchildren. So are the rest of my nieces and nephews, Mitchell, Donna, Dena, Tim, Clint, Danielle, Chris, Jennifer, Jada, Teaver, and Heidi. I have to thank them for adding so much joy to my life.

15

People have a strange way of looking at stars. Just the fact that we refer to certain people as "stars" is a little weird. I have had women follow me into rest rooms and then stand amazed as I actually used the facilities for their intended purpose. I've even reminded them on occasion, "Yes, stars do pee."

It's all a part of the "life in a fishbowl" that goes along with success. There was a time when I was the third most photographed person in the world after the Pope and Madonna (not the Madonna usually associated with the Pope). Unlike Madonna, who has made a career out of shocking the public, I have tried to live and let live. That seems to be the one thing certain elements of the public won't allow.

I have to be very careful what I say in public. Everywhere I turn there's always somebody with a tape recorder or a notepad, and every word I say has the potential to come back to haunt me. Words and phrases can be taken out of context. They also have a way of looking very different printed in black and white. Perhaps the tone of voice you use or a preliminary assurance makes it clear that you're only joking.

I was really hurt recently when something I said was taken to be anti-Semitic. It came out of a conversation with Sandy Gallin, who is Jewish, about a new TV show I am developing. The show is all about the Deep South, fundamentalist Christians in particular. There I was trying to explain to some of the Jewish writers about Pentecostalists, the whole holy-roller talking-in-tongues thing. I said something like, "I can imagine how hard it would be for a Jew to write this. It would be like a hillbilly trying to write the story of Judaism." I think everybody there knew what I was talking about and understood, but it somehow got blown out of proportion in a magazine article. I know how personal a thing people's religion is to them, and I would hate to think I had offended anybody by a thing like that. If I did, I truly want to apologize.

There is a popular notion (mainly among people who make their living by prying) that a person who chooses to be a star gives up the right to privacy. Both publicly and privately, I think that's a crock, and you don't have to pick through my garbage to find that out. Just because some people choose to make a living by singing (or playing a sport or whatever) doesn't mean they're obliged to open their whole lives for public viewing. If I wanted to do that, I would say, "Here's my latest album—oh, and here's a pair of my dirty drawers." Our society takes great measures to ensure the privacy of serial killers being executed for their crimes, but someone who has the audacity to try to entertain the public is probed at like some kind of germ under a microscope. Sometimes you really feel violated.

Sandy Gallin and I have a history of doing some pretty wild things to try to shock, embarrass, or amuse each other. Once in a restaurant at a fairly private table, I took out my famous pair and put them on a platter on the edge of the table. "Here you go, Sandy," I said, "I'm laying 'em out for you." That platter was cold, but I'll do anything for a good joke on Sandy. Thank God the press wasn't there for that one.

Once when we were on vacation, Sandy's wild side got a hold of him. He started in singing to me in a big loud voice, show tunes from *The Sound of Music*. People started to stare, but they didn't know Sandy. Next thing you know, he's up and going to tables all over the restaurant, singing to the patrons like he was Florence Henderson. Sandy has a good voice, and I think some of the people even started to think he was actually the live entertainment. They applauded for him, and of course he took big bows. Some of them even wanted to tip him. I think he made $2.75, although he would claim in the trades he had made twice that much.

One thing that makes my relationship with Sandy so special is that each of us is able to accept, or I should say put up with, a lot from the other that would drive most normal people crazy. A lot of people are put off by Sandy's manners, if he has any. He struts around his house in his jockey shorts, no matter who is there, and makes a big deal out of pampering himself. He's always shuffling meetings around to make time for this guru or that yoga teacher, and that's if you're lucky. He's just as likely to have somebody give him a manicure or, God forbid, a pedicure during a meeting.

Some people don't feel comfortable discussing bigmoney deals with strangers in the room, especially if those strangers are cutting the hair, painting the toenails, or massaging the butt of the person they're trying to talk to. I think that's Sandy's way of wearing power. I think he gets off on the thought that if people want to meet with him, they'll just have to do it on his terms. He has always reminded me of a character Al Pacino would play in a movie. You might not be in a hurry to deal with him again, but you are not likely to forget the experience.

I remember when Sandy was very ill with metastatic melanoma and was scheduled for surgery. There was cause for real concern, and we were not at all certain he would come through the operation. Everyone was fawning over him saying, "poor Sandy, poor Sandy." He was eating it up. It was just the kind of drama he craved. He was holding court like the queen of Sheba, perched up in his bed, surrounded by his hairdressers, as happy as a pig in poop. When I got there, he put on an especially pitiful look, knowing I could see right through it. "What are you doing, getting coiffed for God?" somebody asked him. We all laughed. As it turned out, Heaven was not to get a look at Sandy's do after all. I like to think my prayers helped, but it is just as likely God wasn't up to having such an eccentric angel as a permanent guest just yet.

I came to a point in my life where I wanted to do another TV show. The idea seemed like a good one at first. I thought I had learned from my little show in Nashville. I wanted to do something like that, only with a bigger budget and better guests. I was naive enough to think that what I wanted would somehow matter to the people in network television.

Looking back, the show was doomed from day one. A huge machine was put together made up of people, money, equipment, money, scenery, and more money. But it was all designed to produce a show that didn't exist. Every person involved with the show, with very few exceptions, was determined to revive variety the way it had been in its heyday. That form of variety is dead and by all indications is going to stay dead. Even if it could be revived, I am not the person to do it. That kind of television is as far removed from my personality as it can be. I am not Carol Burnett. Carol Burnett was, in my opinion, the greatest performer that classic television variety ever knew. Yet even she could not make it work in her latest attempt in today's television market.

The first mistake on the ABC version of "Dolly" was to hire old-time variety writers and producers. To them, this was like a new lease on life, a chance to relive their glory days, maybe even buy a new toupee. To me, it was a disaster. From day one, they had me wearing beaded gowns and standing in a spotlight singing old standards like "Someone to Watch Over Me." I was a little embarrassed from the beginning because I simply didn't know any of their old standards. The Broadway sophistication of Cole Porter and Gershwin had never been very big on Locust Ridge. About the only exposure I had ever had to this kind of music was from Willie Nelson's *Stardust* album, so I sang mostly those songs, after spending hours learning them and how to sing them. Even that was silly to me because Willie had just done that.

Sandy Gallin loves that stuff himself, and he loves me even more, so he was blinded to what was going on for the most part. It is difficult to tell what other Hollywood television people knew and when, if ever, they realized something was wrong. There are very few truly talented and creative people in television; the rest of them tend to hang on to their coattails. They're harmless enough if they are simply "along for the ride," but they can all too often actually drag the talented person backward.

The ratings for the first show were great, close to a forty share. In a way, that was unfortunate because it

made the variety-resurrection team appear to be right.
The truth was that people had tuned in out of curiosity and because the show had been hyped through
the roof. The ratings fell steadily after the premiere
until they leveled off at about a fourteen share,
which I think represents my core of true fans who
would watch me if I went on TV and milked a goat.
Come to think of it, milking a goat would have been
more entertaining than some of the stuff that
machine put out.

There were a very few people involved with the
show who understood me and what I needed to be
doing. Unfortunately, they were not the ones making
the decisions. Occasionally a bright spot would come
along. There was one segment that was created about
midway through the run called "Dixie's Place" that
felt more comfortable. I played a waitress in a diner, a
real kind of person I could relate to. Even at that, it
called on me to be something of an actress rather than
just letting me be me. Most of those segments were
written by Buddy Sheffield, who has become one of
my dearest and best friends. He is a wonderful writer,
comedy and otherwise. He even wrote some songs for
the Dixie segments, one of which I later recorded with
Tammy Wynette and Loretta Lynn on the *Honky
Tonk Angels* album. That song, "Sittin' on the Front
Porch Swing," is one of my all-time favorites.

Meanwhile, the machine whizzed along, and every
old fart in Hollywood who had ever done variety was
brought in at one time or another. Writers came and
went. Flash was made flashier, stale was made staler,
Dolly got lost. I remember sitting in some of those
writer/producer meetings and being absolutely
amazed. Of the nine or ten men in the room, five had
hair transplants, four had some kind of nervous tic,
and three had both. It was like a tic fest. Sometimes I

would hear things brought up and I would wait for everybody to laugh at how ridiculous it was, but the laugh never came. The laugh was on me when the ridiculous idea actually got done.

There were some laughs involved with the show. Unfortunately they were not shared with the home audience. One day I was standing with my stage manager, Sandy Prudden, and Buddy Sheffield watching as Kermit the Frog (with the help of the late Jim Henson) sweetly sang a song. Sandy was always a big joker. He sidled up to me and said, "Isn't it amazing the way Kermit can sing like that with somebody's hand up his ass." Without missing a beat, I came back with, "Shoot, that ain't nothin'. I did that for seven years on 'The Porter Wagoner Show.'"

By far the most successful shows were the few episodes where we took the show on the road. A Thanksgiving show back home, a show in Hawaii, one in New Orleans, and one in Nashville came a lot closer to allowing my personality to come through. But the production schedule was grueling. That kind of thing couldn't be done on a weekly basis. If anybody had really analyzed it, it wasn't because of the places we went to, although they have a certain allure. The trick was that the format of those shows put me with real people and just let me happen. That's what I do best. That could have been done in the studio just as easily, if the right decisions had been made.

By the time the show was canceled, I was glad. I wanted it to be over. I was physically and emotionally drained.

I thank God that I have loyal fans. The ABC fiasco didn't cause me to lose them, but it didn't make me any new ones either. Taking nothing away from Sandy Gallin and Jim Morey, God will always be my real manager. He never closes a door without opening a window. If my TV show had gone on, I would have missed many wonderful opportunities that have come my way since then. I believe that when you pray in earnest and really look for answers, you'll find them. If you're really able to get in touch with God and your own subconscious, which I believe are inseparable, you will be able to "separate the wheat from the chaff" and your true way will be made clear to you. My network TV show sucked chaff.

If Sandy and Jim (Sandy's management partner) did one thing right with respect to the show, it was in making the deal when the show was originally sold. Because I had a two-year deal, the network had to pay me many millions of dollars to cancel the show. I had "failed up" in a big way. I still want to do TV when I find the right vehicle. I believe I have. It's called "Heavens to Betsy," and it will be on CBS this fall. Wish me luck.

If there's one bit of advice I could give to young people trying to break into show business, it would be this: Don't assume that the people on the inside know what they're doing. He may have a big office and a fancy suit. He may have the power to hire you or not. But he probably has no idea whether or not you have any talent. Even if he has an opinion, he probably has to clear it with guys in even bigger offices with even more expensive suits (and even less of a clue). There's a joke around Hollywood about a writer who runs into a studio executive over the weekend. "What did you think of the script I turned in Friday?" the writer asks. The studio exec answers in all seriousness, "I don't know. So far I'm the only one who's read it."

Although the ratio may be better than in some other businesses, show business is still essentially a man's world. As a woman, that can be difficult to deal with. Especially if you are a five-foot-two blonde with

a hick accent. In addition, the difficulty factor is mul-
tiplied by two for every cup size. In short, being a
woman in show business is like being a bird dog in
heat. If you stand still, they'll screw you. If you run,
they'll bite you in the ass. I have learned to use all of
that to my advantage.

There are basically two kinds of men you have to
deal with in business: the ones who want to screw you
out of money, and the ones who want to screw you,
period. The second guy is the easiest to deal with. If I
catch a man who is not looking into my eyes as he
talks to me, I have scored two really big points with
him already. A smart woman can take a man who
thinks with his small head and quickly turn the
would-be screwer into the screwee.

I should point out that I am not interested in screwing anybody (professionally). I never want anything
more than what's fair. The problem is, I never want
anything less either. In the old-boy school of business,
if a woman walks away from the table with what's
rightfully hers, the man feels screwed anyway. I have
to admit that adds to the satisfaction of making a fair
deal. "How was it for you, old boy?"

Many an old boy has found out too late that I look
like a woman but think like a man. It is a great mistake to assume that because I look soft, I do business
that way. Just like the first prostitute who realized she
was "sittin' on a gold mine," I know what I have to
sell, and nobody goes prospecting in my gold mine
without first buying the mineral rights.

A southern woman who looks soft and pretty on
the outside but is as strong as forged metal on the
inside is called a "steel magnolia." I am proud if people think of me as one. I am also proud that I had a
part in making a film that pays tribute to those
strong women. *Steel Magnolias* was a fine film with

something to say, and I have always thought it should have been a bigger hit. Although I was very pleased with the final product, the making of the movie was not always a piece of cake.

From day one, people were predicting trouble on the set because the cast included so many strong actresses with distinct and different personalities. That trouble never developed. We all got along fine. The only person who made it less than a wonderful time for me was the director, Herbert Ross.

He didn't particularly like me or Julia Roberts at the start and was very hard on us. He had originally wanted Meg Ryan to play the part Julia had, but he couldn't get her. Julia Roberts was not the big star she is now, and I think Herbert Ross resented having to use her.

He told me I couldn't act. This was not news to me, and I told him so. "I'm not an actress, I'm Dolly Parton. I'm a personality who has been hired to do this movie. You're the director. It's your job to make me look like I'm acting." By the end of the film, we had all made peace and become friends.

I felt an extra drive to do the film justice because of the writer, Bobby Harling. The film was based on a true story, and the girl who died had been Bobby's real-life sister. She was apparently a big fan of mine and loved the song "I Will Always Love You." I never knew her, but I wanted to do well for her and for Bobby.

I felt at home in the character of Truvy, a somewhat redneck hairdresser. I have always thought that if I hadn't made it in show business, I would have been a hairdresser. I have always loved fiddling with hair and makeup and have learned a lot of beautician's skills out of necessity. In case you haven't noticed, I wear big hair. There were many scenes where I actually had to do hair on camera for extended periods of time. This was often in close-up, and there was no way to fake it. For the sake of reality, they had me actually train with real beauticians. There were even brave people from Natchitoches who volunteered to have me do their hair, although I doubt many of them knew exactly how courageous they were.

I couldn't help but be a little amused at the way they tried to "tone me down" for the part of Truvy. They would do everything they could to dress me in plainer colors, make my hair a little less flamboyant, et cetera, but it was a hopeless pursuit. I just told them, "Heck, there's a big, crazy, larger-than-life personality in here. It's painted with broad strokes, and it's going to come through no matter what you do to the broad it's painted on."

As I said, I am proud of *Steel Magnolias*, proud that I held up under difficult working conditions and that I held my own in the company of some very fine actresses. I am also proud for Julia Roberts and the way she kept on going. It thrills me to see the great success she has had since then.

Something else that fills me with pride is Dollywood, my theme park in Pigeon Forge, Tennessee. I can remember looking up at the Hollywood sign the first time I was in L.A. and thinking I would like to change that *H* into a *D*. Of course I have been criticized for having my own theme park, and a lot of people think it is just a big ego trip, but they are all people who haven't been there.

The theme park is much more about the mountains and the culture of the people who live there than it is about Dolly Parton. Dolly Parton simply happens to be the most famous hillbilly from those particular hills, and a lot of people are curious about me and my life. There is plenty there to satisfy that curiosity, but there is also plenty that celebrates the spirit of a people who made a life for themselves in that very stingy countryside. These are my real people, the seed from which I sprang. I saw Dollywood as a chance to honor them.

The people who work there are mostly real hillbillies, and yes, some of them are related to me. You can see them doing what they do best, whether that is making music, making handcrafted dulcimers, soap, quilts, or whatever. I know it sounds like I'm doing a commercial, but I told you right up front I'm proud of the place, so there. As much as the park itself, I am proud of what it has done for the economy of the area. I love the fact that I am able to give something back and provide so many people with jobs where none existed before. Of course, the Great Smoky Mountains were there for a couple of million years before I came along, and they are still the main attraction in the area, which is as it should be. If Dollywood can give some people a little extra incentive to visit there, then I am absolutely tickled.

Dollywood gives me another kind of pleasure too. When I was a kid, I always loved the county fair, the lights, the peanut hulls on the ground, and the big flashy attractions. When Dollywood was being planned, I told them I wanted to have every element of a county fair there for kids to enjoy year-round.

I especially remember the sideshows. They would have a big banner outside to sucker people in. Sometimes the attraction would be a real freak of nature like a two-headed calf or some other kind of oddity that we are all curious about, whether we admit to that little morbid side of ourselves or not. A lot of the time, though, it would just be a joke. I remember one that boasted, "See the Man-eating

Fish!" When you paid your quarter and went inside, all that was there was a man sitting at a table eating fish sticks. There were always some in the crowd who complained that it was a rip-off, but I thought a good joke was well worth a quarter and if somebody was clever enough to do you out of it, he deserved it.

When I was a teenager, a carnival came to town with one sideshow that advertised the "Alligator Girl from the Nile." Well, you know I had to see that. So I talked a couple of girlfriends into going in (my particular little morbid side likes company). There was a man outside selling tickets and shouting about the incredible sights that awaited anybody with a quarter for admission. This "barker" certainly did justice to his title; he had obviously yelled for so many years, his vocal cords must have resembled the fringe on a leather Nudie suit. What was left of his voice sounded like a dog baying at a coon. "See the alligator girl from the Nile. She has crocodile skin and crawls on her belly like a snake," he barked in tones that made a kid want to believe it could be true. We paid our quarters, pushed back the crusty flaps of the old tent, and ventured inside. At a time like that there is a combination of hope that the thing could be true and fear that the thing could be true that is the very definition of mystery. I clung to the back of the shirt of the girl in front of me, and the girl behind me did the same to mine. We wanted to experience the wonders of the universe, but we wanted to be able to beat a hell of a fast retreat if those wonders turned out to be more than three teenage girls could handle.

Then our eyes adjusted to the light and wonder turned to amazement of a different kind. There in a tank, actually a cheap backyard swimming pool, was my own cousin Myrtle (name slightly changed so that she still sends me a Christmas card). She was wearing a swimsuit, and it looked like they had glued green-dyed cornflakes onto her skin to give her that "crocodile" look. She was acting up a storm, flailing her head from side to side and snarling her best alligator growl. "Hey, Myrtle, it's me, Dolly," I said, tapping on the glass. She pretended she hadn't heard me and kept right on with her splashing and slashing and snarling.

The last I had heard of Myrtle, she had run off with a traveling "holy roller" preacher or somebody and was last seen somewhere in Ohio. Now here she was back as the Alligator Girl from the Nile. I could understand her completely. After all, I wanted to leave the mountains too, and I wanted attention. She probably thought I was making fun or blowing her cover, but I just wanted to say, "Hello, I understand. Be the alligator girl. Be whatever your dreams and your luck will let you be. Wear your green cornflakes with pride. Snarl at the crowds, and do your best to make them flinch. Give them a quarter's worth of wonder."

The story was circulating around town a couple of days later that Myrtle's daddy had found out about her and had come to the fair and snatched her right out of the pool and thrown her in the back of his pickup. I guess he didn't understand about wonder. Of course as soon as she found an open window, she was off again on whatever adventure she could find. Go for it, Myrtle. Dreams may be as fragile as soggy cornflakes, but chase them anyway, and store away as many of them as you can in that special place that makes you you. After all, today's alligator girl is tomorrow's storyteller, and both are precious in their own way.

I tried to put as much of that special kind of wonder into Dollywood as was possible, and I think I have succeeded fairly well. Millions of tourists seem to agree with me. It has been a great business venture for me. I have wonderful partners who know business as well as I know dreams, and each of us appreciates the other for what we have to give.

Many special angels have come into my life as a result of putting Dollywood together. My partners, the Hershend brothers, Jack and Pete, are wonderful people. I'm proud to call them friends outside of business. That's true of Jack's wife, Sherry, and Pete's wife, Jodee, as well. Terry Garrison, along with my brother Bobby, was instrumental in getting us all together. Ted Miller is the one who made it all happen. When I see them and all of the other "Dollywooders" working so sweetly, hand in hand, it seems like a part of God's perfect plan. Then there's the good that it's done through the Dollywood Foundation, helping the schoolkids, meeting medical needs, not to mention jobs for thousands of people. I can't help but think of it as part of some greater purpose.

16

People often ask me, "What's it like to make a record?" or "What's it like to make a movie?" The answer is that there is no clear-cut answer. There are as many answers as there are records and movies. Because show business is a creative field, it is carried out by creative people who by their very nature are oddballs. I don't mean that in a negative way: The fact is, creative people are just different. So the experience of working with one creative person or another can be as different as plowing is from making biscuits.

I have always found it true that the more real talent a person has, the more secure he is in that talent and the less likely he is to be a jerk. Most of the tantrums people throw don't really come out of anger with others as much as from an insecurity within themselves. Some of the nicest, genuinely warmest people I have dealt with have been those with the greatest talent and success. And some of the biggest jerks have been people on the perimeter of success who have bluffed their way to where they are.

While making one movie or record is bound to have elements in common with the making of another, you never really know what to expect. Every movie I have made has been a unique experience. The difficulty or ease involved in making a film never seems to be reflected in the finished product. One movie that was an absolute joy to make was *Straight Talk*. I am as proud of it as of anything I have ever done.

I love James Woods. People had warned me that he could be difficult to work with, but to me he was a thrill to be around, although I never saw him off the set. He is very talented and intelligent, and I respect him for those things. What I remember him for is that he is a great kisser. I don't know what it is that makes one man able to kiss so much better than another. If I did, I would put that in a book that would sell a helluva lot better than this one. Whatever it is, James Woods has it in spades.

The movie gave me a chance to use other parts of myself as well. I was able to contribute to it as an actress (or at least a personality), as a songwriter, and as a singer. The character was one that was very close to me. I was also able to inject a considerable amount of what might be called "homespun wit" into the script. Someone would say "if we could do so-and-so," to which I would say something like, "If a frog had wings, it wouldn't bump its ass when it jumps." The rest of the cast and crew would break up in hysterics. The next thing I knew that line was being spoken by my character in the film.

I felt I learned a lot from the director, Barnett Kellman. I appreciated that he was willing to share what he knew with me and that he had a nice way of doing it. I hope I get to work with him again.

Every creative experience is different, and I wouldn't have it any other way. That, to me, is what's so compelling about show business. I was in some place of business the other day, and there was a sign that said, REPETITION IS THE MOTHER OF SKILL. That may be, but it's also the father of boredom. Whatever my career has been, it hasn't been boring.

Although I still do not consider myself an actress, I will say that I have become more comfortable in front of a camera. I might also say that this only applies to cameras I put myself in front of intentionally. The tabloid photographers still seem to dog my steps everywhere I go. Sometimes they can be a real nuisance, especially when it's not just me they're shooting pictures of. For example, the time I was caught coming out of a clinic after some minor cosmetic surgery, Judy and my friend and hairdresser David Blair were more upset about being in the pictures than I was.

David Blair, by the way, is worth his weight in gold to me, more than that. He is a sweet southern boy from Rayne, Louisiana, and has been my hairdresser for many years. It seems funny to describe him as my hairdresser, since he is such a dear friend, but oh, he does love hair. He said he used to watch me years ago on "The Porter Wagoner Show" with all of those big piled-up dos I used to wear and think, "I'd love to get my hands on her hair." Now he does, almost every day. I think he even sleeps with it when I'm out of town.

That's a joke, of course, but he could if he wanted to. I do wear wigs. Someone once threatened to pull my hair, and I said, "Lord, some woman in Hong Kong will scream bloody murder." I sometimes make the joke about me standing on a hilltop with my hair blowing in the wind—and me too proud to run after it. I am awfully proud that I have David to do that job. Everybody always wants to know, "How long does it take to do your hair?" How should I know? I'm never there.

The other friend who makes me look like I have taste (I have admitted I don't) is Tony Chase. He designs all of those wonderful clothes I wear on TV, onstage, on the town, and even on this book cover. I feel privileged to have him do my clothes, because he's designed for a lot of really big stars and is very much in demand.

When I met him it was like heaven had opened its doors to me. He has a knack for designing gowns and outfits that have all of the sparkle and spangle I crave but are still in the best of taste. You wouldn't believe how heavy those beautiful beaded gowns are, though. I think some of them actually weigh more than forty pounds. What with the other weight-distribution problem I have, it's a wonder I don't have back problems like they're always saying in the tabloids.

While we are on the subject of looking good: Yes, I have had cosmetic surgery. If you've read this whole book just to find that out, then I'm glad I made your nosy butt wait this long. I have had little "nature enhancements" for a number of years. I have had nips and tucks and trims and sucks, boobs and waist and butt and such, eyes and chin and back again, pills and peels and other frills, and I'll never graduate from collagen.

I try to handle each little "problem" as it comes along. I wouldn't want to be one of those people who go in for a major face-lift and then come back the next day looking like a different person. I have personally seen women whose skin is so tight they have to sit down to blink their eyes.

I feel like it is not only a right but an obligation for a woman, especially a woman in the public eye, to look as good as she can. Whatever you are comfortable with and can afford, you should do. It reminds me of the story about a woman who refers to her crow's feet as "laugh lines" only to have another woman remark in a catty tone, "Honey, nothing's that funny." I have always said that "We all have our drawbacks, but some of us are drawed back further than others."

Having had plastic surgery is something I am not embarrassed about. I have done it and will do it again when something in my mirror doesn't look to me like it belongs on Dolly Parton.

It may look like vanity, and maybe some of it is, but to me it has more to do with feeling good about yourself. I feel it is my duty to myself and my public. My spirit is too beautiful and alive to live in some dilapidated old body if it doesn't have to. And I don't. It's like keeping up a racehorse or a show dog. I'm more like a workhorse than a thoroughbred, but I don't want to look like it any more than I have to.

So, thank God for wonderful people like Iris Zorn of New York. She's Aunt Iris to me, although she's actually Sandy's aunt. She has pointed me toward some brilliant people to help keep this old horse in shape, people like Dr. Fred Martens, Dr. Richard Stark, and Dr. John Kral. She knows everything about cosmetics, including cosmetic surgery.

My two main miracle workers in L.A. are Dr. Frank Kamer and Dr. John Grossman of Los Angeles. I have put my face in Dr. Kamer's hands, literally. He does his best to make me look good. He's a great-looking man himself, and I've had a crush on him for years. "Won't you just kiss the face you've been so kind to?" I beg him, but he just keeps cutting and pasting.

Dr. Grossman is in charge of my body, although he also does beautiful work on the face and neck. I like to have both doctors work on me at the same time, because I don't want to be put under any more than I have to be. But if I had to go around lookin' like a dog, I would definitely want to be put to sleep. With the earthquakes in L.A., I think I'll start having them work on me at their clinic in Denver. I can think of nothing worse than waking up with a half-assed face job and a half-faced ass job.

Of course, the big question in everybody's mind is, "Have you had your breasts worked on?" Let's just say that some of Dr. Grossman's work has been very uplifting. People were always saying to me, "Show me your boobs," and I got tired of having to pull my skirt up to do it. Dr. Lawrence Birnbaum also deserves some of the credit for my "body and fender" work.

Another regular doctor is my dermatologist, Dr. Arnold William Klein, whom I call Sweet William. He can take care of anything having to do with the skin and gives me a light peel every now and then and is the one who gets rid of my wrinkles with collagen. Dr. Klein is a big, huggy teddy bear. He will kiss the face that Kamer made and pat the butt that Grossman tucked.

I think it's a part of God's work in this modern age that we have such wonderfully skilled people and technologies to keep us beautiful. When I say, "Seek ye your own salvation," that applies to your physical as well as your spiritual being.

I am currently involved in a project that I hope will help millions of women feel better about the way they look and ultimately themselves. I am developing a line of cosmetics with Revlon called The Dolly Parton Beauty Confidence collection. I have always loved cosmetics, and I have spent my whole life finding out what really works. Now I want to share that with the public.

I'm also coming out with what I call Dolly's

Dailies and Nighties. I love sexy underwear, and I personally have always wanted to put out a line of really good bras for big-busted women. My Grandpa Jake is in heaven now. I hope he's getting a kick out of seeing me go into business hawking the very things he used to chastise me for. I think by now he knows that they're just a part of making a woman feel like a woman. That's important for men too. After all, there are plenty of charities for the homeless. I support them too, but isn't it time somebody helped the homely?

The same philosophy I have about being obligated to look my best applies to just about everything in life to me. I feel we have a responsibility to be and do all we can in this world. Sandollar, the company I founded with Sandy Gallin, continues to grow and is realizing many of the dreams I had for it in the beginning. We have produced a lot of television and movies. One thing Sandy and I are both very proud of is the Academy Award for the special film *Common Threads, Stories from the Quilt*. The film made a powerful statement about AIDS, and Sandy deserves the credit for having the vision to see it through.

Everybody thinks the name Sandollar came from the combination of Sandy and Dolly, and I have let them think that. In truth, the actual sea creature called a sand dollar has been special to me for a long time, somewhat like the butterfly. It has great spiritual significance to me, and those who have studied its design know that many symbols of Christianity are represented on the sand dollar. The white doves of peace, the lilies of Easter, and the dogwood petal, associated with the cross upon which Christ died, can all be found in the intricate etching on the side of this simple creature. Its roundness is also a symbol of eternity. So Sandollar was actually a name I sort of "slipped by"

Sandy Gallin. All these years he never knew he was working for a Christian organization.

While Christianity and its symbols are powerful parts of my own life, I am not one of those who believes that a person has to embrace them to be a decent and worthwhile human being. Spirituality is the most intimate part of a person's makeup, and it's strictly up to the individual to choose how to express it.

I have known wonderful, caring people who never professed to believe in God, and I have known evil people who have cloaked themselves in the outward appearance of godliness. I believe that a person who is truly good is in touch with God whether he is consciously aware of it or not. Because I believe we are a part of God and God is a part of us, I cannot see it any other way. God is always there, inside us. We either deal with the other people we come in contact with through the love he bestows us with, or we don't. Either way, it doesn't change the fact that he's there and we all have equal opportunity to use his power. I keep on trying to use that power to the best of my ability.

There have been times when God has spoken to me and I didn't pay attention. I had a lot of reservations about doing *The Best Little Whorehouse in Texas*. Some of my most deeply religious friends and fans didn't want me to do it simply because it had the word *whorehouse* in it. They felt it was glorifying prostitution. I didn't really see it that way. I thought of it more as a human story, and the occupation of the women involved was incidental. Still, something didn't feel right to me about it, and as it turned out, I would have saved myself a lot of heartache if I had not gone against that instinct.

Instinct, of course, is another part of what I consider

God to be. As you now know, that was at a time when my lines of communication with God were not completely open. Since then I have always tried to see that he gets a clear channel.

I have recently released an album called *Honky Tonk Angels* along with Tammy Wynette and Loretta Lynn. I coproduced it with my friend Steve Buckingham, a very talented guy. Tammy and Loretta are two women I can relate to completely, and I have always thought we should record together. I joked to them that perhaps we should call the album *Jurassic Park* because we are all such dinosaurs. We all broke into the business around the same time, within a few years. I have always followed their careers, not so much out of competition as out of respect.

At the time we came along, there weren't enough women in country music to make you feel all that competitive. One of the main reasons for doing the album was as a tribute to women like Kitty Wells who did so much to open doors for the rest of us, even if she had to beat some of them down.

When Kitty started out, country music was very much like the honky-tonk bars it was played in, a place for men to go and play and be away from their wives. Kitty and Patsy Cline broke into that private club and left the door open for me, and I will always be grateful for that.

We asked Kitty to sing with us on *Honky Tonk Angels*. At the time she first came out with that record it caused a huge commotion in Nashville. The "boys' club" couldn't believe that a woman had had the audacity to suggest that philandering men might be responsible for their own actions. Up until that time, it was a lot easier for them to tell themselves that they had been lured into cheating by loose women. Kitty pointed out that they were the ones who had slipped off their wedding bands and gone into the bar in the first place. Right on, Kitty.

Of course, the *Trio* album, the one with Linda Ronstadt and Emmylou Harris, was one of the crowning achievements of my career and something I am very proud of. I sounded better with those two incredible voices than I ever have, before or since. We are working on another album together.

That may seem simple, but it isn't. There are three busy schedules to coordinate and other personal and business problems to deal with. I admit that I have been the problem with this latest effort. It is simply a matter of timing. I am in the middle of starting up a new TV series and have had difficulty setting aside the time it would take to not only finish the album but promote it properly.

The press has a way of playing one party against the other in a situation like this. I don't want anybody to get the idea that Emmy, Linda, and I are enemies; that is far from the truth. We have great respect and admiration for each other, as artists and human beings. As this book goes to press, I am still hopeful that all can be worked out for the second *Trio* project to go forward. If not, then I apologize to those fans who were waiting for the album. If you don't already have it, go out and buy the first album. It is well worth the price, and if my mentioning it here makes Emmy and Linda a few bucks, maybe they won't be pissed at me for screwing up the one we're working on.

"Watch her smile. She thinks she's happy." That's what a lot of my celebrity friends and some other people think when they see me laughing and having a good time. They think I'm simpleminded because I seem to be happy. Why shouldn't I be happy? I have everything I ever wanted and more. Maybe I am simpleminded. Maybe that's the key: simple. Their lives are so complicated, it's hard for them to imagine a grown person enjoying herself. I have always wanted to do what I'm doing now, and I appreciate God and the public for allowing me to do it.

I don't understand how some people can work their whole life to get where they want to be, making the money they want to make, and then turn on the public and on themselves. They get to believing they're some kind of gods and lose sight of the one that made us all special in his eyes. Even though I'm a big star now, I still put my pants on the same way: both legs at a time. I'm ready to leap into them and get on with it, get out in the world and claim my spot. I have the means now to truly enjoy life. Great places to go, great things to do, great people to be with. Why wouldn't I be happy? It would be an insult to God to be this blessed and not realize it.

I've had hard times, been through a lot; we can't grow otherwise. So look on the bright side. It may sound cliché, but there is always somebody who is worse off than you are. I never have to search very far myself. All I have to do is look at those ungrateful turds who don't know how to be happy.

I often wonder what God was thinking when he made me. I hope I get the chance to ask him someday. I hope he gets as big a kick out of my life as I do sometimes. I'm definitely one of his more mischievous angels. If God can forgive me, so can you. So don't get your Calvins all in a twist when I tell you some of the meanness that I've been into.

Once I was on safari with my band in Africa. We were all in open jeeps riding across the savannah. My band and crew, all people I love and respect and who hold me in high regard, were in the jeep behind mine. When people know me too well, when they think I'm too goody-goody, too predictable, that's when I act up. I stood up in the jeep, dropped my drawers, and mooned the whole crowd. It was more of a total eclipse, since I was still fat at the time. I got mixed reviews but a large laugh just the same. They still talk about it today.

One night during the filming of *Nine to Five* I was on my way back to the Bel Air Hotel in a limo with Judy Ogle, Janet Knutsen, Jason Pirro, Gregg Perry, and Susie Glickman. On the way, we passed by Tom Jones's house. He was hotter than a firecracker at the time, and I said, "I wonder how Tom would feel if I just got stark naked and streaked right through his front yard?" Well, I was just talking, but before long people started to say "dare" and "double dare," words like that that make me lose control.

There's a feeling that comes over me at a time like that. It's that same kind of thing that would make a kid cut her own hair or shave her eyebrows off with her daddy's razor. "Jason, stop the car," I said, and before I knew what was happening, I felt the cool grass of Tom Jones's yard on my bare feet. Of course, that was a perfect complement to my bare ass parading around in the swankiest part of L.A. for all to see.

Then, just as quickly, I got that feeling Adam and Eve must have had when they realized they were naked. I got back in the car, grass-stained, guilt-stained, and feeling wicked. I don't know if Tom Jones saw me that night. I do know that shortly after that he put up a large wall around his property.

If it weren't for laughter, I would have died years ago, so I try to find it in every situation. I went to see the Judds' show in Lake Tahoe. They had arranged for me to have a chair backstage to watch from the wings. I love them and I loved their show. They finished the last set and walked off the stage.

Well, while they were waiting to come back for

their encore, I got that devilish feeling. I got up and ran out onstage and took their bows. Then I just kept going to the other side of the stage. The Judds were on the floor laughing, and the crowd didn't know what to think. Naomi said, "Girl, that took some nerve to do that." They knew I wasn't trying to steal their thunder. It was just the spirit of the moment, one of those times when I act on impulse to avoid a case of the "shouldas" later on. Sometimes it can backfire, and you end up with egg on your face. But, I'll take egg face over "shoulda" any day.

Sometimes I like to run naked in the moonlight and the wind, on the little trail behind our house, when the honeysuckle blooms. It's a feeling of freedom, so close to God and nature. Sometimes Judy runs with me. The full moon is my best time. It's a good feeling to have no makeup, no wig, no high heels, just my little stubby self. Just God's little Dolly Parton again.

In my imagination, I dance with the angels, do high fives with them, twirl and play tag. I love to shout at the light and rejoice and praise God. How can I not? How can I not sing, not dance, not feel this music? It's like the old shouting and rejoicing in the church back home. I just get overwhelmed by the spirit and the joy of it.

Since I believe in my own spirit so strongly, I have to believe that the spirits of others can visit me as well. I've had some very unusual encounters with the spirit world. Some I can't say I fully understand. I can describe them to you, but I can't explain them. I don't know their meaning. All I know is they may have helped shape who I am today. Life is full of magical moments and unanswered questions. So I've always tried to perceive everything with an open, inquisitive mind—because I don't want to miss anything. Try to read these stories that same way.

Shortly after my baby brother Larry died, there was an odd occurrence. The whole family had just settled down safely into bed, and all of us kids had finally stopped our fussing. The house was locked up, and all was still—until we heard someone come in the front door. Someone, or something, moved and rambled around our beds as we lay there listening. Then it walked on through the house to Mama and Daddy's room. They said it seemed to just stop by the door.

We all got up. Even the little ones seemed to sense that something strange had happened. The door was still locked and barred from the inside. My brother, who had been sleeping on the couch, said he felt a faint breeze, as if someone had passed closely by him. We looked at Mama and Daddy for answers. For once, they didn't have any. They told us not to speak of this to anyone, because it was strange, and people didn't believe in ghosts.

Mama feared it might have been the death angel coming for someone. She thought that maybe he changed his mind because she was always praying so hard for God to protect us. Some thought it might have been Larry's ghost, since his grave was right up on the hill. Many years later, after I'd read books about the supernatural, I wondered if it was my own trauma about Larry's death that might have created this strange energy force. They say that young children who are extremely sensitive and quietly troubled can cause such things. Whatever it was, we all sensed it. And nobody ever really had a true explanation of it.

Another strange occurrence happened when Carl and I were at our first home in Antioch. We usually shared the house with Judy and a sampling of my brothers and sisters, but they had gone back to East Tennessee for a while. One night we locked the doors and windows, as we routinely did when living in the city, and went off to bed. We soon began to hear noises in the kitchen. We heard the familiar sounds of cabinets opening and water running. We weren't too disturbed because we knew Judy had a key. When we heard footsteps up the stairs and water turning on in the bathroom, I said to Carl, "I guess Judy and the kids have come back early." And I rolled over to sleep.

In the wee hours of the morning, I got up to wee-wee. Just as I entered the bathroom, the hot water came on full force, all by itself. I screamed in horror, and Carl came running. Now, that was a hard faucet to turn on anyway, and it always took a while for the water to heat up. I was scared. But Carl mumbled with a sleepy tongue, "Oh, hell. Judy or one of the kids has left that damn water on."

I went to Judy's room only to find she hadn't been there. And the kids were gone too. Nobody else was in the house. I went downstairs, and all the doors were still locked and chained. But there was one window above the sink that was open just a little bit. I remembered closing it before bedtime, so I was uneasy.

As usual, Carl had an answer for everything. It was the neighbors, or rats, or built-up water pressure in the pipes, or whatever. I needed some comfort, because I had a serious case of the willies. So I bought Carl's explanation and went to sleep willie-free.

Very soon after that night, my Aunt Dorothy Jo told me something odd. She said, "I believe that Mama visited me last night." Her mother, my Grandma Rena, had recently passed away, at least her earthly self had. Aunt Dorothy Jo explained, "I felt Mama's presence real strong, standing right by my bed." Then my willies came back a hundredfold as she went on to say, "This morning, I found the kitchen window open."

I still don't know what happened, but it made me feel that much more certain that there are spirits and angels with us. I'll leave it to you to figure out. There have also been some curious events that profoundly affected me on a personal spiritual level.

One hot Sunday afternoon when I was thirteen, I was starting to feel a need to get in touch with God, but the house was full of relatives. I went back to lie down on Mama and Daddy's bed to pray and meditate. It also just happened to be a lot cooler back there. So I lay on my stomach and listened to the comforting sounds of voices and laughter that all started to seem so far away. I felt calm, holy, and very clean. And I felt that if I could go to heaven right then, they would surely let me in, and I would be safe. So I actually asked God to take me on to heaven that day.

I began feeling as if I were rising. And it was wonderful. I saw bright lights. I got completely swept up in this peaceful floating feeling. Till I had risen totally out of my body, and it scared the pee out of me. I guess I didn't really mean it when I said I wanted to go to heaven, or I wasn't really expecting it to happen. I got scared. I jumped up suddenly, looking like I had been somewhere, and I brushed myself off as if I had some spiritual dust on me. But the very instant that I got up and broke that spell, I felt sorry.

I have always regretted interrupting that experience. I wish that I could go back to that moment, because I really believe that I could have had a wonderful spiritual encounter. Someday maybe I can relive it. I remember that it was the most unbelievable feeling of love and light and peace that I've ever known. And it was similar to the way my mama described her near-death experience. I know that Mama was never the same after that. Now she has no fear of death and looks forward to going back to that light someday. And so do I.

One of the most unusual experiences I've had I shared with Judy. We were both going through a difficult and very draining period in Los Angeles. We needed to restore ourselves emotionally and physically and decided to take a trip up to Napa Valley. We loaded up the car with food, clothing, cameras, et cetera. Well, I said we were depressed. We filled up the tank to head off for our five-day adventure.

We discovered some wonderful places. We explored the old missions all around Santa Barbara. We were mostly alone as we traveled up the coast, with just the quiet trees looking down over the misty sea. Eventually, I remember tall, tall mountains looking down into magical valleys. To me, it was like stepping right into the Old Testament. We were swept up in the spirit of the place. And I do mean spirit, not "spirits." We weren't drunk. We were only going to see the vineyards, not necessarily partake of them. We were both just marveling at the overwhelming feeling of the place. And then, suddenly, we came back to our senses and found we were still in the parking lot at the Bel Air Hotel.

I don't understand it. It was five days later, and it appeared we hadn't moved. Our luggage was still intact. The same gas was still in the tank. And our food was still warm.

I don't expect you to understand, because even Judy and I have never been able to explain this experience. Maybe it was just something that we both needed desperately. I do know that this was shortly before I went into a very dark depression. And maybe God was preparing me for this. I felt so close to him during this sort of spiritual trip that we took. Then, in my darkest days soon afterward, he seemed so far away that I couldn't find him. But, maybe, through this journey, he had instilled in me an extra bit of strength, so that I could hold on. I'll never be sure. I do know that both Judy and I can still recall certain moments from that trip. And they seem to come back at the times when we need it the most.

Throughout my life, my love relationship with God has been the most important. I've had many a jealous friend and lover over my relationship with him. My love for God goes far beyond the physical, although the physical has always been a great weakness. It has been a delicate balancing act for me. Otherwise, I might have flown away years ago.

I feel I have a divinely inspired and ordained mission, and every day I try to find that higher purpose. Some of what I say or do might seem a little weird, sacrilegious, even blasphemous. I assure you, from where I stand, with my God as I know him, it is not.

I am not a *very* religious person, although I grew up with a very religious background. I am highly spiritual, and there is a great difference. Often, I feel religion is so organized and categorized that it loses sight of the true love of the spirit. But I ain't preaching, I'm just talking. "Let every man seek his own salvation" is one of my favorite scriptures. Whatever will make you your better self and allow you to serve God better, to fulfill your mission, that is your salvation.

A lot of people say, "What is my mission, my higher purpose? I just get by day to day. I don't know how to live. I don't know how to die." In the words of one of my favorite old country songs, "Everybody wants to go to heaven, but nobody wants to die." Everybody wants to be rich, but nobody wants to work. Everybody wants to be happy, but nobody wants to sacrifice. We get so caught up in the accumulation of goods that we forget our higher good.

Personally, I love the work and the challenge. That is the joy of life for me, that and enjoying the good when you have attained it and sharing it with others. You have to work at being happy, just like you have to work at being miserable. Don't fight change so much. Change is good. I don't even mind the change of life, because I know it's taking me forward, into the next dimension.

I see someone I love in everybody I meet. Everybody seems like a brother, a sister, a lover. I see parts of myself in them. The less I like a person, the more I usually see myself in them. Part of learning to love them is to admit the weakness in yourself. But I know they all have the God core. It's that light that I search for, in life and in people.

Passion and freedom and a passion for freedom are the ingredients that make me me. To be married yet free, bonded yet unbound—that is balance and truth.

For most of my life I had a childlike faith that everything would be all right. There have been times when that faith let me down, or at least appeared to. I was moving so fast, I met myself coming back. The faith is still there. The child is still there.

When I was seven or eight, a woman considered by some in our part of the country to be a saint or a prophet laid her hands on me in church one day. Her eyes were closed. She didn't know whose child she was touching. She said out loud in a clear voice, "This child is anointed."

I didn't know that word. Disjointed, yes. Anointed, no. I asked Mama what she meant by that. "You have a mission," she said. "God has placed his hand on you, picked you to do some special things in this world, praise him and maybe help people." I took that to heart because Sister Leona and Mama had said so. It made me feel special and safe; after all, God had his hand on me. Maybe that gave me an unfair advantage, made my faith easier to keep. I don't think so. God's hand is on us all. His voice, even clearer than Sister Leona's, is speaking to each of us every day. The key is to learn to listen.

At all of my properties I have a little chapel, a place I can go to talk to and, more importantly, listen to God, although I can do it anywhere. I close my eyes and picture myself surrounded by radiant light. I dance with a circle of angels. They don't have faces, just forms of light, like a string of paper dolls. The light is healthy and energizing to me. I affirm often, "I am dancing with the light. I am encircled by the light of God. Nothing can harm me. I am happy. I am radiant. I am free. I am safe in the love and the light of God."

Every day I visualize God picking me up by the heels, holding me upside down until all of the bad, negative things fall out into that circle of light. Then he stands me up, and I picture streams of light coming through the top of my head, filling my whole body until I too am a being of light. Then we stomp all of the negative things into a fine white powder and blow it away with the wind of our dancing feet.

I believe that God is in you too. Maybe you don't. I've known a lot of atheists, but I've never known a happy one. Don't make God a burden. He's the lifter of burdens. Lay your burdens on him, and go free and be happy.

You say you don't know how to pray? The Lord said, "Pray after this manner: Our Father, who art in heaven. Hallowed be thy name. Thy kingdom come, thy will be done on earth, as it is in heaven. Give us this day our daily bread, and forgive us our trespasses, as we forgive those who trespass against us. Lead us not into temptation, but deliver us from evil. For thine is the kingdom, and the power, and the glory forever, Amen."

Saying the Lord's Prayer always makes me feel good. Another part of the Bible I love is the Twenty-third Psalm: "The Lord is my shepherd. I shall not want. He maketh me to lie down in green pastures. He leadeth me beside the still waters. He restoreth my soul. He leadeth me in the paths of righteousness for his name's sake. Yea, though I walk through the Valley of the Shadow of Death, I will fear no evil. For thou art with me. Thy rod and thy staff, they comfort me. Thou preparest a table before me in the presence of mine enemies. Thou anointest my head with oil. My cup runneth over. Surely goodness and mercy shall follow me all the days of my life. And I will dwell in the house of the Lord forever."

Every day I count my blessings. Then I count my money. Yes, I have made a lot of money. I don't think about the money first. I think of God first. I assume the money's going to come if the work is good. I don't begrudge God his money either. My accountants do sometimes. I believe in tithing ten percent (of gross earnings), but I always get it back a thousandfold. Don't confuse tithing with charity. They are two different things. Charity should go beyond tithing. That's just a given. Once, as a child, I met Colonel Sanders, the chicken king. He was a sweet man, and as we parted company he looked me right in the eye and said, "You always pay your tithe."

Here's an exercise you might try. Get yourself three notebooks and sit down and tell God everything. In one, put everything negative, all of your frustration, your anger, who's ticking you off, what you're not getting that you feel you deserve. Be honest. Let it all out.

In the second book, write down all of the good things in your life, even little things like the joy a pet might bring you or a favorite plant, smells, anything that gives you pleasure. Try to find something good about all of the people in your life, "My mother has nice skin" or "My husband has good hair." Try especially hard to find positive things about the people who are troubling you or disappointing you. You'll be surprised.

Then, in your third book, write down your wishes, your dreams, your desires, all that you could or should have done. Even write down your sexual fantasies. Nobody else is going to see this, and sex is a much bigger part of what we want than most of us will admit.

When you're done, hold your books up to the light. Sunlight is good, but imaginary God light is better. Ask God to consider all of the things you've written down. Ask him to clean up your life, past, present, and future. Ask for forgiveness and direction. Then tear out just the pages of the books that you've used and burn them in a bucket or a fireplace or somewhere. Don't even try this unless you can be completely alone, with no distractions. As your thoughts burn, think of it as "holy smoke"—tiny, almost invisible particles that will go up to God for him to put back together in the way they should be.

Now look at the pages left in your books. Those are the clean white paper on which you can write the rest of your life. You should feel cleansed, forgiven, rejuvenated, perfect. I always do.

There are many books and writers that have been helpful to me: the Holy Bible first and foremost, Robert H. Schuller's works, especially *Possibility Thinking*. I love *The Magic of Believing* by Claude Bristol. Catherine Ponder has been influential with

The Dynamic Laws of Prosperity and *The Dynamic Laws of Healing*. Norman Vincent Peale's work and Edgar Cayce's *The Sleeping Prophet* have been meaningful as well. I believe that God is in all of those works. I pray that he is in mine as well.

As I sit reflecting on my life, my mind goes back to that little girl who had found God in the old empty church and bragged so proudly to the man in the truck, "I'm on the road to paradise." The longer I live, the more apparent it becomes to me that paradise is not a goal at the end of the road, but the road itself. As a believer, I know that the true paradise awaits me in the next life. But I also believe that it is each person's right, and in fact his duty, to try to come as close as he can get to it in this life.

The journey is on a road, not a highway. We don't travel this road in a fine car, or even in the most humble horse-drawn wagon. We walk it each step of the way with the dust of the rugged road clinging to our bare feet. Although we seldom realize it at the time, that dust is more precious to us than gold dust. It is the dust of experience, of error and forgiveness, of risk and reward. Maybe from the dust that has collected on my feet you can sift out a few specks of gold that will be of value to you on your road.

More important than the road itself are the people we meet along the way. That is the real key to life. That is what really separates us from the other animals, our relationships to other people and the love we share with them. You can say, "I love my work" or "I love my dog" or "I love chocolate," but you can only really love another human being and the God that dwells within them.

The poet Emily Dickinson said, "The only thing I know about love is that love is all there is." Love is what it has always been about. The reason for wanting to be a star was to be able to create more love and share it with more people. Maybe a person who wants to be a star is doing it as much to be loved as to give love. So what? Isn't that fair? The biggest heartaches in my life have all been because I wanted people to love me more than they were willing or able to. People are not perfect. They will sometimes take your love and give nothing back or, worse yet, use it against you. But they are still all there is. They are the greatest of God's creations. Loving one another is our only reason for being.

Lord, I have gotten mushy here toward the end. I don't mean to sound like the inside of a Hallmark card. I do think, though, that it's time we learned to use the word *love* without cringing. Maybe then we'll be able to actually do it without making a big deal out if it, to have it be as much a part of our daily lives as eating or sleeping.

One of my favorite expressions is "Angels fly because they take themselves lightly." To me, that means they're not held down by the weight of their own self-importance. They don't ever think of themselves as angels. They just are. Angels are very special to me. I'm not for a moment suggesting that I am an angel, but I have certainly known some.

The most important verse in the Bible to me is "Now abideth faith, hope and love." Some versions of the Bible say "charity," but it is properly translated "love." It goes on to say, "The greatest of these is love." Faith, hope, and love are the three most important words in my life. I believe it is faith that helps you achieve those things you hope for and that love is the reason for all of it. That is my "unfinished business."

I still have love to give and get in this world, and I am excited about that prospect. No one can say how many years God will give us on this earth, but I know that every day he gives me I will cherish as a special privilege, a new opportunity to love. There's plenty of life and love left in Dolly Parton. I plan to enjoy every blessed second of it.

QUESTIONS AND ANSWERS

I have always been asked so many questions. I'm sure I have not covered in this book all of the things that you may want to know, so I thought I'd include a question-and-answer section of real questions by real people. I personally had the most fun with these. I hope they'll be fun, as well as informative, for you.

What are your plans for the future?

I'm starting my own line of cosmetics and wigs; Dolly's Dailies and Nighties; my new CBS-TV series "Heavens to Betsy"; more movies (hopefully my book will be made into one), a Broadway musical, children's stories, videos, and albums; a line of foods called Dixie Fixins, cookbooks; and in my spare time. . . .

Can you give me more information about weight control and plastic surgery?

For advice on plastic surgery and surgeons, call the American Society of Plastic and Reconstructive

Surgeons Referral Service at 1 (800) 635-0635. The Obesity Research Center (which I am personally familiar with) is at the Columbia University Weight Control Unit at St. Luke's–Roosevelt Hospital Center, New York, NY 10025, (212) 523-8440. There are also new drugs and surgical procedures available if you are 90 to 100 pounds overweight. The center or your own doctor can give you more information on these.

Did emotional problems as a child lead to your weight problem?

No. I do not overeat because my mother slapped me when I was five. I overeat because I'm a damned hog.

Have you ever done drugs or alcohol?

I have never abused it. I have seen too many lives destroyed by drugs and/or alcohol. My weakness is food. I'll take a sandwich and a shake over a joint and a jug anytime.

How do you feel about life in general?

Sometimes it drives me crazy. Sometimes it drives me on.

Do you suffer from PMS?

You mean the poisonous manhating shrew syndrome. Lord, yes, when I was filming *Steel Magnolias* the director's biggest fear was that all we women would have simultaneous PMS. We never did, but we could have, since Shirley MacLaine said we were all the same person in another life.

Do you still have a home and restaurant in Hawaii?

No, one of my dearest family friends and godfather

to my niece Rebecca, Heine Fountain, and I opened a restaurant in Hawaii called Dockside Plantation. I was unable to go to Hawaii as much as planned, so I sold my house and the restaurant. I love Hawaii, and the people there are really special to me.

How do you look without your hair and makeup?
   Like hell!

What's the best-kept secret about Dolly Parton?
   That I own the *National Enquirer*!

How would you define love?
   Love is something sent from Heaven to worry the hell out of you.

How do you feel about bald men?
   I love bald men. Just because you've lost your fuzz, don't mean you ain't a peach.

What's one of your most awkward moments?
   One of the most embarrassing things I can remember unfortunately lasted a lot more than a moment. At one time, Sandy Gallin had commissioned the artist Andy Warhol to do five paintings of me to hang over his mantel. When the paintings arrived, Sandy couldn't stand them. I wasn't especially crazy about them either. We had expected them to look something like the ones of Marilyn Monroe, but these were in a different style and looked harsh and severe. These looked more like Bill Monroe!
   Sandy didn't want the paintings. More important, he didn't want to pay for them. Sandy is cheap. Sandy thought that Andy Warhol would be more sympathetic to me, so he sent me to try to finagle a way out of paying for them. I hate that kind of thing. I would

rather shoot myself in the foot than confront some-body over a thing like that. I didn't know what to do, so finally I just said to Mr. Warhol, "Look, Sandy's too cheap to pay for these pictures and they're not exactly what he had in mind. So, could you take them back?" He did.

The last laugh was on Sandy. After Warhol died, each one of the five paintings sold for many times what Sandy would have paid for them. He would have made a million dollars on them if he had kept them.

Is it still possible for you to get excited about your career, or are the thrills all in the past for Dolly Parton?

I can get just as excited about doing something today as I could when I cut my first little record at age twelve. One of the biggest thrills of my entire life hap-pened just recently when Whitney Houston's version of "I Will Always Love You" became the most played song of the year. I was so proud when I went to New York to pick up my award. You couldn't have hit me in the butt with a red apple I had it so high in the air, but humble at the same time.

Were you always a dreamer?

I'm sorry. What did you ask me? I was daydream-ing. Seriously, yes, I have always been a dreamer. It used to drive my mother crazy. She used to always say, "You and your dreams." I hope to someday write a book by that name. I can remember telling her when I was just about knee high, "Mama, someday I'm going to buy you a house so big it'll take you two days to walk from the living room to the kitchen. And you'll be wearing diamonds as big as biscuits."

What's the eeriest thing that ever happened to you?

Once, years and years ago, I went with my daddy up to Greenbriar, Tennessee, where most of his people were born and lived and died. We were walking through a little graveyard way back in the mountains and looking at the tombstones. Daddy was telling me about all of the people and how they were related to me. We turned down a row of graves and I saw something that took my breath. There was a small grave with the name Dolly Parton on it. That was the strangest sensation I have ever had. My dad said he thought it had been a stillborn child of Pink and Dicey Parton, some distant relatives. You can't really imagine how that feels unless you've seen your own name on a grave.

How poor were you really?

Well, I'll put it this way. The ants used to bring back food they'd taken from us because they felt sorry for us.

What is your shoe size?

Well, my feet are small for the same reason my waist is small—things don't grow in the shade. Seriously, I wear a size six medium shoe.

How can you claim to be so God-fearing and have such a dirty mouth?

I don't really talk dirty to be dirty. It's just a way of communication. Some people are just born cussers. I don't even realize I'm doing it. If I have offended anybody with any of my language in this book, all I can say is "Tough titty!"

Is it true that you and Whitney Houston got into a feud over the song "I Will Always Love You"?

I heard she said it was her song and you said it was yours and that she refused to sing it with you.

Absolutely not. I don't know how those stories get started. She was thrilled to have the song to sing, and I was even more delighted to have such a fine singer do my song in such a special way. We were both very grateful for the big hit the record turned out to be, and to David Foster and Kevin Costner, who produced it.

I read somewhere that a sheik offered five million dollars to spend the weekend with you. Is that true?

Do you think if I had done that I would tell you? Now, excuse me while I go and vacuum the sand out of my drawers.

Do you ever think you'll get out of show business and just do God's work?

Well, God and I have a great relationship, but we both see other people. I truly believe that God is in everything I do and that all of my work glorifies him. I don't think you have to be a religious fanatic to do God's work. However, if you are going to be a fanatic, I guess a religious one is the best kind to be.

Do you believe in reincarnation?

No, and I didn't believe in it when I lived before either. Seriously, I don't know if I have lived before or will live again. Since there's no way to tell, I feel like the best thing for me to do is to make the most of this life that I possibly can.

Have you ever cheated on Carl Dean?

That's for me to know and you and Carl Dean to find out.

Have you ever been with a woman?

All my life. I love women. My mother was a woman.

Did you and Porter ever have sex?

Hundreds of times, but not with each other.

What do you sleep in?

A bed; what do *you* sleep in? Actually, I usually sleep naked unless it's in the cold of the winter. Then I'll sleep in a flannel gown or one of Carl's flannel shirts. If it's a special occasion and I'm feeling especially sexy, I'll wear a provocative little negligee . . . but not for very long.

Will there ever be a Whorehouse 2?

There will always be a whorehouse somewhere, but I won't be in it.

Are your fingernails real?

They're real expensive, and real long.

Do you look more like your mother or your father?

That depends on whether or not I have makeup on. Actually, I have my mother's features and my father's coloring.

If you could tell teenagers one thing, what would it be?

I would say always act like it's raining and wear your rubbers. Now I've embarrassed myself, and that's hard to do. I would say, stick to your dreams, stick to your guns. Have faith in yourself.

Do you sleep on your back?

That depends on the man I'm with. Sometimes I'll

sleep on *his* back. But I do have two natural pillows on the front.

How do you feel about premarital and extra-marital sex?
I never had sex I didn't like.

Have you ever considered suing the tabloids?
Yes, for printing lies about me in the middle of the magazine instead of on the cover.

Is it true you only see your husband, Carl, a few weeks out of the year?
No, but I may only see him a few days out of every week. Carl is the only man I could live with all of the time, because I don't.

Why do you wear five-inch heels?
Because I can't find six-inch ones. I never liked being short and felt I needed the height to set off my width. Even what I wear for slippers are old worn-out high heels.

What do you want people to say about you one hundred years from today?
Boy, she looks great for her age!

What do you think is your best feature?
I think it's my smile, not my boobs, although they are two of my biggest assets.

Do you think you're different because you're a southerner?
I'm proud of being from the South. At least rednecks and hillbillies are interesting. I'd rather be rocky road than vanilla. Besides, what other kind of person would call an old maid aunt an "unclaimed treasure"?

What is your greatest strength and your greatest weakness?

Loving too much is my greatest strength and therefore giving too much is my greatest weakness.

How long was Porter in your life?

The same length he's always been.

How do you feel about gay rights and gay people?

Well, I believe in "human rights" and the Scripture, "Judge not, lest ye be judged." I have many gay friends who I love dearly. I have also lost some very special friends to AIDS. I believe that being gay is something you are, not something you do.

What do you think of female impersonators, transvestites, and people who have sex-change operations?

Well, I've always said that if I hadn't been a woman, I would have been a drag queen. I have seen men impersonate me, and I consider it flattering. I especially like it on Halloween. Then I can go anywhere in Hollywood and never be noticed. All I know about sex-change operations I've learned from my good friend Jason, who used to be my good friend Suzie.

Do your fans bug you?

Absolutely not! I love my fans, treasure and appreciate them. I save everything they send me. I have a huge room that I affectionately call my "arts and crap" collection. To me, anything that a fan took time to make for me is art, and I would never throw it away. Without Dolly Parton's fans, there would be no Dolly Parton.

Have you ever had voice lessons?

No. My singing comes naturally. Do you honestly think somebody would teach a person to sing like this?

What advice would you give someone who wants to make it in show business?

Believe in yourself. Work hard. Keep your sense of humor and your day job.

Have you ever been asked to pose nude?

Yes, I have agreed to pose for *Penthouse* on my hundredth birthday. Everybody is going to be sorry.

Do you have any pet peeves?

Yes, people who are always late. I value my time, and everyone else's too.

What do you and Carl do to get away?

We take off in our camper or go to our lake house. We might go on a picnic somewhere, and then decide to stay overnight. Then we'll go to a "drive up to your room" motel.

Do you exercise to keep your weight down?

No. If I tried to jog with these boobs, I'd end up with two black eyes. I am physically lazy and don't like exercise of any kind . . . well, one kind.

Does it bother you being short?

No, because I know I would have been very tall had I not gotten so bunched up at the top!

Is there anything else you would like to talk about?

I'm glad *I* asked that question. I did stage this question so I could tell you about my latest album,

Heartsongs: Live from Home. It will be the first release on my new label, Blue Eye Records. I co-produced the album with Steve Buckingham, a very special musical angel and one of my partners in Blue Eye. I've been waiting all my life to do an acoustic album of the songs I grew up lovin' and singin'. The album has songs from the old world—England, Ireland, Scotland, and Wales—as well as songs from the Smokies and some that I have written that were influenced by all these places. It's the album I hope and believe I will be most remembered for, and it goes nicely with this story of my life.

Do you play any musical instruments, other than guitar?

I play my fingernails, too! I also play banjo, piano, harpsichord, and drums.

Which do you like best, singing, writing, or acting?

Without a doubt, songwriting is my greatest source of joy and the best outlet for my creativity.

Do you have any regrets?

Well, I might regret answering this question. Really, no. I have learned something from everything that has happened in my life. I am who I am because of my past experiences, good and bad.

ACKNOWLEDGMENTS

I have so many people to thank for so many things. I had a list of about three thousand. The publisher said that was far too many and narrowed it down to about half. If your name does not appear here, I'll try to get it in my next book of unfinished business. I thank you just the same.

I've asked for at least a blank space at the end so you can write in your name if it is not here.

Axton, Mae Boren
Ayoob, Dick, and staff
Azzara, Leslie
Bailey, Curly Dan
Baird, Ron
Baker, Howard
Baker, Lois
Baker, Mike
Baldwin, Jack
Bales, Walter
Ball, Anita
Ball, Wayne
Bankston, Scott
Barnard, J. Thomas
Barnes, Christie
Barnett, Donna Chappell
Barr, Nan
Bates, Jim and Judy
Baum, Carol
Beatty, Tony
Beckham, Bob
Beer, Bonnie
Beland, John
Bell, Ken
Bennett, Greg
Benson, Ed
Benson, Ray, & Asleep at the
    Wheel
Benzaken, Piny
Beranato, Bob
Berman, Gail
Berner, Fred
Binkley, Bayron
Biosyan, Hilda
Birnbaum, Lawrence
Black, Clint
Blair, David
Blalock, Jo
Bledsoe, Ron
BMI staff
Bob Northern Sign Co.

Bogen, Joe
Bolotin, Craig
Bono, Mike
Boone, Claude
Booke, Alexandra
Borowski, Ginny
Bossart, Peter A.
Bowling, Lowell
Bradley, Connie
Bradley, Jerry
Bradley, Mark
Bray, Charlene
Breeden, Joe and Virginia
Breneman, Phil
Brennan, Attracta, and family
Brewer, Sis
Brewster, Bud
Brewster, Willie G.
Bright, Laura
Broderick, Gary
Brokaw, Wendy
Brooks, Bobby
Brooks, Clyde
Brown, Art
Brown, Melissa
Brown, Tony
Bryant, Del
Buckingham, Steve and Andy
Buckley, Kaye
Bunch, Ray
Burke, Delta
Burkhimer, Don
Burnham, Burt
Burton, Byrd
Butler, Al
Butler, Brett
Butler, Carl and Pearl
Buttrey, Dan
Byrd, Jerry
Campbell, Archie
Campbell, David

Klein, Gary
Knutsen, Janet
Koch, Ed
Kochel, Nancy
Kohan, Buz
Kohen, Rhea
Koppelman, Charles
Kowalski, Deborah
Kragen, Ken
Kral, John
Kraski, Mike
Krenz, Jano
Kretchmer, John
Kriss, Judy
Laboy, Cliff
Ladanyi, Greg and Laura
Laginestra, Roco
Lagler, Rene
Lamb, Charlie
Landy Gardner & The Christ Church Choir
Lane, Bill
Lane, Penni
Lane, Steve
Lapping, Kelly
Larson, Mark
Lavender, Shorty
Lavigne, Randy
Lawhead, Scott
Layton, Joe
Lebowitz, Fran
Lefkoff, Larry
Leonard, Nan
Leonard, Scotty
Leuschner, Renate
Levin, Jerry
Lewis, Jon
Lewis, Mike
Limato, Ed
Lincoln, Alan/Steve Holmes and crew

Lincoln, Jimmy, Minnie, and Beth
Lipman, Macey
Logan, Hugo
Logan, Jack
Long, Ellen
Long, Hubert
Lopez, George
Loveday, Edna
Loy, Deborah Wagoner
Ludwig, Arlene
Luman, Joyce
Lyon, Linda
Maffatone, Tony
Magid, Beverly
Majd, Mac
Mangatal, Shana
Manis, Clay, and family
Manis, Hubert
Mann, Barry
Maples, Steve
Marden, Jeff
Mark Allen Travel
Martens, Dr. Fred
Martin, Hank
Martinez, Albino
Marusyk, Wayne
Massenburg, George
Mathis, Larry
Mattea, Kathy
Mattingly, Jimmy
Maxwell, Michael
May, Sheila
Maynard-Sprouse, Dona
McCann, Jim, Caitlin, and Connor
McCarter sisters
McCarthy, Amie
McClelland, Angel
McConnell, Bill
McElhiney, Bill

Roman, John
Rosenblum, Mel
Rosenman, Howard
Roskin, Sheldon
Ross, Herbert
Ross, Tony, and staff
Roth, Ann
Roth, Don
Rouse, Jack
Rovick, Jody
Rowe, Debbie
Rowe, Pam
Rowley, Marjean
Rubinstein, Jerry
Rutledge, Tom
Sager, Carol Bayer
Sajulga, Leroy
Salestrom, Jim
Sammeth, Bill
Sancio, Rose
Sandollar staff
Sanger, Dave
Sanicola, Hank and Jackie
Sarsfield, Helen and Jim
Sasser, Senator Jim
Satterfield, Lawayne
Saveanu, Ligiea
Scalamandre, Jill
Scarborough, Carla
Scheffey, Dan
Scheibner, Adrianna
Schreibner, Carson
Schribner, Phil
Schuler, Ed
Scott, Alana and Patrick
Scott, June
Scottie, Tony, Ben, and Fred
Seay, Ed
Sechler, Steve
Secretaries at Gallin-Morey
Segel & Goldman

Seitz, Chuck
Sells, Carolyn
Severs, Mike
Sexton, Ann and Doug
Sexton, Jennifer
Sheffield, Buddy
Sheffield, Heather
Shelton, Vicki
Sheslow, Stu
Shestack, Jon
Shimabuku, Lloyd, Lauren, and Courtney
Shockley, Mike
Shockley, Roy
Shulman, Mitzi
Sidle, Ken
Silver Dollar City staff
Siman, Scott
Simmons, Roy
Simmons, Scooter
Singers, Lea Jane
Sinor, Colleen
Skaggs, Ricky
Sklar, Lee
Smarr, Rod
Smelcer, Geraldine
Smiley, Alan
Smiley, Delores
Smith, Andrea
Smith, Debbie
Smith, Fred
Smith, Gary "Bud"
Smith, Howard
Smith, Jay, and family
Smith, Jim
Smith, Orriel
Smith, Ronnie
Smith, Sandy
Smith, Wendell
Sobel, Bill
Soelberg, Paul

Solters, Lee
Somers, Phil
SONY/Columbia Records
Sotiropoulos, Alexander
Southwick, Lenny
Sova, Peter
Sovine, Roger
Speeks, Red
Spencer, Cynthia
Spurlock, C. K.
Stamper, Pete
Stanley, Ralph
Stapp, Jack
Stark, Ray
Stark, Richard
Starlite Limousine
Steiner, Armin
Stevens, Tony
Strahm, Shirlee
Struble, Edgar
Strzelecki, Henry
Suchman, Pamela
Sullivan, Oot
Summer, Bob
Summers, Cary
Sutherland, Dave
Tandy Rice and Top Billing
Tanner, William
Tardy, Carmella
Tardy, Eugene
Tarlow, Dick
Tate, Della
Taylor, Cheri
Teaster, Irlene
Tewksbury, Joan
Thiemeyer, Fleur
Thomas, Dr. Robert F.
Thomilson, Claude—WIVK
Tillis, Pam
Tomlin, Lily
Tomlinson, J. T.

Tornell, Heidi
Tosti, Blaise and Lucia
Townsend, Carmen
Townsend, Scott
Trasher, Pat
Trashy Lingerie
Trew, Glen
Tribble, Dave
Triplett, Joyce
Trotter, Skip
Tucker, Tanya
Tullis, Kyle
Turley, Joe
Turner, Bill
Turner, Dale
Turner, Grant
Turner, Steve
Tyson, Janet
Uhrig, Paul
Uncle Fred
Uncle Lester
Underwood, Marty
Valencia, Sally
Vampa, Amedeo
Van Gelder, Steve
Van Itallie, Ted
Vandervort, Bill
Vanston, C. J.
Van Winkle, Little Robert
Varallo, Frances
Vicari, Tommy
Villanche, Bruce
Vito, Rick
Von Furstenberg, Diane
Wade, Gary
Wade, Sid
Wagner, Jane
Wagon Masters
Wagoner, Porter
Wagoner, Richard
Waldo, John

Walker, Cas
Walker, Karen
Ward, Judy
Warden, Ann
Warden, Beau
Warden, Charlie, and family
Warden, Don
Watkins, Bruce
Watson, Dot and Estelle
Waugh, Irving
WDLY employees
Weber, Shelly
Weiner, Dan
Weinstein, Paula
Weinstein, Riva
Welch, Ken and Mitzi
Wellons, Mary Lyda
Wells, Bud
Wells, Dennis
Wells, Kent
Wells, Kitty
Wells, Ted
Wells, Vernon, and staff
Wendell, Bud
Wendy Bagwell and the
   Sunliters
West, Albert
Weston, Jack
Whaley, Hazel
Wheeler, Dave
Whitaker, Clayton
Whitfield, Jeff

Whitfield, Tom, and staff
Wilburn, Linda, and family
Wilde, Cynthia
Willard's Jewelers
Williams, Bob
Williams, Glenn
Williams, Margie
Williams, Mike
Willis, Jack
Willoughby, Juliet
Wilson, Cheryl
Wilson, Norro
Winfrey, Ernie
Winkler, Henry
Wolff, Peter
Wolfson, Nancy
Wood, Del
Wood, Jeanne
Worley, Paul
Wright, Steve
Wunch, Roy
Wynn, Steve
Yetnikoff, Walter
Young, Everett and Loretta
Young, Jan
Young, Red
Zable, Lois
Zaentz, Alan
Zorn, Iris and Joe

P.S. Thanks for all the pictures
from family, friends, and fans.

Discography

"Puppy Love" and
"Girl Left Alone" (Single)
DOLLY PARTON
  Gold Band
  1960

Hello, I'm Dolly
DOLLY PARTON
  Monument
  MLP-8085
  Feb. 1967

Just Between You and Me
DOLLY PARTON/PORTER
WAGONER
  RCA Victor
  LSP-3926
  Jan. 1968

Just Because I'm a Woman
DOLLY PARTON
  RCA Victor
  LSP-3949
  April 1968

Just the Two of Us
DOLLY PARTON/PORTER
WAGONER
  RCA Victor
  LSP-4039
  Sept. 1968

In the Good Old Days
DOLLY PARTON
  RCA Victor
  LSP-4099
  Feb. 1969

Always, Always
DOLLY PARTON/PORTER
WAGONER
  RCA Victor
  LSP-4186
  July 1969

My Blue Ridge Mountain Boy
DOLLY PARTON
  RCA Victor
  LSP-4188
  Sept. 1969

The Fairest of Them All
DOLLY PARTON
RCA Victor
LSP-4288
Feb. 1970

*Porter Wayne and
Dolly Rebecca*
DOLLY PARTON/PORTER
WAGONER
  RCA Victor
  LSP-4305
  March 1970

As Long As I Love
DOLLY PARTON
  Monument
  SLP-18136
  April 1970

A Real Live Dolly
DOLLY PARTON
  RCA Victor
  LSP-4387
  July 1970

Once More
DOLLY PARTON/PORTER
WAGONER
  RCA Victor
  LSP-4388
  Aug. 1970

The Best of Dolly Parton
DOLLY PARTON
  RCA Victor
  LSP-4449
  Nov. 1970

Golden Streets of Glory
DOLLY PARTON
RCA Victor
  LSP-4398
  Feb. 1971

Two of a Kind
DOLLY PARTON/PORTER
WAGONER
  RCA Victor
  LSP-4490
  Feb. 1971

Joshua
DOLLY PARTON
  RCA Victor
  LSP-4507
  April 1971

*The Best of Dolly Parton &
Porter Wagoner*
DOLLY PARTON/
PORTER WAGONER
  RCA Victor
  LSP-4556
  July 1971

Coat of Many Colors
DOLLY PARTON
  RCA Victor
  LSP-4603
  Oct. 1971

*The World of Dolly Parton
(2-Record Set)*
DOLLY PARTON
  Monument
  KZG-31913
  1972

The Right Combination:
Burning the Midnight Oil
DOLLY PARTON/PORTER
WAGONER
  RCA Victor
  LSP-4628
  Jan. 1972

Touch Your Woman
DOLLY PARTON
  RCA Victor
  LSP-4686
  March 1972

Together Always
DOLLY PARTON/PORTER
WAGONER
  RCA Victor
  LSP-4761
  Sept. 1972

Just the Way I Am
DOLLY PARTON
  RCA Camden
  CAS-2583
  Oct. 1972

Dolly Parton Sings, My
Favorite Songwriter, Porter
Wagoner
DOLLY PARTON
  RCA Victor
  LSP-4752
  Oct. 1972

We Found It
DOLLY PARTON/PORTER
WAGONER
  RCA Victor
  LSP-4841
  Feb. 1973

My Tennessee Mountain
Home
DOLLY PARTON
  RCA Victor
  APL1-0033
  March 1973

Love and Music
DOLLY PARTON/PORTER
WAGONER
  RCA Victor
  APL1-0248
  July 1973

Bubbling Over
DOLLY PARTON
  RCA Victor
  APL1-0286
  Sept. 1973

Mine
DOLLY PARTON
  RCA Camden
  ACL1-0307
  Oct. 1973

Jolene
DOLLY PARTON
  RCA Victor
  APL1-0473
  Feb. 1974

Porter 'n Dolly
DOLLY PARTON/PORTER
WAGONER
  RCA Victor
  APL1-0646
  May 1974

Love Is Like a Butterfly
DOLLY PARTON
  RCA Victor
  APL1-0712
  Sept. 1974

The Bargain Store
DOLLY PARTON
  RCA Victor
  APL1-0950
  Feb. 1975

The Best of Dolly Parton
DOLLY PARTON
  RCA Victor
  APL1-1117
  July 1975

Say Forever You'll Be Mine
DOLLY PARTON/PORTER
WAGONER
  RCA Victor
  APL1-1116
  Aug. 1975

*Dolly: The Seeker & We
Used To*
DOLLY PARTON
  RCA Victor
  APL1-1221
  Sept. 1975

All I Can Do
DOLLY PARTON
  RCA Victor
  APL1-1665
  Aug. 1976

You Are (UK)
DOLLY PARTON
  RCA International
  INTS-5044
  1977

*New Harvest—First
Gathering*
DOLLY PARTON
  RCA Victor
  APL1-2188
  Feb. 1977

Here You Come Again
DOLLY PARTON
  RCA Victor
  APL1-2544
  Oct. 1977

Heartbreaker
DOLLY PARTON
  RCA Victor
  APL1-2797
  July 1978

Great Balls of Fire
DOLLY PARTON
  RCA Victor
  APL1-3361
  May 1979

Dolly, Dolly, Dolly
DOLLY PARTON
  RCA Victor
  AHL1-3546
  April 1980

Porter & Dolly
DOLLY PARTON/PORTER
WAGONER
  RCA Victor
  AHL1-3700
  June 1980

9 to 5 (and Other Odd Jobs)
DOLLY PARTON
  RCA Victor
  AHL1-3852
  Nov. 1980

Heartbreak Express
DOLLY PARTON
  RCA Victor
  AHL1-4289
  April 1982

*The Best Little Whorehouse
in Texas*
VARIOUS—SOUNDTRACK
  MCA Records
  MCA-6112
  July 1982

*Dolly Parton's
Greatest Hits*
DOLLY PARTON
  RCA Victor
  AHL1-4422
  Oct. 1982

Burlap and Satin
DOLLY PARTON
  RCA Victor
  AHL1-4691
  May 1983

The Great Pretender
DOLLY PARTON
  RCA Victor
  AHL1-4940
  Jan. 1984

Rhinestone
VARIOUS—SOUNDTRACK
  RCA Victor
  ABL1-5032
  May 1984

Once Upon a Christmas
DOLLY PARTON/
KENNY ROGERS
  RCA Victor
  ASL1-5307
  Dec. 1984

Real Love
DOLLY PARTON
  RCA Victor
  AHL1-5415
  Feb. 1985

*Dolly Parton
(Collectors Series)*
DOLLY PARTON
  RCA Victor
  AHL1-5471
  1985

Think About Love
DOLLY PARTON
  RCA Victor
  AHL1-9508
  March 1986

Trio
DOLLY PARTON/EMMYLOU
HARRIS/LINDA RONSTADT
  Warner Bros.
  1-25491
  Feb. 1987

Rainbow
DOLLY PARTON
  CBS Records
  FC-40968
  Nov. 1987

White Limozeen
DOLLY PARTON
  CBS Records
  44384
  May 1989

Home for Christmas
DOLLY PARTON
  CBS Records
  CK-46796 (CD)
  Sept. 1990

Eagle When She Flies
DOLLY PARTON
  Sony (CBS)
  CT&CK 46882
  March 1991

Straight Talk
DOLLY PARTON
  Hollywood Records
  HR-61303-2 & 4
  March 1992

*Slow Dancing with
the Moon*
DOLLY PARTON
  Columbia/Sony
  7464 53199
  Feb. 1993

Honky Tonk Angels
DOLLY PARTON/LORETTA
LYNN/TAMMY WYNETTE
  Columbia
  53414
  Nov. 1994

Heartsongs: Live from Home
DOLLY PARTON
  Columbia
  66123
  Sept. 1994